1973

The Study of
Attitude Change

ook he kept

The Study of
Attitude Change

Edited by

Richard V. Wagner
Bucknell University

John J. Sherwood
Purdue University

Brooks/Cole Publishing Company
Belmont, California
A Division of Wadsworth Publishing
Company, Inc.

Preface

The Study of Attitude Change is the first of a series of books, each of which will provide undergraduate and graduate students with the opportunity to study a particular social psychological problem in some depth. The subject of attitude change has been chosen because it seems to be at the heart of those problems that are truly social psychological in nature.

The selection of articles for this volume is based on our desire to present not only original and representative statements of the major theoretical approaches to the study of attitude change but also a sample of the research engendered by each theoretical approach. We have juxtaposed theoretical and research articles: first, a theoretical statement; then, a research study that follows from the theory and tests its adequacy.

We begin with our own introductory chapter, which outlines the general parameters of the study of attitude change. This is followed by Katz's statement of the functional approach to the study of attitude change, and then by a sample of the research that this theoretical orientation has generated (Chapters 2 and 3). Cognitive dissonance—surely one of the most heuristic of the cognitive consistency orientations to attitude change—together with a review of dissonance research, is examined in an article prepared especially for this volume (Chapter 4). Cognitive consistency is further illustrated by the theoretical articles of Rosenberg (Chapter 6) and Osgood and Tannenbaum (Chapter 7), both of which include research to support their theoretical ideas. A learning theoretical approach is presented in an article by Janis and Hovland, and that is followed by research by Elms and Janis (Chapters 8 and 9).

Two other types of papers appear in the book. First, we have included two articles that illustrate how the same study can be interpreted differently by advocates of two different theoretical persuasions. Thus, in Chapter 5, Bem reinterprets well-known research deriving from dissonance theory; and Brehm (Chapter 10) looks again at research derived from the Yale learning position. Second, we have included two articles that are of general interest to students of attitude change. In Chapter 11, McGuire discusses "resistance to persuasion"—an issue implicit but seldom discussed in most studies of changing attitudes. Finally, there is Hovland's well-known and discerning analysis of the conflicting results derived from experimental and survey studies of attitude change (Chapter 12).

We wish to acknowledge the valuable suggestions of those who reviewed the original proposal for this volume, particularly: Daryl J. Bem, Carnegie-Mellon University; Chester A. Insko, University of North Carolina at Chapel Hill; Victor H. Vroom, Carnegie-Mellon University; Lawrence S. Wrightsman, Jr., George Peabody College for Teachers; and Robert B. Zajonc, University of Michigan. Helpful criticism was also provided by Barry E. Collins, University of California, Los Angeles, who reviewed the manuscript in its final form; and Consulting Editor Edward L. Walker, University of Michigan.

Richard V. Wagner
John J. Sherwood

Contents

1

The Study of
Attitude Change:
An Introduction

Richard V. Wagner

The concept of attitude has been a constant companion of the social psychologist since the early years of the twentieth century. According to Allport (1954), the concept initially emerged from Thomas and Znaniecki's (1918) extensive analysis of the emigration of the Polish peasant. Thomas and Znaniecki gave attitudes a central place in describing the adaptation of Polish peasants to changes in their lives when they settled in the United States.

Because attitudes — that is, evaluations of objects, ideas, and people — are part of the repertoire of human behavior, the psychologist must include their study within his domain. For him, the value of the concept of attitude is in its implications for studying complex human behavior. Certainly attitudes are less relevant to the type of research that involves studying only simple behavioral responses. If the psychologist wants to study visual acuity, for example, he can ask a research subject to press a button when he recognizes a stimulus being flashed on a screen. In this type of research, his evaluation of the stimulus may well be irrelevant. Thus, the psychologist would be unconcerned about attitudes. But when he is studying more complex social behavior, the subject's evaluation of a social stimulus may be a crucial determinant of his response to it.

"Attitude" is often defined as a predisposition to behave in a particular way toward a given object. Assuming that man acts according to his predispositions, there is no better way to predict his response to a stimulus than to know his attitude toward it. A second and more common definition of "attitude" is "a predisposition of the individual to evaluate some symbol or object or aspect of his world in a favorable or unfavorable manner" (Katz, 1960, p. 168). This definition also implies that if we know a person's attitude toward an object, we can predict his response to that object with some degree of certainty. If you like a person, it is a fairly good bet that you will approach him in some manner — talk with him, visit him, or choose to play tennis with him. If you dislike him, you are likely to avoid him. If attitudes do predispose a person to respond in particular ways to particular stimuli, then it is also important to study attitude change; that is, we not only want to know that he will probably act in a given way, but we also want to know the processes involved in any alteration in his behavior.

To the extent that the psychologist conceives of attitudes as aids in predicting behavior, he must investigate the conditions under which they are and are not good predictors. Numerous investigations — for example, LaPiere (1934) — have pointed out very clearly that people do not always act in accordance with the attitudes they express. In LaPiere's study, two couples, one Caucasian and the other Chinese, traveled across the country. When they stopped for the night at hotels and inns, they were refused lodging only twice during the trip. Several months later the managers of these hotels and inns were asked by mail whether they would accept Oriental guests. The vast majority of the managers replied that they would *not*.

That psychologists have been somewhat remiss in acknowledging and fulfilling the responsibility to study the predictability of attitudes is perhaps understandable in view of the complexity of the problem. One simple indication of the difficulties involved in determining the predictive validity of an attitude is the fact that attitudes seldom exist as separate entities. They are usually parts of complex attitude constellations or value systems. For example, if you have a negative attitude toward Professor Scrooge, the simplest prediction would be that you would avoid him. Does this mean that we can predict with 100 percent certainty that you will turn away from him when he walks up to speak to you? Certainly not; it would be impolite to do so. Besides, he might mention this incident to Professor Nutcracker, from whom you are currently taking a course, and you might think this would prejudice the latter against you. Other relevant attitudes and values, then, prevent you from making the response that is most likely to follow from your attitude toward Professor Scrooge; your attitude toward impolite behavior and your concern about Professor Nutcracker's evaluation of you modify your behavior toward Scrooge. There are, moreover, other factors, such as the intensity of the evaluation of the object, that tend to complicate the use of attitudes to predict behavior. In a paper presented later in this volume, Katz and Stotland (1959) discuss this problem and present one approach that may help us to overcome this stumbling block.

The Nature of Attitudes

An attitude is composed of *affective, cognitive,* and *behavioral* components that correspond, respectively, to one's evaluations of, knowledge of, and predisposition to act toward the object of the attitude. If one were to consider, for example, a person's general attitude toward a given politician, the *affective* component would refer to the person's evaluation of the politician, such as how nice a guy he is and how good a job he has done; the *cognitive* component would include the person's knowledge or beliefs (correct or incorrect) about the politician, such as what legislation he supports; and the *behavioral* component would refer to the person's predisposition to act toward the politician, such as writing to him or voting for or against him.

These components can vary in the degree to which they comprise a particular attitude. For example, the affective component of an attitude can vary in its intensity — a person may feel moderate or extreme like or dislike of socialism. The cognitive component of his attitude toward socialism can consist of only a simple belief, such as "Socialism is akin to communism," or it can consist of hundreds of facts and beliefs. The behavioral component can vary in the number of actions that he is predisposed to carry out — he may merely discuss socialism with his best friend, or he may discuss it with everyone, write to his congressman, picket, and vote for or against socialist political candidates.

Attitude should be distinguished from three related concepts with which it is often confused: *opinion, belief,* and *value.* The difference between an attitude and an opinion is quite simple: An opinion is merely the verbal expression of an attitude. The difference between an attitude and a belief is slightly more complex: An attitude always includes evaluation of an object (the affective component), whereas a belief does not. One is expressing a belief about a woman, for example, when he says, "Her measurements are 36-26-36." The belief becomes an attitude when he adds, "I *like* those measurements!"

The difference between an attitude and a value is one of inclusiveness or scope: Attitude refers to an orientation toward one object, whereas value implies an orientation toward a series or class of related objects. Thus, a value is often a collection of attitudes. For example, one may have a particular religious value system that is the constellation of all of one's individual attitudes toward various facets of religion.

Attitude Change

The study of attitude change is the attempt to identify and understand the processes underlying the modification of attitudes. Happily, studies of attitude change have necessarily included formulations about other crucial aspects of attitudes, such as how they originally develop and how they are related to values, personality, and the social environment. This section presents a brief overview of four contemporary approaches to attitude change: (1) the functional approach, (2) learning theory, (3) perceptual theory, and (4) consistency theory.

In this overview some of Louis Fischer's experiences are used as case studies. Louis Fischer is an American correspondent and frequent traveler to Europe and the Soviet Union. In 1949, he wrote about his attraction to and later disenchantment with Soviet-style communism. His report describes distress over conditions in Europe and America after World War I, his gradual attraction to the communist ideology in Russia, and his attempts to reconcile discrepancies between his idealized hopes for the Soviet system and many of the discouraging features he heard about or witnessed — such as persecution of dissenters, restrictions on the press, and repressive actions of the secret police. He greatly admired the Spanish Loyalists during the Spanish Civil War. His ultimate disenchantment with Russian communism followed the Russian-German Pact in 1939, which he saw as an agreement to subject other nations to dictatorship. In his report, Fischer presents many instances of changes in his own and in others' attitudes toward communism, and he describes many of the incidents that precipitated these changes. Because of their clarity, some of these instances are used here to illustrate the major principles emphasized by the four approaches to attitude change.

The Functional Approach

The functional approach to attitude change suggests that attitudes develop and change as they serve to promote or support goals of the individual; that is, attitudes are instrumental to the person's satisfaction of his needs. For example, a functional explanation of the fact that during the Great Depression some workers developed positive attitudes toward communism is that communism promised to satisfy their need for relief from extreme poverty.

There have been two major attempts to present a functional explanation of attitude change. The first was proposed by Katz and Stotland (1959) and further elaborated by Katz (1960); the second was suggested by Kelman (1961). The functional approach to attitude change is represented in this volume by Katz's

(1960) theoretical statement and illustrative research by Katz, Sarnoff, and McClintock (1956).

Katz and Stotland's theory of attitude change. Katz and Stotland argue that attitudes develop and change because they satisfy psychological needs of the individual, so that the psychologist must be aware of what need is being served by an attitude in order to predict the nature of the change. Katz postulates four different motivational bases of attitudes. The first is the *instrumental* function, which is based on the assumption that a person seeks to maximize rewards and minimize punishments; that is, he develops positive attitudes toward those objects or ideas that are rewarding or lead to reward and negative attitudes toward those that are punishing or lead to punishment. The above illustration of workers developing positive attitudes toward communism because communism seemed to represent an opportunity for relief from poverty is an example of the instrumental function of attitudes.

The *ego-defensive* function is based on the individual's desire to protect himself from those self-perceptions that he finds painful to recognize. In the Freudian sense of unconscious defense mechanisms, he develops attitudes toward specific objects when holding such attitudes helps to camouflage feelings that threaten his self-esteem. An example is the person who has a low evaluation of himself but does not want to admit it and therefore clings to an ideology that disguises his feelings of weakness, one that is itself strong and so provides him with the mask of strength that he needs to protect his self-esteem.

The *value-expressive* function is based on the individual's desire to present attitudes consistent with his central values. In this instance, he is willing to reveal those aspects of himself and his values that he evaluates highly, as opposed to an ego-defensive attitude, which implies an attempt to conceal certain personal characteristics. Fischer's description of his own conversion to communism is an example. He deplored the suffering brought about by war and by the "powerful few" who were exploiting the masses. He "preferred fresh sweeping winds to stale stagnant air . . . [and] liked the Soviets because they were an experiment in the interest of the downtrodden majority, because they destroyed the privileges of the powerful few . . ." (p. 205). Fischer's support of the communist cause was, then, his means of expressing his own social values on international politics and economics.

The *knowledge* function is based on man's need to acquire information and to organize it in a way that gives meaning to a potentially chaotic environment. Inconsistencies abound in our psychological worlds. In order to make some sense of all the inconsistencies facing us, we often make "best guesses" and generalizations about objects or people when there is insufficient information available for us to make completely accurate judgments. Filling in the gaps in our knowledge in this way helps us to understand our environment with greater ease.

Beginning with this classification of the motivational bases of attitudes, Katz (1960) then analyzes the manner in which such attitudes are changed. For example, he suggests that an instrumental attitude will change if the object of the attitude loses its inherent rewarding capacity or its instrumentality in attaining another valued goal. Thus, some Soviet farmers turned actively anticommunist when their farms were threatened by the regime's policy of collectivization. In his analysis, which appears later in this book, Katz describes other ways in which attitudes change.

Kelman's theory of attitude change. Kelman (1961) proposes a "three-process" theory of attitude change, which is particularly concerned with situations in which one person attempts to influence the attitudes of another. Two of these processes concern the relationship between the agent of the attempt to influence and the recipient of the attempted influence; the third concerns the relationship between the change advocated and the attitudes already held by the recipient. The first process, *compliance,* occurs when the recipient changes his attitude in order to obtain a favorable reaction or avoid an unfavorable reaction from the influencer. After the onset of the purges in Russia in the 1930s, Fischer notes that many of his friends who had previously been willing to discuss with him the positive and negative aspects of the Soviet regime were no longer willing to do so for fear of incurring the wrath of the secret police. It would seem that they were complying by refusing to mention any of their former doubts about the system. However, compliance may often mean that the individual simply changes the public expression of his attitude while privately disagreeing with what he said − or, as in the instance noted by Fischer, by publicly refusing to criticize Soviet communism while privately remaining critical of it. Change under these circumstances may persist only as long as the influencer remains present. In fact, one may argue that this is not attitude change at all but rather behavioral change in a particular situation.

The second process of attitude change, *identification,* occurs when the person adopts the attitudes of others with whom he has gratifying personal relationships. Although Fischer does not report any such instances, some people might have become communist sympathizers because their friends or people they admired were sympathetic toward the cause. People often find it "satisfying" to be like others they admire. This type of attitude change is more likely to persist because, unlike compliance, it is not dependent upon the presence of the influencing agent. The attitudes of people one admires become one's own.

The third process described by Kelman is *internalization.* This is acceptance of influence when the direction of change is consistent with the attitudes or values that the recipient already holds. Internalization is similar to Katz's value-expressive function, in which the person is gratified by expressing attitudes that support his basic value systems. Because of Fischer's general anti-war, anti-poverty, anti-exploitation values, it was much easier for him to accept the Soviet doctrines than it would have been had his values been more oriented toward a capitalistic economic and political system.

The way in which attitude change occurs depends upon the particular function that the attitude serves. Under conditions of compliance, a favorable reaction by the influencing agent is crucial to the maintenance of the attitude. If the favorable reaction were altered or supplanted by another agent, presumably the attitude would change. For example, if the secret police in Russia had been disbanded, it is very possible that some of the people Fischer describes as being afraid to criticize the Soviet regime might have spoken out against it once again. Or, if they had been convinced that they would not be punished, they might have been more open about their actual attitudes.

In the case of the identification process, attitude change occurs either when the person with whom one has identified changes his own attitude, in which case the identifier will change in a similar manner, or when "being like" the other person is no longer satisfying. Fischer reports such an instance: "The communists and their fellow-travellers had denounced anybody who predicted a Soviet-Nazi agreement; they said it was inconceivable. On the eve of its signing, they heatedly refused to believe it. When it became official, they defended it. They defended it because they automatically defend everything Moscow does" (p. 224-225).

These people had apparently identified with the communist leaders in Russia, and when the leadership expressed its new attitude toward Nazi Germany, their attitudes changed accordingly.

Finally, an internalized attitude can change when the person becomes aware that it is not consistent with the value system he espouses. Fischer opposed dictatorship and international aggression. As a result, the signing of the Soviet-Nazi Pact in 1939 was too much of an inconsistency for him to bear, and he became "officially" disenchanted with the Soviet system.

Learning Theory and Attitude Change

A second major approach to the study of attitude change focuses on principles and explanations derived from a learning theory approach to behavior as found in general experimental psychology. Hovland and his associates have been the main proponents of this orientation. They make predictions about attitude development and change on the basis of well-known psychological principles of learning. For example, Hovland and others have conducted several studies of the effect of primacy and recency on attitude change: If two sides of an argument are presented, is an individual likely to be influenced more by the first presentation or by the second? This question can be derived directly from studies of proactive and retroactive inhibition and facilitation: To what extent does learning one set of facts help or hinder learning a second set of facts? Which set will be remembered better? What are the contingencies determining which set will be retained better?

Unfortunately, the learning theory approach lacks a clear, concise statement of its basic tenets. Perhaps the most expedient way of describing the nature of the approach is to provide a summary of the initial comprehensive work in this tradition — Hovland, Janis, and Kelley's *Communication and Persuasion* (1953).

In this monograph the authors report on research concerned with four major aspects of attitude change: (1) the communicator or source of new information about an object of an attitude; (2) the nature of the communication, subdivided into appeals to the audience's motives and the organization of the arguments; (3) audience predispositions, subdivided into the predisposition to conform to particular groups and individual personality factors; and (4) responses of the audience to the communication, subdivided into overt expression of acceptance of the new opinion and degree of retention of opinion change. The authors note that these are the four basic aspects of any persuasive procedure: Who says what to whom with what effect. However, they also fit neatly into a learning theory framework. The first two, the communicator and the communication, are aspects of the stimulus that is presented to a person or an audience and that, modified by characteristics or predispositions of the audience, leads to certain responses by the audience.

Beginning with the first aspect of the stimulus, the source of a communication, Hovland, Janis, and Kelley show that characteristics of the source can affect attitude change by presenting studies (Hovland and Mandell, 1952; Hovland and Weiss, 1951; Kelman and Hovland, 1953; Weiss, 1953) of the credibility of the communicator. Credibility was considered in two respects — expertness and trustworthiness of the person or medium presenting an appeal to an audience. The basic design of the studies was to present to two different groups of subjects the same magazine or newspaper article but to attribute them to sources that differ in their credibility. For example, one group might be told that an article evaluating the United States educational system appeared in *Pravda,* while a second group is told that this article appeared in the *Harvard Educational Review.*

The results of the studies described were that sources low in credibility were perceived by audiences as being more biased in their appeal than those high in credibility. Thus, sources high in credibility had significantly greater immediate effect than those low in credibility, although this difference in effect disappeared when subjects' change in attitude was measured four weeks later. Finally, subsequent analyses confirmed that these effects were the result of differences in credibility rather than of differences in such factors as amount of attention paid to or understanding of the material presented.

Turning to the second aspect of the stimulus, Hovland, Janis, and Kelley consider two different ways in which motivational aspects of the communication itself can affect attitude change. The first of these, arousing fear through the communication, draws extensively on an investigation by Janis and Feshbach (1953). The experimenters presented high school students with three forms of a communication — an illustrated lecture on dental hygiene — that differed in the degree of appeal to the fears of the audience. Strong appeals to fear were characterized by references to the pain from toothaches and the secondary diseases that can be instigated by poor condition of teeth. Weak appeals referred to cavities and discoloration of teeth.

The results of the study show that the minimal appeal to fear had much greater positive effects in producing change in dental hygiene, much less of an emotional effect on the audience, and much greater resistance to counter-propaganda than did the moderate or strong appeals. The authors attribute the lack of effectiveness of maximal appeals to fear to the high degree of emotion aroused in the recipients of the communication, which leads them to ignore the importance of the threat.

A second motivational variable reported is salience of group norms. Kelley's (1955) study was used to illustrate the effect that heightened awareness of one's group membership has on resistance to persuasion counter to the group's norms. Specifically, he gave one group of Catholic students neutral reading material and another group material designed to increase the salience of their church membership. Then the students were subjected to persuasive arguments counter to the norms of the Catholic Church. Generally, students for whom salience was high were more resistant to the counterarguments than were those for whom salience was low.

The general organization of the communication to an audience was considered in several respects. Hovland and Mandell (1952), for example, found that students who received an argument in which the conclusions were explicitly drawn changed their attitudes more than those for whom conclusions were not drawn. Further theoretical discussion was made about the relative effects of drawing or not drawing conclusions when the arguments are simple rather than complex, when the audience is more rather than less intelligent, and when it is more rather than less ego-involved in the topic being argued.

Presenting one-sided versus two-sided arguments was investigated in a series of studies. In one (Lumsdaine and Janis, 1953), the experimenters conclude that giving people advance rationales (two-sided presentation) for disregarding later counterpropaganda is more effective in producing sustained attitude change than when no such preparation (one-sided presentation) is given. Other examples of research suggest that one-sided and two-sided presentations differentially affect the acceptance of the implications of subsequent information (Janis, Lumsdaine, and Gladstone, 1951) and that, in general, people of higher intelligence are more persuaded by two-sided arguments than they are by one-sided arguments (Hovland, Lumsdaine, and Sheffield, 1949).

Hovland, Janis, and Kelley describe several analyses of two types of variables having to do with the characteristics of the audience receiving persuasive communications. The first type that they consider is individual differences in desire to belong to groups to which a communication is relevant. Kelley and Volkart (1952), for example, investigated the amount of resistance to attitude change among Boy Scouts who valued their membership in the organization to varying degrees. They found that those Scouts who most valued their membership were most resistant to arguments contrary to the norms of the Scout organization.

The second variable that they analyzed is the personal persuasibility of the recipient of a communication. Most of the early research (for example, Janis, 1954) was concerned with discovering the personality characteristics that make one person generally more persuasible than another. Among other factors, low self-esteem, a low incidence of neurotic anxiety and obsessional symptoms, and a high degree of depression and inhibition of aggression have been found to be associated with high persuasibility. Hovland and Janis' *Personality and Persuasibility* (1959) is devoted entirely to reports of extensive research on this topic.

Turning to response variables, Hovland, Janis, and Kelley discuss two: (1) the effects of active participation or involvement in the process of persuasion on the acceptance of the persuasive communication, and (2) the length of time that acceptance of the communication will persist. Active participation in the process essentially involves having the individual express arguments on an issue in favor of the side with which he disagrees. This can take such forms as having the person role-play (for example, having a representative of the management of a business act as if he were a union steward in a bargaining session, which often results in an increase in his "understanding" of the workers' point of view) or merely having him write an essay advocating a point of view to which he is opposed. Generally, studies of this variable have found that people who actively participate in ways such as these are more willing to accept the arguments that they have been forced or asked to espouse than are those who are passively exposed to the arguments. There are a number of qualifying factors involved, however. For example, studies by Kelman (1953) and by Janis and King (1954) suggest that the greater the amount of improvisation the individual includes in his participation, the more he accepts the point of view that he has espoused.

Hovland, Janis, and Kelley's discussion of the duration of the effects of persuasion considers primarily the incidental finding in some studies that opinion change *increases* over time — a phenomenon they call the "sleeper effect." This became evident in the Hovland and Weiss (1951) study comparing the effects on attitude change of communicators high and low in credibility; the initially minimal change effected by the source low in credibility increased over a four-week span, essentially equalizing the effect that sources high and low in credibility had on the subjects' attitudes. A study by Kelman and Hovland (1953) suggests that this phenomenon should be attributed to a dissociation of the source and the content of the persuasive message; for subjects reminded of the source of the argument three weeks after its initial presentation, the "sleeper effect" disappeared.

Many studies derived from the learning theory approach to attitude change can be found in a series of monographs published by Hovland and his associates at Yale (Hovland and Janis, 1959; Rosenberg, Hovland, McGuire, Abelson, and Brehm, 1960). An article from one of these monographs appears later in this volume. Another paper by Hovland also appears in which he presents a critical evaluation of methods used in most studies of attitude change and specifically compares, and attempts to resolve the discrepancies between, the results of studies using real issues in real-life situations (such as studies of voting behavior) and studies conducted in the relatively artificial laboratory setting.

Perceptual Theory and Attitude Change

A third approach to attitude change concerns the individual's perception of the object, person, or idea that he is evaluating. Asch (1952) and Sherif and Sherif (1956) have been major proponents of this orientation. They suggest that attitude change is primarily a reinterpretation or redefinition of the object of the attitude. This approach is illustrated by the following statement by Louis Fischer: "At the time, I did not realize that Stalin's bad taste and the GPU's [secret police's] bad behavior were deadly germs. I thought they were sores on a healthy body which was building new cities and creating new values. I thought the favorable was fundamental and the unfavorable ephemeral. Hope distorted judgment. Seeing did not interfere with believing" (p. 213). Fischer is saying, in essence, that *now* he sees "Stalin's bad taste and the GPU's bad behavior" as fundamental defects in the system. He has changed one of the characteristics of the object of his attitude — its degree of fundamentalness. He now judges these objects in terms of this new characteristic, so that the bad taste and the bad behavior are for him qualitatively different from what they were.

No article on the perceptual theory of attitude change appears in this volume primarily because of the absence of a clear, concise statement of its basic principles.

The Consistency Principle and Attitude Change

The application of the consistency principle to the analysis of attitudes began with Heider's (1946) statement on attitude and cognitive organization. His formulation was framed in terms of the relationship between three elements, person P, other person O, and object X, all from the point of view of person P. There are four possible ways in which P's perception of the relationship between himself, another person, and an object could be consistent, or *balanced* (see Figure 1): (1) P likes O, P likes X, and P perceives that O likes X (for example, P sees that he and his friend like the same movie); (2) P likes O, P does not like X, and P perceives that O does not like X (P sees that he and his friend dislike the same movie); (3) P does not like O, P likes X, and O does not like X (P sees that he and his enemy disagree about the merits of a movie); (4) P does not like O, P does not like X, and O likes X (this is the same as (3) except that who likes and who dislikes the movie are reversed). In all four of these cases, the system P-O-X is balanced, so that there is no motivation to change any of the relations among the elements.

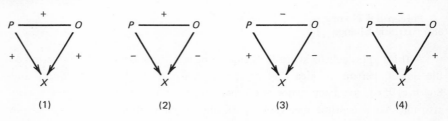

Figure 1

Were two friends to disagree about an object (P likes O and X but perceives that O does not like X), or were two enemies to agree about an object (P does not like O, likes X, and perceives that O likes X), then the system would be unbalanced. Thus, there would be a tendency for P to change one or more of the relationships so as to achieve balance. In a system in which a person perceives that he and his friend disagree about an object, balance would be attained if the person altered his attitude or perceived that his friend had altered his attitude toward the object so that they now agreed. Basically, according to Heider, balance exists when the signs in a triad (P-O-X) are all positive or when two are negative; imbalance exists when one or all three signs are negative.

Following Heider's original statement, a series of balance theories appeared that served to extend and refine his original ideas. Newcomb's (1953) theory of *symmetry* is an attempt to account for the development of *inter*personal relationships. He considers the actual relationship between two people's attitudes toward an object rather than the relationship from one person's point of view. Newcomb suggests that imbalance leads to a "strain toward symmetry," which results in communication between the two people about the object.

On the basis of his model, Newcomb tested predictions about the effects of symmetry and asymmetry on the relationships between people and on the attitudes they hold toward various objects (Newcomb, 1961). Specifically, he analyzed the development of friendships in a boardinghouse inhabited by transfer students who were, at first meeting, strangers to one another. His initial prediction was that the greater the agreement between two people (P and O)[1] about a series of objects (Xs), the greater would be their attraction to each other. He predicted further that once the P-O friendships were established, the strain that persisted because of the remaining disagreements about some Xs would be resolved in one or both of two ways: (1) by changes in P's or O's attitudes toward these Xs (over time, P and O would come to agree even more than they had originally), and (2) by distortions in P's and O's perception of the other's attitudes toward these Xs (over time, P and O would perceive themselves to be more in agreement than they really were). The results of Newcomb's study supported these hypotheses and helped to establish the value of consistency theories in studies of attitude change.

Cartwright and Harary (1956) and Harary (1959) noted some limitations of Heider's model and attempted to treat them in terms of a mathematical theory of linear graphs. The application of graph theory allowed the two researchers to treat systems of any number of elements, not just the three used by Heider. They accomplished this by using "cycles." A cycle is begun at any given element, follows a path of relations through at least two other elements, and ultimately returns to the starting point. For example, let us consider four people, A, B, C, and D, and the relations among them. Figure 2 (1) depicts this system when all four like one another. There are five cycles in this system:

[1]Newcomb uses the letters A and B to refer to people in his model. To avoid confusion and remain consistent with Heider, we have substituted P and O.

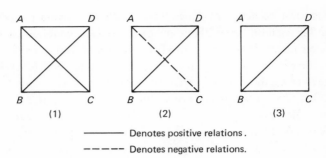

Denotes positive relations.
Denotes negative relations.

Figure 2

A-B-C-D, A-B-C, A-C-D, B-C-D, and A-B-D. In the total system comprised by A, B, C, and D, only these five cycles exist because no cycles may overlap completely; D-A-C is merely a duplication of A-C-D.

In addition to treating any number of elements, a second advantage of the graph model is that it allows one to consider "degrees of balance," which are defined as the proportion of cycles in balance relative to the total number of cycles possible. A balanced cycle is one in which there are an even number of negative relations or no negative relations. (This is essentially the same as Heider's definition.) Consider the four people in Figure 2 (2). Two of them, A and C, do not like each other, while the others do. Two of the five cycles (A-B-C and A-C-D) are *not* balanced (one negative relation, A-C, in each), and the other three are. According to Cartwright and Harary, this system is 60 percent balanced, and there would be motivation to achieve a greater degree of balance one way or another.

A third advantage of the graph model is that a distinction is made between a *negative* relationship and *no* relationship — a distinction left unclear by Heider. Compare the situation depicted in Figure 2 (2) with that in Figure 2 (3). In the former, A and C dislike each other, whereas in the latter, A and C have no relationship (perhaps because they do not know each other or simply feel neutral toward each other). Making this distinction, Cartwright and Harary consider Situation 2 (2) to be only 60 percent balanced and Situation 2 (3) to be 100 percent balanced (all three cycles — A-B-C-D, A-B-D, and B-C-D — are balanced). Cartwright and Harary, therefore, contend there will be more discomfort or a greater motivation to change attitudes in Situation 2 (2) than in 2 (3).

These and other extensions and elaborations of Heider's original formulation have helped to make balance theory a viable, heuristic approach to attitude change. In addition, Cartwright and Harary have opened the door for the application of this approach to systems other than the cognitive systems that were the original focus of Heider's model. For example, one can see that Cartwright and Harary's model can be applied to the analysis of cliques. Newcomb has already begun studies of social systems, as was noted in the description of his research on the formation of friendships.

Abelson and Rosenberg. Another important extension of basic balance theory has been presented by Abelson and Rosenberg (1958). They use a model based on matrix algebra to consider systems including more than three elements and have suggested an analysis that allows one to predict with some accuracy what relations will change in an unbalanced system (Rosenberg and Abelson, 1960).

Rosenberg (1960a) has extended the idea of consistency to the analysis of the relations between the affective and cognitive *components* of a *single* attitude. He postulates that if a person feels very positively about an object, he should also believe strongly that this object leads to or is positively associated with his basic values. Conversely, if a person believes that a given object leads to or is positively associated with his basic values, then he should feel very positive toward that object. The latter postulate is seen in Fischer's affiliation with Russian communism. His affiliation developed because he perceived the Soviet system as being potentially capable of attaining goals that he held dear: "I liked the Soviets because they were an experiment in the interest of the downtrodden majority, because they destroyed the privileges of the powerful few . . ." (p. 205).

Rosenberg's idea of the "structural consistency" of one attitude differs from the usual approach to consistency among various attitudes. One of Rosenberg's articles outlining his approach appears later in this volume. It should also be noted that his formulation has many similarities to the functional approach, described earlier. The idea that consistency occurs because an object leads to the attainment of one's values is basically a statement about the function of that object.

Osgood and Tannenbaum. Osgood and Tannenbaum's (1955) theory of *congruity* represents an attempt to *quantify* the relations between elements. The elements in their system are an *object* of an attitude, a *source* of information about that object, and an *assertion* by a source about the object. The definition of "congruity" is similar to the definition of "balance": the existence of two or no negative relations among the three elements. Hence, a negative statement by a positively evaluated source about a negatively evaluated object is congruent, whereas a positive assertion by the same positive source about a negatively evaluated object is incongruent. A good example of congruence can be seen in

Fischer's comment about conservative and reactionary opposition to the Soviet system. A negative source (conservatives and reactionaries) is making a negative assertion (opposition) about a positive object (the Soviet system). This is congruent for Fischer. Laudatory comments by conservatives and reactionaries about the Soviets would have been incongruent for him and thus would have made him uncomfortable.

Osgood and Tannenbaum postulate that change will occur when incongruity exists, and they attempt to predict the direction and amount of this change. Their model was developed primarily for use in the analysis of attitude change when new information (an assertion) is received by a person. Using this model, they have demonstrated empirically that quantification of attitude change is a realistic possibility. The article by Osgood and Tannenbaum that appears later in this volume presents a more specific statement of their model and includes examples of their research.

McGuire. McGuire (1960 a, b) has also attempted to quantify attitude change. His theory proposes two processes of consistency. First, some attitudes will be consistent according to the rules of logic. For example, if a man knows that a car has the best engine available and if he likes cars that perform well, he should have a positive attitude toward that particular car. Second, some attitudes will be consistent with "wishful thinking." For example, if a boy loves a girl, he is likely to evaluate most of her characteristics very positively, to the point of distorting reality to conform to what he "wishes" she were like.

McGuire suggests that the individual attempts to resolve discrepancies between attitudes based on wishful thinking and those based on logical relations between objects. Fischer provides an excellent example of inconsistency between two propositions. Logical thinking led him to perceive "Stalin's bad taste and the GPU's [secret police's] bad behavior" as indications of flaws in the Soviet system. Wishful thinking led him to believe that "building new cities and creating new values" were fundamental assets of the system. How such inconsistencies are resolved depends on the relative importance of each of these propositions. McGuire attempts to quantify the differential importance of inconsistent propositions and thereby to predict the nature of the resolution of the inconsistency. Apparently, the proposition based on wishful thinking was more important than the other in this comment by Fischer: "I thought the favorable was fundamental and the unfavorable ephemeral. Hope distorted judgment. Seeing did not interfere with believing" (p. 213). The inconsistency was resolved by calling one proposition "fundamental" and the other "ephemeral."

An article presenting McGuire's theoretical framework and research on inducing resistance to attitude change, which differs from the approach presented in this section, appears later in this volume.

Festinger's theory of cognitive dissonance. The last consistency theory to be reviewed here is Festinger's (1957) theory of cognitive dissonance, perhaps the one that is best known and that has stimulated the most research. The elements in his theory tend to be propositions, such as "Smoking causes cancer" and "I smoke," rather than definitive statements of evaluation of objects, such as "I like Bill." Two objects or propositions are dissonant when one implies the opposite of the other. Often these implications demand logical translation or assumptions by the holder of the attitude. For example, the statements "I just traded my old car for a new one" and "My old car is better than my new one" are dissonant because, presumably, one trades in an old car only if one is dissatisfied with it and/or feels the new one is better. Because the second statement ("My old car is better") does not conform to such logic, it produces dissonance, which, according to Festinger, results in a drive to reduce the discomfort that dissonance causes the person.

Festinger feels that dissonance arises when decisions are made. Making a decision between various alternatives results in dissonance to the extent that the alternative chosen has negative features and the alternatives rejected have positive features. For example, if one has to choose between two equally valued college courses, greater dissonance will exist than if the choice is between a highly and a lowly valued course.

Festinger and some of his associates (Festinger, 1957, 1964; Brehm and Cohen, 1962) have suggested various ways in which dissonance may be reduced, which can be described with some illustrations from Fischer's treatise. Dissonance may be reduced *cognitively.* Fischer notes that once his pro-Soviet choice was made, he attempted to resolve the dissonance created by the negative features of his choice: "Developments which seemed detrimental to Russia were regarded as ephemeral, dishonestly interpreted, or canceled out by more significant and countervailing developments" (p. 205). Dissonance may also be reduced *behaviorally.* A second way in which Fischer attempted to resolve the dissonance resulting from his pro-Soviet decision was to act so as to seal the commitment. He and his family moved to Moscow, and he wrote articles in partisan magazines. Finally, dissonance may be reduced by *selective exposure* to information about the dissonant elements. Fischer helped to maintain his faith in the progress promised by Soviet communism by making frequent visits to construction sites of dams, power stations, and factories. In a sense, he was selectively exposing himself to scenes that supported his view of the assets of the Soviet system.

A more extensive exposition of dissonance theory and research is presented later in this volume.

Organization of the Book

This volume is designed to consider the major theoretical approaches to the study of attitude change. In this chapter, we have attempted to present an introduction to the theme of the book and to lay the groundwork for an understanding of the articles that follow. In doing so, we have not treated a number of important empirical issues. Examples of some issues in the study of attitude change that have not been assimilated into a particular theoretical approach and that are not treated here are the effect of distraction, the order of arguments in persuasive communication, and the measurement of attitudes. The selection of articles was predicated by our desire to present representatives of the major theoretical approaches to the study of attitude change and a sample of the research emanating from these approaches.

The functional approach to attitude change is represented by Katz's (1960) statement and is followed by illustrative research by Katz, Sarnoff, and McClintock (1956).

The consistency theories are represented by a chapter on dissonance theory and a review of some of the most significant research derived from that theory, by Osgood and Tannenbaum's (1955) theoretical formulation and supporting research, and by Rosenberg's (1960a) analysis of consistency between affective and cognitive elements of attitudes.

The learning theory approach is presented in an article by Janis and Hovland (1959) and in research by Elms and Janis (1965), which is followed by a comment by Brehm (1965). Also included is McGuire's (1964) theoretical formulation and research on producing resistance to attitude change, which differ from his two-process theory of attitudinal consistency, described earlier in this introduction.

Two additional articles appear. Bem (1965) presents a unique reinterpretation of dissonance theory, including a specific analysis of the most prominent studies cited as support for dissonance theory. And Hovland (1959) describes some disagreements in attitude research that he attributes to methodological differences between experimental and survey studies of attitude change.

2

The Functional Approach to the Study of Attitudes

Daniel Katz

This is the foremost statement of the functional approach to the study of attitude change. Katz asserts that attitudes can perform four major functions for the personality of the individual. His analysis indicates that knowing the functional basis and dynamics of an attitude suggests the procedures most likely to lead to a change in that attitude. The value of this excerpt lies in Katz's detailed discussion of attitude change as it relates to attitudes based on each of the four functions that he specifies.*

Four Functions Which Attitudes Perform For The Individual

The major functions which attitudes perform for the personality can be grouped according to their motivational basis as follows:

1. *The instrumental, adjustive, or utilitarian functions* upon which Jeremy Bentham and the utilitarians constructed their model of man. A modern expression of this approach can be found in behavioristic learning theory.

2. *The ego-defensive function* in which the person protects himself from acknowledging the basic truths about himself or the harsh realities in his external world. Freudian psychology and neo-Freudian thinking have been preoccupied with this type of motivation and its outcomes.

3. *The value-expressive function* in which the individual derives satisfactions from expressing attitudes appropriate to his personal values and to his concept of himself. This function is central to doctrines of ego psychology which stress the importance of self-expression, self-development, and self-realization.

*The paper following this editorial introduction is excerpted from D. Katz, The functional approach to the study of attitudes, *Public Opinion Quarterly*, 1960, *24*, 163-204, by permission of the author and the publisher.

4. *The knowledge function* based upon the individual's need to give adequate structure to his universe. The search for meaning, the need to understand, the trend toward better organization of perceptions and beliefs to provide clarity and consistency for the individual, are other descriptions of this function. The development of principles about perceptual and cognitive structure have been the contribution of Gestalt psychology.

Stated simply, the functional approach is the attempt to understand the reasons people hold the attitudes they do. The reasons, however, are at the level of psychological motivations and not of the accidents of external events and circumstances. Unless we know the psychological need which is met by the holding of an attitude we are in a poor position to predict when and how it will change. Moreover, the same attitude expressed toward a political candidate may not perform the same function for all the people who express it. And while many attitudes are predominantly in the service of a single type of motivational process, as described above, other attitudes may serve more than one purpose for the individual. A fuller discussion of how attitudes serve the above four functions is in order.

1. The Adjustment Function

Essentially this function is a recognition of the fact that people strive to maximize the rewards in their external environment and to minimize the penalties. The child develops favorable attitudes toward the objects in his world which are associated with the satisfactions of his needs and unfavorable attitudes toward objects which thwart him or punish him. Attitudes acquired in the service of the adjustment function are either the means for reaching the desired goal or avoiding the undesirable one, or are affective associations based upon experiences in attaining motive satisfactions (Katz and Stotland, 1959). The attitudes of the worker favoring a political party which will advance his economic lot are an example of the first type of utilitarian attitude. The pleasant image one has of one's favorite food is an example of the second type of utilitarian attitude.

In general, then, the dynamics of attitude formation with respect to the adjustment function are dependent upon present or past perceptions of the utility of the attitudinal object for the individual. The clarity, consistency, and nearness of rewards and punishments, as they relate to the individual's activities and goals, are important factors in the acquisition of such attitudes. Both attitudes and habits are formed toward specific objects, people, and symbols as they satisfy specific needs. The closer these objects are to actual need satisfaction and the more they are clearly perceived as relevant to need satisfaction, the greater are the probabilities of positive attitude formation. These principles of attitude formation are often observed in the breach rather than the compliance. In industry, management frequently expects to create favorable attitudes toward job performance through programs for making the company more attractive to the worker, such as providing recreational facilities and fringe benefits. Such programs, however, are much more likely to produce favorable attitudes toward the company as a desirable place to work than toward performance on the job. The company benefits and advantages are applied across the board to all employees and are not specifically relevant to increased effort in task performance by the individual worker.

Consistency of reward and punishment also contributes to the clarity of the instrumental object for goal attainment. If a political party bestows recognition and favors on party workers in an unpredictable and inconsistent fashion, it will destroy the favorable evaluation of the importance of working hard for the party among those whose motivation is of the utilitarian sort. But, curiously, while consistency of reward needs to be observed, 100 per cent consistency is not as effective as a pattern which is usually consistent but in which there are some lapses. When animal or human subjects are invariably rewarded for a correct performance, they do not retain their learned responses as well as when the reward is sometimes skipped (Jenkins and Stanley, 1950).

2. The Ego-Defensive Function

People not only seek to make the most of their external world and what it offers, but they also expend a great deal of their energy on living with themselves. The mechanisms by which the individual protects his ego from his own unacceptable impulses and from the knowledge of threatening forces from without, and the methods by which he reduces his anxieties created by such problems, are known as mechanisms of ego defense. A more complete account of their origin and nature will be found in Sarnoff (1960). They include the devices by which the individual avoids facing either the inner reality of the kind of person he is, or the outer reality of the dangers the world holds for him. They stem basically from internal conflict with its resulting insecurities. In one sense the mechanisms of defense are adaptive in temporarily removing the sharp edges of conflict and in saving the individual from complete disaster. In another sense they are not adaptive in that they handicap the individual in his social adjustments and in obtaining the maximum satisfactions available to him from the world in which he lives. The worker who persistently quarrels with his boss and with his fellow workers, because he is acting out some of his own internal conflicts, may in this manner relieve himself of some of the emotional tensions which beset him. He is not, however, solving his problem of adjusting to his work situation and thus may deprive himself of advancement or even of steady employment.

Defense mechanisms, Miller and Swanson (1960) point out, may be classified into two families on the basis of the more or less primitive nature of the devices employed. The first family, more primitive in nature, are more socially handicapping and consist of denial and complete avoidance. The individual in such cases obliterates through withdrawal and denial the realities which confront him. The exaggerated case of such primitive mechanisms is the fantasy world of the paranoiac. The second type of defense is less handicapping and makes for distortion rather than denial. It includes rationalization, projection, and displacement.

Many of our attitudes have the function of defending our self-image. When we cannot admit to ourselves that we have deep feelings of inferiority we may project those feelings onto some convenient minority group and bolster our egos by attitudes of superiority toward this underprivileged group. The formation of such defensive attitudes differs in essential ways from the formation of attitudes which serve the adjustment function. They proceed from within the person, and the objects and situation to which they are attached are merely convenient outlets for their expression. Not all targets are equally satisfactory for a given defense mechanism, but the point is that the attitude is not created by the target but by the individual's emotional conflicts. And when no convenient target exists the individual will create one. Utilitarian attitudes, on the other hand, are formed with specific reference to the nature of the attitudinal object. They are thus appropriate to the nature of the social world to which they are geared. The high school student who values high grades because he wants to be admitted to a good college has a utilitarian attitude appropriate to the situation to which it is related.

All people employ defense mechanisms, but they differ with respect to the extent that they use them and some of their attitudes may be more defensive in function than others. It follows that the techniques and conditions for attitude change will not be the same for ego-defensive as for utilitarian attitudes.

Moreover, though people are ordinarily unaware of their defense mechanisms, especially at the time of employing them, they differ with respect to the amount of insight they may show at some later time about their use of defenses. In some cases they recognize that they have been protecting their egos without knowing the reason why. In other cases they may not even be aware of the devices they have been using to delude themselves.

3. The Value-Expressive Function

While many attitudes have the function of preventing the individual from revealing to himself and others his true nature, other attitudes have the function of giving positive expression to his central values and to the type of person he conceives himself to be. A man may consider himself to be an enlightened conservative or an internationalist or a liberal, and will hold attitudes which are the appropriate indication of his central values. Thus we need to take account of the fact that not all behavior has the negative function of reducing the tensions of biological drives or of internal conflicts. Satisfactions also accrue to the person from the expression of attitudes which reflect his cherished beliefs and his self-image. The reward to the person in these instances is not so much a matter of gaining social recognition or monetary rewards as of establishing his self-identity and confirming his notion of the sort of person he sees himself to be. The gratifications obtained from value expression may go beyond the confirmation of self-identity. Just as we find satisfaction in the exercise of our talents and abilities, so we find reward in the expression of any attributes associated with our egos.

Value-expressive attitudes not only give clarity to the self-image but also mold that self-image closer to the heart's desire. The teenager who by dress and speech establishes his identity as similar to his own peer group may appear to the outsider a weakling and a craven conformer. To himself he is asserting his independence of the adult world to which he has rendered child-like sub-servience and conformity all his life. Very early in the development of the personality the need for clarity of self-image is important — the need to know "who I am." Later it may be even more important to know that in some measure I am the type of person I want to be. Even as adults, however, the clarity and stability of the self-image is of primary significance. Just as the kind, considerate person will cover over his acts of selfishness, so too will the ruthless individualist become confused and embarrassed by his acts of sympathetic compassion. One reason it is difficult to change the character of the adult is that he is not comfortable with the new "me." Group support for such personality change is almost a necessity, as in Alcoholics Anonymous, so that the individual is aware of approval of his new self by people who are like him.

The socialization process during the formative years sets the basic outlines for the individual's self-concept. Parents constantly hold up before the child the model of the good character they want him to be. A good boy eats his spinach, does not hit girls, etc. The candy and the stick are less in evidence in training the child than the constant appeal to his notion of his own character. It is small wonder, then, that children reflect the acceptance of this model by inquiring about the characters of the actors in every drama, whether it be a television play, a political contest, or a war, wanting to know who are the "good guys" and who are the "bad guys." Even as adults we persist in labeling others in the terms of such character images. Joe McCarthy and his cause collapsed in fantastic fashion when the telecast of the Army hearings showed him in the role of the villain attacking the gentle, good man represented by Joseph Welch.

A related but somewhat different process from childhood socialization takes place when individuals enter a new group or organization. The individual will often take over and internalize the values of the group. What accounts, however, for the fact that sometimes this occurs and sometimes it does not? Four factors are probably operative, and some combination of them may be necessary for internalization. (1) The value of the new group may be highly consistent with existing values central to the personality. The girl who enters the nursing profession finds it congenial to consider herself a good nurse because of previous values of the importance of contributing to the welfare of others. (2) The new group may in its ideology have a clear model of what the good group member should be like and may persistenty indoctrinate group members in these terms. One of the reasons for the code of conduct for members of the armed forces, devised after the revelations about the conduct of American prisoners in the Korean War, was to attempt to establish a model for what a good soldier does and does not do. (3) The activities of the group in moving toward its goal permit the individual genuine opportunity for participation. To become ego-involved so that he can internalize group values, the new member must find one of two conditions. The group activity open to him must tap his talents and abilities so that his chance to show what he is worth can be tied into the group effort. Or else the activities of the group must give him an active voice in group decisions. His particular talents and abilities may not be tapped but he does have the opportunity to enter into group decisions, and thus his need for self-determination is satisfied. He then identifies with the group in which such opportunities for ego-involvement are available. It is not necessary that opportunities for self-expression and self-determination be of great magnitude in an objective sense, so long as they are important for the psychological economy of the individuals themselves. (4) Finally, the individual may come to see himself as a group member if he can share in the rewards of group activity which includes his own efforts. The worker may not play much of a part in building a ship or make any decisions in the process of building it. Nevertheless, if he and his fellow workers are given a share in every boat they build and a return on the proceeds from the earnings of the ship, they may soon come to identify with the ship-building company and see themselves as builders of ships.

4. The Knowledge Function

Individuals not only acquire beliefs in the interest of satisfying various specific needs, they also seek knowledge to give meaning to what would otherwise be an unorganized chaotic universe. People need standards or frames of reference for understanding their world, and attitudes help to supply such standards. The problem of understanding, as John Dewey (1910) made clear years ago, is one "of introducing (1) *definiteness* and *distinction* and (2) *consistency* and *stability* of meaning into what is otherwise vague and wavering." The definiteness and stability are provided in good measure by the norms of our culture, which give the otherwise perplexed individual ready-made attitudes for comprehending his universe. Walter Lippmann's (1922) classical contribution to the study of opinions and attitudes was his description of stereotypes and the way they provided order and clarity for a bewildering set of complexities. The most interesting finding in Herzog's (1944) familiar study of the gratifications obtained by housewives in listening to daytime serials was the unsuspected role of information and advice. The stories were liked "because they explained things to the inarticulate listener."

The need to know does not of course imply that people are driven by a thirst for universal knowledge. The American public's appalling lack of political information has been documented many times. In 1956, for example, only 13 percent of the people in Detroit could correctly name the two United States Senators from the state of Michigan and only 18 percent knew the name of their own Congressman (Katz and Eldersveld, 1961). People are not avid seekers after knowledge as judged by what the educator or social reformer would desire. But they do want to understand the events which impinge directly on their own life. Moreover, many of the attitudes they have already acquired give them sufficient basis for interpreting much of what they perceive to be important for them. Our already existing stereotypes, in Lippmann's language, "are an ordered, more or less consistent picture of the world, to which our habits, our tastes, our capacities, our comforts and our hopes have adjusted themselves. They may not be a complete picture of the world, but they are a picture of a possible world to which we are adapted" (1922, p. 95). It follows that new information will not modify old attitudes unless there is some inadequacy or incompleteness or inconsistency in the existing attitudinal structure as it relates to the perceptions of new situations.

Determinants of Attitude
Arousal and Attitude Change

The problems of attitude arousal and of attitude change are separate problems. The first has to do with the fact that the individual has many predispositions to act and many influences playing upon him. Hence we need a more precise description of the appropriate conditions which will evoke a given attitude. The second problem is that of specifying the factors which will help to predict the modification of different types of attitude.

The most general statement that can be made concerning attitude arousal is that it is dependent upon the excitation of some need in the individual, or some relevant cue in the environment. When a man grows hungry, he talks of food. Even when not hungry he may express favorable attitudes toward a preferred food if an external stimulus cues him. The ego-defensive person who hates foreigners will express such attitudes under conditions of increased anxiety or threat or when a foreigner is perceived to be getting out of place.

The most general statement that can be made about the conditions conducive to attitude change is that the expression of the old attitude or its anticipated expression no longer gives satisfaction to its related need state. In other words, it no longer serves its function and the individual feels blocked or frustrated. Modifying an old attitude or replacing it with a new one is a process of learning, and learning always starts with a problem, or being thwarted in coping with a situation. Being blocked is a necessary, but not a sufficient, condition for attitude change. Other factors must be operative and will vary in effectiveness depending upon the function involved.

Arousing and Changing
Utilitarian Attitudes

Political parties have both the problem of converting people with antagonistic attitudes (attitude change) and the problem of mobilizing the support of their own followers (attitude arousal). To accomplish the latter they attempt to revive the needs basic to old attitudes. For example, the Democrats still utilize the appeals of the New Deal and the Republicans still talk of the balanced budget. The assumption is that many people still hold attitudes acquired in earlier circumstances and that appropriate communication can reinstate the old needs. For most people, however, utilitarian needs are reinforced by experience and not by verbal appeals. Hence invoking the symbols of the New Deal will be relatively ineffective with respect to adjustive attitudes unless there are corresponding experiences with unemployment, decreased income, etc. Though the need state may not be under the control of the propagandist, he can exaggerate or minimize its importance. In addition to playing upon states of need, the propagandist can make perceptible the old cues associated with the attitude he is trying to elicit. These cues may have associated with them favorable affect, or feeling, though the related needs are inactive. For example, the fighters for old causes can be paraded across the political platform in an attempt to arouse the attitudes of the past.

The two basic conditions, then, for the arousal of existing attitudes are the activation of their relevant need states and the perception of the appropriate cues associated with the content of the attitude.

To change attitudes which serve a utilitarian function, one of two conditions must prevail: (1) the attitude and the activities related to it no longer provide the satisfactions they once did, or (2) the individual's level of aspiration has been raised. The Chevrolet owner who had positive attitudes toward his old car may now want a more expensive car commensurate with his new status.

Attitudes toward political parties and voting behavior are often difficult to change if there is no widespread dissatisfaction with economic conditions and international relations. Currently, however, the polls show that even Republicans in the age group over sixty are worried about increased costs of medical care and the general inadequacy of retirement incomes. Thus many old people may change their political allegiance, if it becomes clear that the Democratic Party can furnish a program to take care of their needs.

Again the mass media play a role secondary to direct experience in changing attitudes directly related to economic matters. Once dissatisfaction exists, they can exert a potent influence in suggesting new ways of solving the problem. In the field of international affairs, mass media have a more primary role because in times of peace most people have no direct experience with other countries or their peoples. The threat of war comes from what they read, hear, or see in the mass media.

The area of freedom for changing utilitarian attitudes is of course much greater in dealing with methods of satisfying needs than with needs themselves. Needs change more slowly than the means for gratifying them, even though one role of the advertiser is to create new needs. Change in attitudes occurs more readily when people perceive that they can accomplish their objectives through revising existing attitudes. Integration of white and Negro personnel in the armed forces came to pass partly because political leaders and military leaders perceived that such a move would strengthen our fighting forces. And one of the powerful arguments for changing our attitudes toward Negroes is that in the struggle for world democracy we need to put our own house in order to present a more convincing picture of our own society to other countries. Carlson (1956) has experimentally demonstrated that discriminatory attitudes toward minority groups can be altered by showing the relevance of more positive beliefs to such individual goals and values as American international prestige and democratic equalitarianism.

Just as attitudes formed in the interests of adjustment can be negative evaluations of objects associated with avoidance of the harmful effects of the environment, so too can attitudes change because of unpleasant experiences or anticipation of harmful consequences. The more remote the cause of one's suffering the more likely he is to seize upon a readily identifiable target for his negative evaluation. Public officials, as highly visible objects, can easily be associated with states of dissatisfaction. Thus there is truth in the old observation that people vote more against the candidates they dislike than for the candidates they like. In the 1958 elections, in a period of mild recession, unemployment, and general uneasiness about atomic weapons, the incumbent governors (the more visible targets), whether Republican or Democratic, fared less well than the incumbent legislators.

The use of negative sanctions and of punishment to change utilitarian attitudes is more complex than the use of rewards. To be successful in changing attitudes and behavior, punishment should be used only when there is clearly available a course of action that will save the individual from the undesirable consequences. To arouse fear among the enemy in time of war does not necessarily result in desertion, surrender, or a disruption of the enemy war effort. Such channels of action may not be available to the people whose fears are aroused. The experiment of Janis and Feshbach (1953) in using fear appeals to coerce children into good habits of dental hygiene had the interesting outcome of a negative relationship between the amount of fear and the degree of change. Lurid pictures of the gangrene jaws of old people who had not observed good dental habits were not effective. Moreover, the group exposed to the strongest fear appeal was the most susceptible to counterpropaganda. One factor which helps to account for the results of this investigation was the lack of a clear-cut relation in the minds of the children between failure to brush their teeth in the prescribed manner and the pictures of the gangrene jaws of the aged.

The necessity of coupling fear appeals with clear channels of action is illustrated by a study of Nunnally and Bobren (1959). These investigators manipulated three variables in communications about mental health, namely, the relative amount of message anxiety, the degree to which messages gave apparent solutions, and the relative personal or impersonal phrasing of the message. The high-anxiety message described electric shock treatment of the psychotic in distressing detail. People showed the least willingness to receive communications that were high in anxiety, personalized, and offered no solutions. When solutions were offered in the communication, there was more willingness to accept the high-anxiety message.

The use of punishment and arousal of fear depend for their effectiveness upon the presence of well-defined paths for avoiding the punishment, i.e. negative sanctions are successful in redirecting rather than suppressing behavior. When there is no clearly perceptible relation between the punishment and the desired behavior, people may continue to behave as they did before, only now. they have negative attitudes toward the persons and objects associated with the negative sanctions. There is, however, another possibility, if the punishment is severe or if the individual is unusually sensitive. He may develop a defensive avoidance of the whole situation. His behavior, then, is not directed at solving the problem but at escaping from the situation, even if such escape has to be negotiated by absorbing extra punishment. The attitudes under discussion are those based upon the adjustive or utilitarian function, but if the individual is traumatized by a fearful experience he will shift from instrumental learning to defensive reactions.

Arousing and Changing
Ego-Defensive Attitudes

Attitudes which help to protect the individual from internally induced anxieties or from facing up to external dangers are readily elicited by any form of threat to the ego. The threat may be external, as in the case of a highly competitive situation, or a failure experience, or a derogatory remark. It is the stock in trade of demagogues to exaggerate the dangers confronting the people, for instance, Joe McCarthy's tactics with respect to Communists in the State Department. Many people have existing attitudes of withdrawal or of aggression toward deviants or out-groups based upon their ego-defensive needs. When threatened, these attitudes come into play, and defensive people either avoid the unpleasant situation entirely, as is common in the desegregation controversy, or exhibit hostility.

Another condition for eliciting the ego-defensive attitude is the encouragement given to its expression by some form of social support. The agitator may appeal to repressed hatred by providing moral justification for its expression. A mob leader before an audience with emotionally held attitudes toward Negroes may call out these attitudes in the most violent form by invoking the good of the community or the honor of white womanhood.

A third condition for the arousal of ego-defensive attitudes is the appeal to authority. The insecurity of the defensive person makes him particularly susceptible to authoritarian suggestion. When this type of authoritarian command is in the direction already indicated by his attitudes of antipathy toward other people, he responds quickly and joyously. It is no accident that movements of hate and aggression such as the Ku Klux Klan or the Nazi Party are authoritarian in their organized structure. Wagman (1955), in an experimental investigation of the use of authoritarian suggestion, found that students high in ego-defensiveness as measured by the F-scale were much more responsive to directives from military leaders than were less defensive students. In fact, the subjects low in defensiveness were not affected at all by authoritarian suggestion when this influence ran counter to their own attitudes. The subjects high in F-scores could be moved in either direction, although they moved more readily in the direction of their own beliefs.

A fourth condition for defensive arousal is the building up over time of inhibited drives in the individual, for example, repressed sex impulses. As the drive strength of forbidden impulses increases, anxiety mounts and release from tension is found in the expression of defensive attitudes. The deprivations of prison life, for example, build up tensions which can find expression in riots against the hated prison officials.

In other words, the drive strength for defensive reactions can be increased by situation frustration. Though the basic source is the long-standing internal conflict of the person, he can encounter additional frustration in immediate circumstances. Berkowitz (1959) has shown that anti-Semitic girls were more likely than less prejudiced girls to display aggression toward an innocent bystander when angered by a third person. In a subsequent experiment, Berkowitz and Holmes (1959) created dislike by one group of subjects for their partners by giving them electric shocks which they thought were administered by their partners. In a second session, subjects worked alone and were threatened by the experimenter. In a third session they were brought together with their partners for a cooperative task of problem solving. Aggression and hostility were displayed by subjects toward one another in the third session as a result of the frustration produced by the experimenter, and were directed more against the disliked partner than toward an innocuous partner.

Studies outside the laboratory have confirmed the principle that, where negative attitudes exist, frustration in areas unrelated to the attitude will increase the strength of the prejudice. Bettelheim and Janowitz (1950) found that war veterans who had suffered downward mobility were more anti-Semitic than other war veterans. In a secondary analysis of the data from the Elmira study, Greenblum and Pearlin (1953) report that the socially mobile people, whether upward or downward mobile, were more prejudiced against Jews and Negroes than were stationary people, provided that the socially mobile were insecure about their new status. Though it is clear in these studies that the situation frustration strengthens a negative attitude, it is not clear as to the origin of the negative attitude.

Most research on ego-defensive attitudes has been directed at beliefs concerning the undesirable character of minority groups or of deviants, with accompanying feelings of distrust, contempt, and hatred. Many ego-defensive attitudes, however, are not the projection of repressed aggression but are expressions of apathy or withdrawal. The individual protects himself from a difficult or demanding world and salvages his self-respect by retreating within his own shell. His attitudes toward political matters are anomic: "It does not make any difference to people like me which party is in power" or "There is no point in voting because I can't influence the outcome." Threat to people of this type takes the form of a complexity with which they cannot cope. Thus, they daydream when the lecturer talks about economic theories of inflation or the public official talks about disarmament proposals.

The usual procedures for changing attitudes and behavior have little positive effect upon attitudes geared into our ego defenses. In fact they may have a boomerang effect of making the individual cling more tenaciously to his emotionally held beliefs. In the category of usual procedures should be included increasing the flow of information, promising and bestowing rewards, and invoking penalties. As has already been indicated, punishment is threatening to the ego-defensive person and the increase of threat is the very condition which will feed ego-defensive behavior. The enuretic youngster with emotional problems is rarely cured by punishment. Teachers and coaches know that there are some children who respond to censure and punishment by persevering in the forbidden behavior. But what is not as well recognized is that reward is also not effective in modifying the actions of the ego-defensive person. His attitudes are an expression of his inner conflicts and are not susceptible to external rewards. The shopkeeper who will not serve Negroes because they are a well-fixated target for his aggressions will risk the loss of income incurred by his discriminatory reactions.

Three basic factors, however, can help change ego-defensive attitudes. In the first place, the removal of threat is a necessary though not a sufficient condition. The permissive and even supportive atmosphere which the therapist attempts to create for his patients is a special instance of the removal of threat. Where the ego-defensive behavior of the delinquent is supported by his group, the social worker must gain a measure of group acceptance so as not to be perceived as a threat by the individual gang members. An objective, matter-of-fact approach can serve to remove threat, especially in situations where people are accustomed to emotional appeals. Humor can also be used to establish a nonthreatening atmosphere, but it should not be directed against the audience or even against the problem. Cooper and Jahoda (1947) attempted to change prejudiced attitudes by ridicule, in the form of cartoons which made Mr. Biggott seem silly, especially when he rejected a blood transfusion which did not come from 100 percent Americans. Instead of changing their attitudes, the subjects in this experiment found ways of evading the meaning of the cartoons.

In the second place, catharsis or the ventilation of feelings can help to set the stage for attitude change. Mention has already been made of the building up of tension owing to the lack of discharge of inhibited impulses. When emotional tension is at a high level the individual will respond defensively and resist attempts to change him. Hence, providing him with opportunities to blow off steam may often be necessary before attempting a serious discussion of new possibilities of behavior. Again, humor can serve this purpose.

There are many practical problems in the use of catharsis, however, because of its complex relationship to other variables. In his review of the experimental work on the expression of hostility, Berkowitz (1958) reports more findings supporting than contradicting the catharsis hypothesis, but there is no clear agreement about the mechanisms involved. Under certain circumstances permitting emotional outbursts can act as a reward. In a gripe session to allow individuals to express their complaints, group members can reinforce one another's negative attitudes. Unless there are positive forces in the situation which lead to a serious consideration of the problem, the gripe session may have boomerang effects. The technique often employed is to keep the group in session long enough for the malcontents to get talked out so that more sober voices can be heard. Catharsis may function at two levels. It can operate to release or drain off energy of the moment, as in the above description. It can also serve to bring to the surface something of the nature of the conflict affecting the individual. So long as his impulses are repressed and carefully disguised, the individual has little chance of gaining even rudimentary insight into himself.

In the third place, ego-defensive behavior can be altered as the individual acquires insight into his own mechanisms of defense. Information about the nature of the problem in the external world will not affect him. Information about his own functioning may have an influence, if presented without threat, and if the defenses do not go too deep into the personality. In other words, only prolonged therapy can help the psychologically sick person. Many normal people, however, employ ego defenses about which they have some degree of awareness, though generally not at the time of the expression of such defenses. The frustrations of a tough day at work may result in an authoritarian father displacing his aggression that night on his family in yelling at his wife, or striking his youngsters. Afterward he may recognize the cause of his behavior. Not all defensive behavior, then, is so deeply rooted in the personality as to be inaccessible to awareness and insight. Therefore, procedures for arousing self-insight can be utilized to change behavior, even in mass communications.

One technique is to show people the psychodynamics of attitudes, especially as they appear in the behavior of others. Allport's widely used pamphlet (1944) on the ABC's of scapegoating is based upon the technique. Katz, Sarnoff, and McClintock (1956, 1957) have conducted experimental investigations of the effects of insightful materials upon the reduction of prejudice. In their procedure the psychodynamics of prejudice was presented in the case history of a subject sufficiently similar to the subjects as to appear as a sympathetic character. Two findings appeared in these investigations: (1) Subjects who were very high in defensiveness were not affected by the insight materials, but subjects of low or moderate defensiveness were significantly affected. (2) The changes in attitude produced by the arousal of self-insight persisted for a longer period of time than changes induced by information or conformity pressures. In a further experiment Stotland, Katz, and Patchen (1959) found that involving subjects in the task of understanding the dynamics of prejudice helped arouse self-insight and reduce prejudice. McClintock (1958) compared an ethnocentric appeal, an information message, and self-insight materials, with similar results. There was differential acceptance of these influences according to the personality pattern of the subject. McClintock also found a difference in F-scale items in predicting attitude change, with the projectivity items showing a different pattern from the conformity items.

Of practical concern are four general areas in which insufficient attention has been paid to the ego-defensive basis of attitudes with respect to the role of communication in inducing social change.

1. Prejudices toward foreigners, toward racial and religious out-groups, and toward international affairs often fall into this category. The thesis of the authors of *The Authoritarian Personality* that the defenses of repression and projectivity are correlated with racial prejudice has seen more confirmation than disproof in spite of the fact that not all racial prejudice is ego-defensive in nature. In a review of studies involving the California F-scale, Titus and Hollander (1957) report investigations where positive correlations were obtained between high scores on authoritarianism and prejudice and xenophobia.

Of course not all the variance in social prejudice can be accounted for by ego-defensiveness. Pettigrew (1958) has shown that a sample of Southern respondents was almost identical with a sample of Northern respondents on the F-scale measure of authoritarianism, but the Southern sample was much more negative toward Negroes with respect to employment, housing, and voting.

Relations have also been found between authoritarianism and attitudes toward nationalism and internationalism. Levinson (1957) constructed a scale to give an index of internationalism which included such items as opinions about immigration policy, armaments, the "get tough with Russia" policy, cooperation with Red China, our role in the UN, etc. This measure of internationalism correlated .60 with the F-scale. A study by Lane (1955) in 1952 showed that a larger proportion of authoritarians than of equalitarians were against working toward a peaceful settlement of the Korean issue. The authoritarians either favored the bombing of China and Manchuria or else were for complete withdrawal. And Smith and Rosen (1958) found such consistent negative relations between world-mindedness and the dimension of authoritarianism that they suggested in the interest of parsimony the two be considered as slightly different aspects of the same basic personality structure.

2. A related area of attitudes consists of opinions toward deviant types of personalities, e.g. delinquents, the mentally ill, beatniks, and other nonconformers. The problem of the rehabilitation of the ex-convict or the discharged mental patient is sometimes impeded by the emotional attitudes of the public toward individuals with a record of institutionalization.

3. Attitudes toward public health measures, whether the fluoridation of the water supply of a community, the utilization of X-ray examinations for the prevention of disease, or the availability of information about birth control, often have their roots in unacknowledged anxieties and fears. Davis (1959), for example, believes that opposition to fluoridation is not so much a matter of ignorance of the specific problem as it is a function of a deeper attitudinal syndrome of naturalism. Governmental interference with natural processes is regarded as the source of many evils, and this general ideology is tinged with suspicion and distrust suggestive of defensive motivation.

4. Apathy toward political issues and especially toward atomic weapons may reflect a defensive withdrawal on the part of some people. The information officer of a government agency or the public relations officer in charge of a health campaign faces the difficult problem of changing public attitudes which may satisfy different needs for different people. To present information designed to show the dangerous situation we are in may be effective for some people but may prove too threatening for others. What is needed in such cases is research which will get at the reasons why people hold the attitudes they do. There are times when dramatically confronting the public with the dangers of a situation may be more effective strategy than a more reassuring approach. But there are also occasions when the first strategy will merely add to defensive avoidance. Gladstone and Taylor (1958) presented communications to their students, two of which were news stories from the *New York Times*. One reported speeches made by Malenkov and Khrushchev about the peaceful intentions of the Soviet Union but its readiness to crush aggressors. The second news story reported British reactions to the American opinion about the situation in Indo-China. A third communication concerned the H-bomb and its dangers. Students were previously tested on their susceptibility to

being threatened. Those who were threat-prone tended to deny the truth of the points in the communications or to overlook them entirely. For these subjects the communications had no effect on existing attitudes.

The use of mass communication has been better adapted to supplying information and to emphasizing the advantages of a course of action than to changing defensive attitudes. A new field in communication to large publics is the creation of self-understanding, which so far has been pre-empted by personal advice columns. The specifics for this new development remain to be worked out, but they may well start with techniques based upon attitude research of the basic reasons for resistance to an objectively desirable program.

Conditions for
Arousing and Changing
Value-Expressive Attitudes

Two conditions for the arousal of value-expressive attitudes can be specified. The first is the occurrence of the cue in the stimulus situation which has been associated with the attitude. The liberal Democrat, as a liberal Democrat, has always believed in principle that an income tax is more just than a sales tax. Now the issue has arisen in his state, and the group in which he happens to be at the moment are discussing an increase in sales tax. This will be sufficient to cue off his opposition to the proposal without consideration of the specific local aspects of the tax problem. The second condition for the arousal of this type of attitude is some degree of thwarting of the individual's expressive behavior in the immediate past. The housewife occupied with the routine care of the home and children during the day may seek opportunities to express her views to other women at the first social gathering she attends.

We have referred to voters backing their party for bread and butter reasons. Perhaps the bulk of voting behavior, however, is the elicitation of value-expressive attitudes. Voting is a symbolic expression of being a Republican or a Democrat. Party identification accounts for more variance in voting behavior than any other single factor (Campbell, Converse, Miller, and Stokes, 1960). Though there is a minority who consider themselves independent and though there are minor shifts in political allegiance, the great majority of the people identify themselves as the supporters of a political party. Their voting behavior is an expression of this self-concept, and it takes a major event such as a depression to affect their voting habits seriously.

Identification with party is in good measure a function of the political socialization of the child, as Hyman (1959) has shown. An analysis of a national sample of the electorate in 1952 by Campbell, Gurin, and Miller (1954) revealed that of voters both of whose parents were Democrats, 76 percent identified themselves as Democrats, another 10 percent as independent Democrats, and 12 percent as Republicans. Similarly, of those with Republican parents 63 percent considered themselves Republican and another 10 percent as independent Republicans. Attachment to party, Hyman suggests, furnishes an organizing principle for the individual and gives stability to his political orientation in the confusion of changing issues.

Even in European countries, where we assume greater knowledge of issues, political behavior is the symbolic expression of people's values. Members of the Labor Party in Norway, for example, are little more conversant with the stand of their party on issues than are voters in the United States. In fact, the policy of their party in international affairs and armament in recent years has been closer to the views of Conservative voters than to their own. Nevertheless, they consider themselves supporters of the party which reflects their general values.

The problem of the political leader is to make salient the cues related to political allegiance in order to arouse the voters who consider themselves party supporters to the point of expressing their attitudes by voting on election day. One technique is to increase the volume and intensity of relevant stimulation as the election approaches. If the relevant cues could be presented to each voter on election day − for example, a ballot box in his home − then the appropriate behavior would follow. But the citizen must remember on the given Tuesday that this is election day and that he must find time to go to the polls. The task of party organization is to try to remind him of this fact the weekend before, to call him that very day by phone, or even to call for him in person.

Again, two conditions are relevant in changing value-expressive attitudes.

1. Some degree of dissatisfaction with one's self-concept or its associated values is the opening wedge for fundamental change. The complacent person, smugly satisfied with all aspects of himself, is immune to attempts to change his values. Dissatisfaction with the self can result from failures or from the inadequacy of one's values in preserving a favorable image of oneself in a changing world. The man with pacifist values may have become dissatisfied with himself during a period of fascist expansion and terror. Once there is a crack in the individual's central belief systems, it can be exploited by appropriately directed influences. The techniques of brain washing employed by the Chinese Communists both on prisoners of war in Korea and in the thought reform of Chinese intellectuals were essentially procedures for changing value systems.

In the brain washing of Chinese intellectuals in the revolutionary college, the Communists took advantage of the confused identity of the student (Lifton, 1957). He had been both a faithful son and a rebellious reformer and perhaps even an uninvolved cynic. To make him an enthusiastic Communist the officials attempted to destroy his allegiance to his parents and to transfer his loyalty to Communist doctrines which could meet his values as a rebel. Group influences were mobilized to help bring about the change by intensifying guilt feelings and providing for atonement and redemption through the emotional catharsis of personal confession.

To convert American prisoners of war, the Communists made a careful study of the vulnerability of their victims. They found additional weaknesses through a system of informers and created new insecurities by giving the men no social support for their old values (Schein, 1957). They manipulated group influences to support Communist values and exploited their ability to control behavior and all punishments and rewards in the situation. The direction of all their efforts, however, was to undermine old values and to supply new ones. The degree of their success has probably been exaggerated in the public prints, but from their point of view they did achieve some genuine gains. One estimate is that some 15 percent of the returning prisoners of war were active collaborators, another 5 percent resisters, and some 80 percent "neutrals." Segal (1957) in a study of a sample of 579 of these men, found that 12 percent had to some degree accepted Communist ideology.

2. Dissatisfaction with old attitudes as inappropriate to one's values can also lead to change. In fact, people are much less likely to find their values uncongenial than they are to find some of their attitudes inappropriate to their values. The discomfort with one's old attitudes may stem from new experiences or from the suggestions of other people. Senator Vandenburg, as an enlightened conservative, changed his attitudes on foreign relations from an isolationist to an internationalist position when critical events in our history suggested change. The influences exerted upon people are often in the direction of showing the inappropriateness of their present ways of expressing their values. Union leaders attempt to show that good union men should not vote on the old personal basis of rewarding friends and punishing enemies but should instead demand party responsibility for a program. In an experiment by Stotland, Katz, and Patchen (1959) there was suggestive evidence of the readiness of subjects to change attitudes which they found inappropriate to their values. Though an attempt was made to change the prejudices of the ego-defensive subjects, individuals who were not basically ego-defensive also changed. These subjects, who already approved of tolerance, apparently became aware of the inappropriateness of some of their negative evaluations of minority groups. This second factor in attitude change thus refers to the comparatively greater appropriateness of one set of means than another for confirming the individual's self-concept and realizing his central values.

We have already called attention to the role of values in the formation of attitudes in the early years of life. It is also true that attitude formation is a constant process and that influences are continually being brought to bear throughout life which suggest new attitudes as important in implementing existing values. An often-used method is to make salient some central value such as the thinking man, the man of distinction, or the virile man, and then depict a relatively new form of behavior consistent with this image. The role of motivational research in advertising is to discover the rudimentary image associated with a given product, to use this as a basis for building up the image in more glorified terms, and then to cement the association of this image with the product.

Arousing and Changing Attitudes Which Serve the Knowledge Function

Attitudes acquired in the interests of the need to know are elicited by a stimulus associated with the attitude. The child who learns from his reading and from his parents that Orientals are treacherous will not have the attitude aroused unless some appropriate cue concerning the cognitive object is presented. He may even meet and interact with Orientals without identifying them as such and with no corresponding arousal of his attitude. Considerable prejudice in this sense is race-name prejudice and is only aroused when a premium is placed upon social identification. Since members of a minority group have many other memberships in common with a majority group, the latent prejudiced attitude may not necessarily be activated. Prejudice based upon ego-defensiveness, however, will result in ready identification of the disliked group.

The factors which are productive of change of attitudes of this character are inadequacies of the existing attitudes to deal with new and changing situations. The person who has been taught that Orientals are treacherous may read extended accounts of the honesty of the Chinese or may have favorable interactions with Japanese. He finds his old attitudes in conflict with new information and new experience, and proceeds to modify his beliefs. In this instance we are dealing with fictitious stereotypes which never corresponded to reality. In other cases the beliefs may have been adequate to the situation but the world has changed. Thus, some British military men formerly in favor of armaments have changed their attitude toward disarmament because of the character of nuclear weapons. The theory of cognitive consistency later elaborated in this book as the theory of cognitive dissonance (Chapter 4) can draw its best examples from attitudes related to the knowledge function.

Any situation, then, which is ambiguous for the individual is likely to produce attitude change. His need for cognitive structure is such that he will either modify his beliefs to impose structure or accept some new formula presented by others. He seeks a meaningful picture of his universe, and when there is ambiguity he will reach for a ready solution. Rumors abound when information is unavailable.

Summary

In the foregoing analysis we have attempted to clarify the functions which attitudes perform and to give some psychological specifications of the conditions under which they are formed, elicited, and changed. This material is summarized in Table 1.

Table 1.   Determinants of Attitude Formation, Arousal, and Change in Relation to Type of Function

Function	Origin and Dynamics	Arousal Conditions	Change Conditions
Adjustment	Utility of attitudinal object in need satisfaction; maximizing external rewards and minimizing punishments	1. Activation of needs 2. Salience of cues associated with need satisfaction	1. Need deprivation 2. Creation of new needs and new levels of aspiration 3. Shifting rewards and punishments 4. Emphasis on new and better paths for need satisfaction
Ego defense	Protecting against internal conflicts and external dangers	1. Posing of threats 2. Appeals to hatred and repressed impulses 3. Rise in frustrations 4. Use of authoritarian suggestion	1. Removal of threats 2. Catharsis 3. Development of self-insight
Value expression	Maintaining self-identity; enhancing favorable self-image; self-expression and self-determination	1. Salience of cues associated with values 2. Appeals to individual to reassert self-image 3. Ambiguities which threaten self-concept	1. Some degree of dissatisfaction with self 2. Greater appropriateness of new attitude for the self 3. Control of all environmental supports to undermine old values
Knowledge	Need for understanding, for meaningful cognitive organization, for consistency and clarity	1. Reinstatement of cues associated with old problem or of old problem itself	1. Ambiguity created by new information or change in environment 2. More meaningful information about problems

3

Ego-Defense and Attitude Change

Daniel Katz
Irving Sarnoff
Charles McClintock

From Katz's theoretical statement on the functional approach to attitudes, we now turn to one of the experiments upon which his statement was based. As Katz indicates, attitudes based on the ego-defensive function are by far the most elusive and the most resistant to change. Most of the research efforts by Katz and his associates have been devoted to the study of ego-defense and attitude change.

Note that in the following research study, first published four years prior to the theoretical statement, the authors suggest only three motivational bases of attitudes — reality-testing (knowledge), reward and punishment (instrumental-adjustive), and ego-defensive. The fourth motivational basis attributed to attitudes — value expression — apparently had not yet been formulated.[*]

In a previous paper the theoretical framework for a program of research on the motivational bases of attitude change was set forth (Sarnoff and Katz, 1954). It was postulated that no single theory of motivation could adequately account for all of the ways in which attitudes are formed, maintained, and altered. It was held that identical attitudes often stem from a variety of differing motivational sources. Specifically, it was felt that any attitude could be regarded as serving one or more of three major motivational determinants: (1) reality-testing and the search for meaning: the need to acquire consistent knowledge about the external world, (2) reward and punishment, including the need to gain social acceptance and to avoid social disapproval, and (3) ego-defense: the need to defend against inner conflict.

*The paper following this editorial introduction is slightly abridged from D. Katz, I. Sarnoff, and C. McClintock, Ego-defense and attitude change, *Human Relations*, 1956, *9*, 27-46, by permission of the senior author and the publisher, Plenum Publishing Company.

Because of the complexity of human functioning, it is probable that all three sets of motivational determinants contribute to the development of every attitude. Nevertheless, they tend to contribute in a differential manner. It follows, therefore, that the most effective techniques of attitude change would be those aimed at the particular motivational sources that support the attitude under investigation.

The attitudinal focus of our research, our major dependent variable, is anti-Negro bias. In keeping with our theoretical position, we postulated that negative attitudes toward Negroes could stem from any of the three motivational contexts previously listed (Sarnoff and Katz, 1954). Hence the bias might: (1) reflect exposure to a limited and inaccurate range of information about Negroes, (2) reflect conformity to prevailing social pressures, or (3) represent the use of Negroes as social media for such ego-defensive purposes as the projection of unconscious and unacceptable impulses.

The work of Adorno *et al.* (1950) gives priority to the basis of prejudice in personality mechanisms. We should grant this priority for anti-Negro attitudes that greatly distort the actuality of the attitudinal object under conditions minimizing the operation of the other two motivational patterns. Where there is ample opportunity for reality-testing and interaction, as in a Northern college population, we should assume that misinformation about Negroes based upon old stereotypes is not the primary factor in most of the subjects. We should assume that where the social rewards and punishments for the maintenance of prejudice have been relaxed, as in a Northern college population, this type of motivational pattern would again not be the primary factor. But where these conditions do not hold we should expect that prejudice could be maintained at a high level without being based upon ego-defensiveness.

It is difficult to test theories about the genetic acquisition of attitudes without longitudinal studies of personalities over time. A profitable attack upon this motivational problem can be made, however, by using the traditional experimental procedure of introducing different manipulations and testing their effects. Thus, our basic assumption was that to the extent attitudes have different motivational roots, they will be influenced in corresponding fashion by different experimental manipulations. Accordingly, two different influence procedures were devised.[1] The one attempt was *informational* and was directed at the cognitive reorganization postulated by the Gestalt approach. It presented information about Negroes in a neutral or perhaps slightly favorable framework of cultural relativity. Crockett (1953) has shown the importance of cognitive structure in changing attitudes. In his experiment, greater attitude change

---

[1]In this experiment no attempt was made to manipulate the second motivational pattern through reward or punishment. In a combination of the rational and reward approaches, Rosenberg (1953) has shown that individuals' attitudes can be predicted from their hierarchy of values and the perceived instrumentality of certain activities for achieving these values. In a follow-up of this study, Carlson (1953) demonstrated that attitudes can be changed by changing the perception of their instrumental function for moving the individual toward his preferred goals.

occurred when people were given a rationale for the announced group norm than when the group norm was presented without a rationale. The other attempt was *interpretive* and was designed to give insight into the mechanisms and motivations of an ego-defensive nature that could be the basis of prejudice. G. W. Allport used this type of approach in his *ABC's of Scapegoating* (1944).

Since we assumed that anti-Negro bias in our experimental population would be related more to ego-defensiveness than to other motivational factors, we also assumed that the influence procedure of the interpretive sort would produce more favorable attitudes toward Negroes than the informational procedure.

In addition to this overall expectation concerning the relative effectiveness of these influence procedures, our theory holds that such procedures will have a differential effect upon individuals of differing degrees of ego-defensiveness. Thus, in comparison with less defensive individuals, highly ego-defensive persons should resist change on the basis of the interpretive approach because it is too threatening to them. Janis and Feshbach (1953) have shown that high fear arousal is not a favorable condition for changing attitudes. Cooper and Jahoda (1947) have found that highly prejudiced people will react defensively and block and distort the materials directed at caricaturing their beliefs. Moreover, these highly defensive persons should be relatively unmoved by the informational approach since it by-passes the essential emotional core of their anti-Negro attitudes. On the other hand, as compared with the highly defensive individuals, low ego-defensive persons should be more open and receptive to new information about Negroes, and, lacking as strong an emotional need to persist in their distorted perceptions of Negroes, they should develop more positive attitudes toward Negroes once the facts are presented to them. Hence, in addition to the greater effectiveness of the interpretive approach compared with the informational materials, the predictions are: (1) that the people who are in the middle ranges in ego-defensiveness will show the most positive change to the interpretive approach, with the low group next, and with the high group showing the least change, and (2) that the low ego-defensive group will show the most positive change to the informative approach, with the middle group next, and the high group last.

Procedure

Subjects for this study were 243 female college students at Michigan State Normal College. They were all volunteers solicited as members of sorority and dormitory groups. These groups were then assigned to one of two experimental treatments or to a control situation. The subjects were asked to participate in a series of three sessions, which took place at the Normal College during the spring of 1953. The first two sessions were separated by an interval of one week. The third session was held six weeks after the second. All data were gathered in a group setting.

For the first session, each subject was given a booklet that contained measures of personality and attitudes toward Negroes, including the F-scale, a specially designed TAT card, a twenty-item check list of statements pertaining to the subject's emotional functioning, a Bogardus social distance scale, and a Negro stereotype scale. All booklets were identical and subjects were free to leave as soon as they had finished filling out the materials.

At the outset of the second session, subjects assigned to the two experimental situations were presented with different sets of written influence materials aimed at inducing more favorable attitudes toward Negroes. One experimental treatment consisted of an interpretation of the relationship between mechanisms of ego-defense and anti-Negro attitudes. The other experimental treatment presented information about Negroes in a setting of cultural relativity. The control group was not exposed to any influence procedure.

Immediately after reading the influence materials, subjects in both experimental groups were requested to fill out another set of the same attitude questionnaires as they had answered a week before. Similarly, but without prior presentation of influence materials, the control group also filled out the same questionnaires.

To begin the third session, all subjects (both experimental and control) were again required to fill out a set of the original attitude scales.

Personality Measures

Ego-defensiveness. Since there is no generally accepted measure of ego-defensiveness as it relates to prejudice, a TAT card in the tradition of Murray was designed.[2] It was hoped that a pictorial representation of the attitudinal object would evoke the motivational matrix associated with the subject's attitudes toward the object.

Instructions accompanying the card were as follows: "Please take the picture out and place it beside the folder. Then make up a story about it. Be sure to

[2]The card presents an unstructured social situation with two female figures sitting in chairs at a table in the foreground and two female figures standing in the background. The ethnic identity of the seated figures is ambiguous. Standing in the background and turned slightly toward each other, with their faces seen by the viewer, are a Negro girl and a white girl. There are no definite expressions on their faces although their features are drawn in detail. All four figures are dressed in the fashion of college girls and the two standing figures appear to be of college age. Two empty chairs are shown at the table near the seated girls.

cover these three main questions: (1) What is going on in the present situation? (2) What has happened in the past? (3) What is going to happen in the future? Tell what the people are doing, thinking, and feeling. Try to tell us as complete a story as possible in about five minutes."

The stories based on the TAT card were coded on projection, denial, and extrapunitiveness; and a combined score on ego-defensiveness was computed. Specifically, the code for projection included two categories: (1) attribution of hostile feelings to the Negro girl, and (2) attribution of hostile feelings to non-principals (seated figures) with respect to the Negro girl. Extrapunitiveness was defined as perceiving one or more characters in the picture as playing a punitive role. Failure to identify the Negro girl as a Negro and omission of essential story elements required by the instructions were code categories for denial. Two coders independently coded for these specific categories, and the inter-coder reliability was computed on the basis of the number of agreements vs. the number of disagreements in terms of assigning persons to High, Middle, and Low Ego-Defensive groups. For an N of 60 TAT protocols randomly selected from the total test population, there were 51 agreements (85 percent) and 9 disagreements (15 percent). None of the 9 disagreements were more than one unit away in terms of our three-point scale. That is to say, no individual was scored as low ego-defensive by one coder and high ego-defensive by another.

Conformity. The measure of a need to conform was based on two items, which were part of a twenty-item check list. This list consisted of statements pertaining to the subject's emotional functioning. Subjects were presented with the list and the following instructions: "The following are a number of things which often trouble people. Please check (✓) all those items which apply to yourself at the present time." The two conformity items were: "It makes me uncomfortable to be different"; "People can pretty easily change me even though my mind is already made up on the subject." A need to conform was considered present if a subject checked one or both of the above items.

Attitude Measures

Negro stereotypes. This Likert-type scale consisted of 15 anti-Negro statements in a twenty-one-item questionnaire. Six pro-Negro statements were interspersed in the questionnaire in order to prevent subjects from developing a rigid response set. Subjects were requested to express the extent of their agreement or disagreement with each statement. Examples of the statements follow:

1. The refreshing aspect of Negro music is its rhythm and spontaneity.

5. Cleanliness and courtesy are characteristics which are noticeably lacking in the behavior patterns of most Negroes.

8. Superstition and ignorance are characteristics which alienate Negroes from other groups.

9. Most Negroes let situations of complete equality go to their heads. They find it impossible to control their excessively strong sexual and aggressive desires.

Negro Bogardus. The preceding Negro Stereotype Scale tends to approach anti-Negro attitudes from the standpoint of the subject's perception of the attitudinal object. In order to get an attitude measure with more affinity to the action level, we utilized a modern version of the Bogardus social distance scale. This scale specifies the levels of social intimacy to which a Negro would be admitted by the subject.

Influence Procedures

1. Interpretation. This material consisted of eleven double-spaced type-written pages entitled "Emotions and Attitudes." In the first part of this presentation, we described in general terms the dynamics of scapegoating, projection, and compensation with respect to the development of anti-minority attitudes. We then presented a case history of a college girl to illustrate how these mechanisms of defense were basic to her ethnic prejudices. In doing this, we attempted to maximize identification of the subjects with the hypothetical case.

2. Information. This untitled presentation, nine double-spaced type-written pages in length, attempted to evoke a frame of reference, cultural relativity, in which the attitudinal object and information concerning it could be perceived in a new way. Hence, this material was also roughly divided into two parts. The first part, the evocation of the frame of reference, was a presentation of the concept of cultural relativity. This concept is illustrated by a number of references to various societies that have drastically different ways of looking at and reacting to identical human phenomena such as personal disputes and mother-child relationships. The second part is aimed at a re-evaluation of the attitudinal object from the viewpoint of the new frame of reference. Thus the concept of cultural relativity is applied to the negative attitudes and unfavorable circumstances that have confronted Negroes in America. The article then goes on to explain the apparent differences between whites and Negroes in social terms and to point out that whenever Negroes have had genuine equality of opportunity, they have performed as well as whites. A number of outstanding Negroes in various professional fields were listed to illustrate the social contributions already made by Negroes. The attempt here is to produce cognitive restructuring that will take account of the new information and to make the conditions for such restructuring favorable by first evoking a new and acceptable frame of reference for the evaluation of the cognitive object.

Control Variables

It is generally desirable to control attitude-change studies by breaking cases according to original attitude position. Change toward the positive end of the scale may have different qualitative meanings for people occupying different positions along the scale. It may be easier to move people who are already favorably disposed to the ideas in the influence attempt than those who have opposed views. On the other hand, there is much less room to move for those already near the favorable end of the scale. In this study we did not have enough cases to control by original attitude position. But we did relate the amount of change to the original position of the subjects and found no significant differences between the number of people changing and the original attitude position that they held.

While it was assumed that ego-defensiveness was the main motivational pattern for the majority of the subjects as the basis for prejudiced attitudes, a very high correlation between original attitude position and degree of ego-defensiveness would raise the question of the identity of the processes being measured. Therefore, ego-defensiveness was broken against original attitude position. The results show that people who are higher in ego-defensiveness tend to be higher in prejudice but there is no statistically significant relationship between these factors.[3]

[3]Methodological note:

a. Scores on the Negro Stereotype Scale were computed on the basis of the subject's responses to the fifteen negative stereotype items. The positive stereotypes were not used for this analysis.

b. For both the Negro Bogardus and Negro Stereotype Scales, + indicates change favorable to the attitude object, Negro, − indicates change unfavorable, and 0 indicates no change toward the attitude object, Negro.

c. Because of the relative infrequency of 0 change on the Negro Stereotype Scale from Sessions 1 to 3, the 0 and − categories are combined in the tables, except for Table 1.

d. Statistical analysis was based on the use of chi square corrected for continuity.

e. In the computation of chi square, the 0 and − change categories were combined. Results should thus be interpreted in terms of positive change versus non-positive change.

f. All probabilities reported have been computed on the basis of one-tail tests. That is, they have all taken into consideration the directional predictions made.

Results and Interpretation

1. The approach utilizing interpretive materials proved to be a more powerful influence attempt in producing positive attitudes than the approach utilizing informational materials. Table 1 shows that significantly more people changed in the direction of favorable beliefs about Negroes over a six-week period (Sessions 1 to 3) after exposure to the interpretive approach than after exposure to the informational treatment. Though there was some positive change in the group receiving the informational material, it was not significantly greater than in the control group.

Table 1.   Change on Negro Stereotypes, Sessions 1-3 (N = 243)

Direction of Change	Approach		
	Interpretation	Information	Control
+	55	49	21
0	4	11	5
−	18	33	14
N.A.	14	13	6
Total	91	106	46

Interpretation/Information	$x^2 =$ 5.60	$P = .01$
Interpretation/Control	$x^2 =$ 3.38	$P = .03$
Information/Control	$x^2 = <1.00$	$P = $ N.S.

The second measure of the dependent variable, a slightly modified Bogardus scale, proved much more stable over the six-week period. Again, however, there was a significant difference between the people subjected to the interpretive approach compared with those subjected to the informational approach, and again it was in the expected direction (Table 2). Since the control group also shifted over time, the difference between the interpretive approach and the control group is not, however, significant. The ratio of favorable to unfavorable change is three to one for the interpretive approach and two to one for the control situation, but the number of cases is too small to make this a statistically significant result. The greater stability of the scores on the Bogardus scale as against the measure of stereotypes (some twenty people did not change in either direction on their stereotype score, whereas 86 did not shift on the Bogardus) is probably due to two factors. The Bogardus scale may have more reliability as a measure, and in addition it may be more difficult to move people on items

Table 2. Change on Negro Bogardus, Sessions 1-3 (N = 243)

Direction of Change	Approach		
	Interpretation	*Information*	*Control*
+	37	30	16
0	28	42	16
−	12	21	8
N.A.	14	13	6
Total	91	106	46

Interpretation/Information x^2 =   3.76 P = .03
Interpretation/Control x^2 = <1.00 P = N.S
Information/Control x^2 = <1.00 P = N.S.
(x^2 computed on the basis of combining 0 and − change.)

relating to a change in behavior than on items of belief having little specific behavioral reference.

The greater effectiveness of interpretation as compared with information can of course be a function of using a greater amount of the one influence than of the other. In other words, we may have done a better job in mobilizing a strong set of interpretation materials than of informational materials. There is, however, suggestive evidence on this point in that the *immediate* effects of the two influence procedures were not significantly different, but over time there was more continuous gain and less backsliding among the people subjected to the interpretive approach than among those subjected to the informational approach. The immediate results (Tables 3 and 4) show that there were no significant differences between the two approaches immediately after their presentation. Both interpretation and information produced positive changes in over half of the group on beliefs about Negro characteristics. Six weeks later, however, the gains produced by interpretation were significantly greater than those produced by the information approach. The findings from the Bogardus scale are less clear-cut but they do tend to support the same trend. The immediate effects of the two approaches are not at an acceptable level of statistical significance, but the effects several weeks later do meet the conventional criterion of less than the .05 level. It would appear, therefore, that the superior power of the interpretation approach lies in its ability to effect more cognitive reorganization over time.

The detailed breakdown of the movements of people from the second to the third session (Table 5) shows that more of the people who changed positively

Table 3.   Change on Negro Stereotypes, Sessions 1-2 (N = 243)

	Approach		
Direction of Change	*Interpretation*	*Information*	*Control*
+	60	60	20
0	13	17	8
−	18	28	17
N.A.	0	1	1
Total	91	106	46

Interpretation/Information	x^2 = <1.00	P = N.S.
Interpretation/Control	x^2 = 4.60	P = .01
Information/Control	x^2 = 1.56	P = .11

(x^2 computed by combining 0 and − change and running against + change.)

Table 4.   Change on Negro Bogardus, Sessions 1-2 (N = 243)

	Approach		
Direction of Change	*Interpretation*	*Information*	*Control*
+	34	31	12
0	36	57	22
−	21	18	12
N.A.	0	0	0
Total	91	106	46

Interpretation/Information	x^2 = 1.10	P = .15
Interpretation/Control	x^2 = 1.28	P = .13
Information/Control	x^2 = <1.00	P = N.S.

(x^2 computed by combining 0 and − change and running against + change.)

after the presentation of the interpretive materials continue to change positively during the following weeks than is true of the people receiving the information materials. Similarly there is a tendency for more backsliding to occur among the subjects receiving the information than among those getting the interpretive materials, though this is not a significant difference.

2. The greater effectiveness of the interpretive approach seems to be differentially related to the ego-defensiveness of the individual subjects (Tables 6 and 7). If the subjects high in ego-defensiveness are excluded from consideration,

Table 5. Consistency of Direction of Attitude Change Based on Change from
Sessions 1-2 and Change from Sessions 2-3 (N = 243)

Positive Change: Sessions 1-2

Direction of Change Sessions 2-3	Approach		
	Interpretation	*Information*	*Control*
+	30	23	7
0, −	25	33	16
Sub-total	55	56	23

Negative or No Change: Sessions 1-2

Direction of Change Sessions 2-3	Approach		
	Interpretation	*Information*	*Control*
+	14	21	9
0, −	9	16	9
Sub-total	23	37	18
N.A.	13	13	5
Total	91	106	46

(Positive Change: Sessions 1-2) [+, (−, 0) change Sessions 2-3]
Interpretation/Information $x^2 =$ 1.52 P = .11
Interpretation/Control $x^2 =$ 2.88 P = .05
Information/Control $x^2 =$ < 1.00 P = N.S.
(Negative Change: Sessions 1-2)/[+, (−, 0) change Sessions 2-3]
Interpretation/Information $x^2 =$ < 1.00 P = N.S.
Interpretation/Control $x^2 =$ < 1.00 P = N.S.
Information/Control $x^2 =$ < 1.00 P = N.S.

then the superiority of the interpretive approach over the informational
presentation becomes even clearer. Forty-four of the middle and low defensive
groups changed positively on their stereotype score over the six-week period,
and only twelve showed no change or shifted negatively under the influence of
interpretive materials. The comparable ego-defensive groups under the influence
of informational materials gave a fifty-fifty split, 33 shifting positively and 33
shifting negatively or showing no change. Similarly, for the low and middle
defensive groups, on the Bogardus scale the information approach moved only
18 subjects positively, with 48 showing zero or minus change; whereas the
interpretation approach shifted 30 people positively, with 26 showing zero or
negative change.

Table 6.   Change on Negro Stereotypes, Sessions 1-3, by Ego-Defensiveness for Interpretational and Informational Approaches ($N = 197$)

Direction of Change	Interpretation			Information		
	Ego-Defensiveness					
	Low	Med.	High	Low	Med.	High
+	24	20	11	16	17	11
−,0	5	7	10	16	17	15
N.A.	6	4	4	6	4	5

Approach	Defensiveness	x^2	P
Interpretation	High vs. low	4.00	.02
	Middle vs. high	1.57	.10
	Middle vs. low	<1.00	N.S.
	Middle and low vs. high	3.92	.02
Information	No significant relations between high, middle, low	—	—
Interpretation vs. information	Low vs. low	5.83	.01
	Middle vs. middle	2.67	.05
	High vs. high	<1.00	N.S.

The difference in changed stereotype scores between the high ego-defensive people and the combined middle and low group is significant for the interpretation approach but the corresponding difference for the information approach is slight and insignificant. The same findings hold when the Bogardus scale is used as the dependent variable. In general, then, the prediction of change as a function of the relationship between influence process and personality mechanism seems confirmed. The more detailed predictions, however, are in need of revision in a number of respects, as the following specific findings suggest.

Within the group receiving the interpretation approach, the subjects scoring high in ego-defensiveness were less amenable to change both on the measure of beliefs about Negroes and on the Bogardus scale than were the subjects scoring in the middle and low ranges on ego-defensiveness. The original prediction was that the high ego-defensive people would be more resistant because of the difficulty of breaching their defenses with anything less than prolonged individual therapy. This hypothesis was thus confirmed. It was predicted, however, that the middle group in defensiveness would show the most change under the interpretation approach, since it was expected that the low group would not be characteristically using the defense mechanisms under exposure or would at least have more insight into these mechanisms. This prediction was not

Table 7. Change on Negro Bogardus, Sessions 1-3, by Ego-Defensiveness for
Interpretational and Informational Approaches (N = 197)

Direction of Change	Interpretation			Information		
	Ego-Defensiveness					
	Low	Med.	High	Low	Med.	High
+	16	14	7	8	10	11
0	10	10	8	14	18	10
−	3	3	6	10	6	5
N.A.	4	4	6	5	4	6

Approach	Defensiveness	x^2	P
Interpretation	High vs. low	1.54	.11
	Middle vs. high	<1.00	N.S.
	Middle vs. low	<1.00	N.S.
	Middle and low vs. high	2.14	.07
Information	High vs. low	1.24	*
	Middle vs. high	<1.00	N.S.
	Middle vs. low	<1.00	N.S.
	Middle and low vs. high	1.32	*
Interpretation vs. information	Low vs. low	4.55	.02
	Middle vs. middle	2.27	.05
	High vs. high	<1.00	N.S.

*Indicates that findings are in the reverse direction from that predicted.
(x^2 computed by combining 0 and − change and running them against + change.)

confirmed, and the low and middle groups· responded equally well to the
interpretation materials and were remarkably alike in their reactions. The failure
to obtain the predicted difference between the low and middle groups may be
due to the lack of sensitivity of the measure, or it may be that in most
populations there are very few people so low in defensiveness that they cannot
profit from exposure to interpretive materials.

Within the group receiving the informational approach there were no
differences between the people of varying degrees of defensiveness on the
measure of beliefs about Negroes. There was, however, a tendency for the
combined middle and low groups in defensiveness to show less change than the
high group on the Bogardus scale. It should be remembered that the
informational materials were presented in an indirect manner through the
activation of a new frame of reference about the problem, namely, the approach
of cultural relativity and historical perspective. Thus there would be a minimal
challenge to the effect-laden defenses of the highly defensive subjects.
Nevertheless, it was assumed that the people lowest in ego-defensiveness would

be the most amenable to change. The theory was that these people did not hold racial attitudes in the service of defense mechanisms and hence could be readily changed if given new facts and new information. Again this prediction was not confirmed and perhaps for the reason already suggested, namely, that we did not have in our population of girls in a normal college enough subjects of the type postulated. It is also possible that the group scoring low in defensiveness may have been relatively more sophisticated and more familar with the "new" information presented. This is speculation, in that there was no control on the "newness" of the materials for any of the subjects. Such controls are desirable, in that experimental influences for some subjects may be forces to which they are already habituated and for others may represent new forces.

3.   There is evidence to indicate that the unpredicted tendency of the high ego-defensive group to change under the influence of information materials was due to the conformity pressures generated in the experimental situation. The prestige of the experimenters from the state university, the resort to "scientific" facts in the presentation, and the general trend in the direction of more liberal attitudes toward Negroes in the academic world may have produced a perception that the *correct* opinions were at the favorable end of the scale. Not only did a majority of the students, subjected to experimental influences, shift in the expected direction but more of the control group shifted in a positive than a negative direction (though not significantly so). In other words, the experiment probably made the issue more salient on the campus, and the resulting interactions made it clear that the majority were clearly positive in their attitudes toward Negro students.

A partial test of this hypothesis, that the high ego-defenders were affected by conformity pressures, was possible through a measure of conformity tendencies obtained from two items in the personality inventory. When this personality measure of conformity is applied to the high ego-defensive group, we find that the positive changers on the stereotype scale had significantly more high conformers among them than had the zero or negative changers. Among the low and middle groups in ego-defensiveness, however, there is no significant relationship between conformity and positive change, though there is a tendency in this direction. Thus the effect of the information approach on the high ego-defenders can be interpreted as due to the conformity aspects of the experimental setting. In general, moreover, the changes produced by the information approach were not significantly greater than the real changes occurring in the control group. It seems plausible, therefore, to account for the effect of the information approach as a function of conformity to the experimenter and to the changes in group norms, rather than as a function of a rational restructuring to take account of the new cognitive materials presented.

The *differential effects* of the interpretive approach upon the high and low ego-defenders cannot be explained away on the basis of conformity, however, for here the difference is not due to differential conformity effects in the two groups. If conformity pressures were to account for the greater positive change among the low and middle defensive groups, then the conformers in these groups should be contributing more to the change than are the conformers in the high ego-defensive group. But the figures in Table 8 indicate that the reverse tendency is manifest. The conformity effect in fact works against finding the differential relationship postulated.

Table 8. Change on Negro Stereotypes, Sessions 1-3, by Ego-Defensiveness for Conformity and Non-conformity within the Interpretational Approach (N = 91)

	Defensiveness					
	Low		Middle		High	
	+	−, 0	+	−, 0	+	−, 0
Non-conformity	11	5	12	5	5	9
Conformity	13	0	8	2	6	1

N.A. = 14

Conformity/Non-conformity

Low Ego Group x^2 = <1.00 P = N.S.
Middle Ego Group x^2 = <1.00 P = N.S.
High Ego Group x^2 =   2.96 P = .04

The greater susceptibility of high ego-defenders to conformity pressures is an integral part of the theory of the authoritarian personality as developed by Adorno *et al.* (1950). These authors include in their syndrome of authoritarian character structure both defensive reactions of repression, projection, and displacement, and conventionalism and conformity. Suggestive evidence about the susceptibility of high F-scores to conformity pressures comes from an experimental investigation by Wagman (1953), in which he used authoritarian suggestion of two types. The one authoritarian suggestion was designed to move a group of subjects in the direction of more liberal attitudes; the second was designed to move another group of subjects in a less liberal direction. Low F-scorers could not be influenced in the direction of greater liberality by authoritarian suggestion, but high F-scorers could be influenced in either direction. Barlow (1954), in a separate analysis of some of the data from the study here reported, found that high scorers in ego-defensiveness were more likely than low scorers to see themselves as very close to the group norm all through the change process.

Summary

In this exploratory study, we tested several hypotheses derived from the theory that social attitudes are supported by one or more of three principal motivational determinants: reality-testing, reward and punishment, and ego-defense. Since identical attitudes have different motivational roots, we assumed that they would be influenced in corresponding fashion by different experimental manipulations. To test this assumption, we devised interpretive and informational techniques that would attack the ego-defensive and reality-testing components of anti-Negro attitudes in a differential manner. We presented these techniques to white college girls in an effort to produce more favorable attitudes toward Negroes. We tested the relative overall effectiveness of the two change procedures as well as their effects upon subjects of various degrees of ego-defensiveness.

In general the findings confirmed the theory that affect-laden attitudes are more effectively influenced through attempting to give insight into the self than through giving insight into the objective nature of the problem. Moreover, the people highest in ego-defensiveness are the most difficult to change through the self-insight procedure. But the prediction that the people lowest in ego-defensiveness would be most easily influenced by informational materials (insight into the objective problem) was not confirmed. The high ego-defenders were as susceptible to change under the informational approach as were the low ego-defenders. The interpretation of this result was that the high ego-defenders were affected by the conformity pressures in the experimental situation rather than by the informational materials themselves.

4

Cognitive Dissonance: Theory and Research

John J. Sherwood
James W. Barron
H. Gordon Fitch

In 1957, Leon Festinger put forth a little, but fascinating, theory in his book *A Theory of Cognitive Dissonance.* The book created an immediate sensation and has produced a decade of feverish research activity. It is a little theory because it is based upon a single principle and because it uses only a few concepts. Furthermore, it does not pretend to be a big theory; that is, it does not pretend to be a theory of behavior or personality. Yet at the same time, it is an important theory in that it is apparently useful in a wide variety of behavioral contexts — from studies of social problems and morality to the swimming of rats, from studies of attitude change and social influence to defense mechanisms. Finally, it is a fascinating theory because researchers have used it to make some "surprising" predictions that do not easily follow from common sense or from other psychological theories.

The theory of cognitive dissonance is frequently referred to as a social psychological theory. That is probably because Festinger is best known as a social psychologist and because the theory has proved to be particularly useful in areas of social psychological concern, such as attitude change, social influence, and conformity. More accurately, however, the theory of cognitive dissonance is a cognitive theory of motivation. The term "cognitive" comes from the Latin word for "knowing" and refers to processes of thought and perception.

In contrast to most of the other chapters in this book, this chapter is not a report of a research effort but a statement of the theory of cognitive dissonance and a review of the research literature that the theory has produced.*

Introduction to the Theory

The basic assumption underlying dissonance theory is that an individual *strives for consistency among his opinions, attitudes, and values.* Festinger replaced the word "consistency" with the more neutral term *consonance.* Similarly, "inconsistency" was replaced with a term having a less logical connotation — *dissonance.* So a restatement of the basic proposition is that there is "pressure to produce consonant relations among cognitions and to avoid dissonance" (Festinger, 1957, p. 9).

The existence of dissonance is assumed to be psychologically uncomfortable. It is an aversive motivational state that impels a person to try to reduce the dissonance and to achieve consonance. In addition to being motivated to reduce dissonance, the person actively avoids situations that are likely to increase the dissonance in his cognitive world.

A state of dissonance exists when a person holds, at the same time, two cognitions that are inconsistent with each other according to his psychological expectations. The two cognitions are said to be dissonant with each other if — for the person — the obverse of one cognition would follow from the other. Thus, if cognition A implies cognition B, then holding A and the obverse of B — that is, not-B — is dissonant. For example, "viewing oneself as an honest person" (A) and "behaving honestly" (B) are consonant, because B follows from A. On the other hand, "viewing oneself as an honest person" and the *obverse* of "behaving honestly" — such as "stealing from the poor box" — are dissonant conditions.

A cognition is any knowledge, belief, attitude, or value that a person holds about himself, about his behavior, or about his environment. Expectations about what cognitive relationships are consonant — that is, what follows from what — are acquired through an individual's experience, the mores of his culture, and his notions about logical relations between events. If a person were to stand in the rain and yet not get wet, the cognitions representing these two facts would be dissonant with each other because people usually learn from experience that getting wet follows from standing in the rain.

The amount or level of dissonance aroused is (1) a function of the ratio of dissonant to consonant cognitions, and (2) a function of the importance of each

---

cognition to the person. Although the precise nature of these functions is an empirical question that is not yet fully understood, the basic relations between amount of dissonance and the cognitions held by an individual are represented by the following:

$$\text{Dissonance} = \frac{\text{Importance x Number of Dissonant Cognitions}}{\text{Importance x Number of Consonant Cognitions}}$$

This heuristic expression is not meant to be precise in terms of specific numbers or measurements but to suggest a number of relationships — for example, that dissonance will be reduced if the number or importance of consonant cognitions in a given situation is increased.

The meaning of "importance" is not clearly explicated in the original theory. A definition that seems to fit the theory is that "importance" refers to the instrumentality of the cognition for the satisfaction of the individual's needs and values, particularly those central to his wider value system. However, at times, situations may become so salient as to attach temporary importance to otherwise peripheral cognitions.

The initial observational basis for Festinger's notion that people actively seek to avoid and reduce dissonance among cognitions came from trying to understand some bizarre rumors that started after a major earthquake in India in 1934. The rumors were recorded in an area where people felt severe and prolonged tremors but did not suffer any injury or witness any damage. These are samples of the rumors: "There will be a severe cyclone in the next few days," "There will be a severe earthquake on the lunar eclipse day," "A flood is rushing toward the province," and "In five days the fatal day will arrive . . . unforeseeable calamities will arise." These observations seem to contradict the widely accepted hedonistic assumption that people avoid unpleasant things, such as anxiety and the prospect of pain.

Some comparable data from people who were actually in an area of death and destruction in another natural disaster show a complete absence of rumors predicting further disaster. The data from the two communities do not agree with so-called common sense. Why should the occurrence of an earthquake — in the absence of death and destruction — be correlated with such frightening and exaggerated rumors, while people who were actually in an area of disaster did not invent such rumors? For Festinger, the rumors fell into place when viewed in terms of relations between cognitions. In the community that experienced only the shock of the earthquake but no suffering and destruction, Festinger assumed that the residents had a strong and persistent fear reaction yet could see nothing to fear. The *feeling* of fear in the absence of an adequate *reason* for fear was dissonant. The rumors predicting future disaster, if believed, provided the residents with cognitions that were consonant with being afraid. The rumors were, according to the theory, "fear justifying" rumors and thus a shared mechanism for dissonance reduction.

Examples of Dissonance Reduction

It is assumed that if a person holds two cognitions that are inconsistent with each other, he will experience dissonance — an aversive motivational state — and he will then try to reduce the dissonance and achieve consonance. Dissonance can be reduced in several ways, including increasing the number and/or importance of consonant cognitions. The fear justifying rumors, an example of the first method, served to reduce dissonance by adding new elements that were consonant with being afraid. An example of changing the importance of consonant cognitions is in the person who — rather than stop smoking in the face of its danger to health — increases the feeling of enjoyment he receives from smoking. He might also add new consonant elements, such as "Smoking is not so deadly as this publicity suggests; I run a far greater risk whenever I drive a car."

The smoker, instead of seeking to enhance the consonant aspects of his behavior, could act to remove the dissonant elements; he could give up smoking and thereby remove one major dissonance-producing cognition. Or he could attempt to minimize the other by distorting or ignoring the claims of medical research on the relation between smoking and health, perhaps by carefully avoiding exposure to articles or arguments discussing the ill effects of smoking.

According to the theory, the individual will choose one or more of all these possible ways to reduce dissonance. As might be expected, there is no unambiguous way of predicting which he will select. However, the general rule for determining the mode of dissonance reduction is that of least effort; that is, the cognition least resistant to change will be changed. Resistance is in part determined by (1) the number of presently irrelevant cognitions with which the changed cognition will become dissonant, thereby creating new dissonance, and by (2) the importance of these newly relevant cognitions in terms of the person's system of values.

Moreover, although dissonance can be reduced by decreasing the number of dissonant cognitions, the theory is not clear on how that can be done. The ease with which reality can be changed (or distorted) depends, among other things, on the concreteness or abstractness of the cognition, the extent to which it is private or public, and the relative ambiguity or clarity of the reality that it represents.

Anyone doubting the efficacy of consistency as a principle of behavior might remember having seen some person suddenly reverse his direction of travel on a crowded sidewalk and then remember having noticed his public attempt to make this seemingly inconsistent behavior seem consistent — for example, he might have consulted his watch with an amazed expression, or he might have made some utterance like "I forgot my briefcase."

Although dissonance theory is undeniably useful in a great many situations, problems are encountered if we attempt to extend the theory beyond the limits originally intended for it. One of these problems stems from the theory's incompleteness, which Festinger acknowledged when he said that "there are generally so many other cognitive elements relevant to any given element that some dissonance is the usual state of affairs" (1957, p. 17). He also states that dissonance is not always reduced — that it sometimes cannot be. A person, for example, might invest a great deal of money in a company that declares bankruptcy soon afterward. The action is irreversible, and the elements are so important to the person that all of the dissonance cannot be eliminated, at least for some time. It would seem, then, that people either (1) *constantly* experience the psychological discomfort or tension that accompanies cognitive inconsistencies and are constantly motivated to dispel it or (2) have some tolerance for a certain level of dissonance, further reduction of which is unnecessary or not particularly satisfying.

If we accept the first alternative above, the goal of the organism would be to reduce *all* dissonance, and the logical end-point of this process would be a completely quiescent state. In other words, the organism would be striving for a condition that contains no imbalance or incongruity. Several other motivational theories have this characteristic, and all of these are challenged by evidence showing that organisms do *not* pursue a quiescent state in which all motivational tensions have been reduced but in fact often seek out higher levels of stimulation, tension, or dissonance. Mild stimulation, tension, or dissonance may actually be pleasurable.

This line of argument would seem to favor Alternative (2). Indeed, the development of various "optimal level of arousal" theories (for example, Berlyne, 1960) clearly indicates that a position advocating the maintenance of a certain amount of dissonance or imbalance is at least tenable. Dissonance theory in its original form did not deal with this problem but assumed that any inconsistency between cognitions would lead to attempts to reconcile it or to restore balance.

Commitment and Volition

The most extensive modification of dissonance theory as originally stated by Festinger has been that of Brehm and Cohen in their book *Explorations in*

Cognitive Dissonance (1962). In their summary of the research literature on dissonance theory at that time, they demonstrated the predictive value of the theory in these situations: (1) the period after a free choice among *attractive alternatives* (decision making in which dissonance is a function of the relative number of favorable cognitions of the unchosen alternatives); (2) instances of forced compliance, in which a person is induced to *behave* in a manner inconsistent with his attitudes; and (3) situations in which a person is exposed to *information* inconsistent with his attitudes.

Brehm and Cohen's primary contribution, however, was in their demonstration of the importance of commitment and volition to the predictions of dissonance theory. According to Brehm and Cohen, "Commitment provides a specification of the conditions under which one cognition follows from the obverse of another. . . . a central kernel of dissonance theory . . . is the notion that *a person will try to justify a commitment to the extent that there is information discrepant with that commitment"* (p. 300). They define "commitment" very simply as a decision (to do or not to do something) or a choice (and thereby a rejection of unchosen alternatives) or active engagement in a given behavior.

Presumably, when a person engages in a course of action discrepant from an attitude that he holds about this action, he will experience dissonance. He may reduce the dissonance by bringing his attitude into consonance or agreement with his behavior; that is, he might change his attitude about the behavior. An example is a high school student who praises ivy league schools and denigrates state universities and afterward discovers he cannot get into an ivy league school. If he then chooses to enter a state university, dissonance theory would predict his attitude toward state universities would become more favorable and, possibly, his attitude toward the ivy league more negative. By his actions he is now committed to a state university, and his actions are dissonant with his formerly critical attitude toward state universities. Of course, one's attitudes toward a state university might change for many other reasons, but in this example the student's entry into the state university is crucial. His entry is contrary to his attitude toward state universities, and it is likely that his attitude will become more favorable in order to be more consonant with the fact that he is now attending the state university.

The crucial variable in commitment is *volition*, which refers to the degree of free choice involved in the decision to behave in an attitude-discrepant way. Thus, to the extent that the student in the example saw himself as being *forced* to attend a state university, the theory predicts he would experience less dissonance and, therefore, less pressure to change his attitudes about state universities than he would if he saw himself as making a *free* and uncoerced choice. A frequent, and non-obvious, finding in research on dissonance theory is the *less* the reward for engaging in an attitude-discrepant behavior, the greater the resultant attitude change is likely to be. Similarly, it has usually been found that the *less* the coercion used to force compliance or commitment, the greater the likelihood of attitude change. Presumably, a person finding himself committed to doing something contrary to his attitudes for a large reward or from coercion can deny responsibility for his behavior. He can externalize the reason he is doing what he is doing; that is, he can say to himself: "I don't really believe in this, but I really had no choice because I cannot afford to refuse such a large reward; therefore, I am justified in doing this even though I believe it is not what I should be doing." On the other hand, a person who receives a minimal reward or very slight coercion cannot justify his attitude-discrepant actions so easily. He is more likely to conclude: "I got myself into this situation, and because I don't normally do things in which I don't believe, there must really be something to the position I am advocating."

An Example of Research:
The Effects of Temptation

Consider a person who is tempted by anticipation of reward to do something he thinks is immoral. If he performs such an act, dissonance will ensue between his knowledge that the act is immoral and his knowledge that he has done it. One way to reduce this dissonance would be to change his attitude – to decide, "It's not really so very bad."

As with other attitude-discrepant behavior that is a consequence of forced compliance, the amount of dissonance created decreases as the strength of the inducing force (temptation) increases. Therefore, one would expect, the *greater* the reward for performing an immoral act, the *less* the dissonance. The cognitions about the large reward received are consonant with performing the act; that is, the immoral act can be in some sense "justified" by the large reward.

How about the person who is tempted but resists? For him giving up the reward induces dissonance. He can reduce this dissonance by increasing the number and/or the importance of cognitions that are consonant with his behavior. If he has refrained from doing something he thinks is wrong – in spite of a reward – he can then convince himself the act is extremely immoral, thus justifying the behavior to which he has committed himself.

Whereas the person who *succumbs* to temptation and commits an act he considers immoral has less dissonance the greater the reward he gains, the person who *resists* temptation has more dissonance the greater the reward he forsakes.

These hypotheses were tested by Mills (1958) in an experiment with sixth graders. They were first given a questionnaire to measure the severity of their attitudes toward cheating. Then they participated in a contest in which they worked individually at a task involving eye-hand coordination. Three experimental conditions were created: (1) high temptation to cheat (offer of a large prize for outstanding performance on the task) together with low restraints against cheating (the students were given the opportunity to cheat while scoring their own performance); (2) low temptation (small prize) together with low restraint; and (3) high temptation together with high restraint (little opportunity to cheat). Cheating could be secretly detected by the experimenter. Some students cheated, some did not. One day later, the students were again asked about their attitudes toward cheating.

The findings generally supported dissonance theory. Attitude change scores showed on the average that those children who cheated tended to become more lenient toward cheating and that those who did not cheat became more critical of cheating. Students who cheated for a small prize became more lenient toward cheating than did those who cheated for a big prize. For the students who did not cheat, those giving up a large prize became more severe in their condemnation of cheating than did those who gave up only a small prize.

Finally, Mills' study showed that the effects of dissonance arousal are limited to cognitions directly relevant to the decision involved. Attitudes were also measured about other aggressive actions unrelated to cheating, but these attitudes were unaffected by the experiment.

The following sections of this chapter will review research that has been generated by dissonance theory. At the outset, it is probably safe to say that this theory has produced more research in the period from 1957 to the present than any other single theory in social psychology. A systematic literature survey (Fitch, 1967) revealed almost 400 separate studies dealing with various derivations and implications of dissonance theory.

The discussion immediately following examines both predispositional and situational factors that influence the arousal or induction of cognitive dissonance and the magnitude of dissonance experienced. We next look at various modes of dissonance reduction and attempt to determine whether or not the experimental evidence supports a particular mechanism of dissonance reduction.

Dissonance theory is then examined in the context of some other psychological theories. Finally, criticisms of dissonance theory are reviewed, and the current status of the theory is examined.

The Arousal of Cognitive Dissonance

Individual Differences

One would expect to find individual difference, or personality, variables related to the amount of dissonance induced in a given situation. It is an empirical fact that individuals engage in different amounts of dissonance reducing behavior, but the research conducted so far on this question has by no means clearly defined the relationships or even specified the variables that are most directly involved. Investigation of this issue seems to be very promising and seems likely to lead to further development of dissonance theory and related theories of cognitive motivation. The problems inherent in the issue, however, make the research challenging, as can be inferred from the difficulties encountered by investigators in the studies conducted to date.

In one of the earliest attempts to develop a measure of individual tolerance for dissonance, Aronson and Festinger (1958) found that none of five tests developed for this purpose effectively discriminated between subjects showing a high amount of dissonance reducing behavior and those showing a low amount. Taking a different approach, they looked at students who changed their major during their junior year in college and reasoned that they must possess an unusually high tolerance for dissonance. The researchers found substantial differences in six areas of a personality inventory administered to these students.

In an exploratory study of individual differences, Stack (1964) studied prospective college students. The subjects rated various colleges both before and after their decision on which college to attend. A measure of the relative amount of dissonance reduction was obtained by measuring the changes in the ratings of the various colleges rated by each student after his own decision had been made. Of the 13 personality variables studied, only three correlated with the measure of amount of dissonance reduction. For females, Rosenzweig's measure of "extrapunitiveness" (the extent to which people blame others for their own feelings of frustration) and their grade point average while in high school were inversely related to amount of dissonance reduction. For males, a measure of risk taking propensity was inversely related to one type of dissonance reducing activity.

In another exploratory effort, Brewster (1966) found no significant association between dissonance and the personality variable known as "field dependence-independence." Gallimore (1965), in a study primarily concerned with discovering dissonance-associated autonomic activity, administered several personality scales in an attempt to discover personality-associated differences in modes of dissonance reduction. None of the personality scales discriminated a preferred mode of dissonance reduction.

Although exploration of the predictive value of traditional personality scales for amount of dissonance has shown them to be largely unsuitable, more success has been achieved with a number of special variables that have some intuitive connection with dissonance induction.

Fillenbaum (1964) studied the relationship between dissonance and degree of open-mindedness as measured by Rokeach's dogmatism questionnaire and found a significant correlation. The more dogmatic subjects experienced higher dissonance. However, he found a comparable correlation in the relevant control condition, so that his results are inconclusive and must simply be considered a stimulus to further research on the question.

Rosen (1961) studied the relationship between dissonance and the variable "category width," which refers to a measure of individual differences in the widths of the cognitive categories people employ when they judge things. Some people regard rather diverse events as equivalent, whereas other people do not. Rosen found that narrow categorizers showed a more extreme preference for supportive, consonant reading material, a preference suggesting that a higher level of dissonance had been induced in these subjects. This finding held for males but not for females.

Harvey (1965) studied the relationship between the cognitive variable "concreteness-abstractness" and dissonance reduction. He found that when subjects argued against their own beliefs about philosophy, the more "concrete" subjects engaged in more dissonance reducing activity. This increase was evidenced by greater attitude change when measured both immediately following and one week after their arguments.

Harvey's theory assumes that the more "concrete" individual thinks in black and white terms and is less able to tolerate contradiction or incongruity between cognitions. It may be that Harvey's measure of "concreteness" contains or approaches in some way a measure of an individual's tolerance for dissonance. The precise relationship between the two variables is presently unclear, but it is worthy of further consideration.

Brasfield and Papageorgis (1965), hoping to discover some relationship between anxiety and dissonance, administered the Taylor Manifest Anxiety Scale (MAS) to 30 subjects and then measured their reaction to a dissonant self-relevant communication. The communication, which was allegedly based on the Holtzman Inkblot Technique, gave (disguised as a test result) a threatening but false profile. As predicted, only the high anxiety subjects accepted the communication, presumably because they experienced more dissonance upon being confronted by the discrediting communication.

Suinn (1965) investigated the same hypothesis in a different fashion. He administered the MAS and two "measures" of dissonance. The expected relationship, that people high in manifest anxiety experience greater dissonance, was found to hold with one of the measures but not the other. In general, the findings of studies on anxiety and dissonance are in line with dissonance theory because dissonance is alleged to have characteristics of psychological tension. Thus, presumably, a person experiencing dissonance would experience an increase in anxiety.

In conclusion, an individual's tolerance for dissonance is not easily predicted from standard personality scales. However, variables such as dogmatism, concreteness-abstractness, and category width seem to be related to differences in the amount of dissonance experienced by different subjects in the same situation. The conceptual relation between these variables and tolerance for dissonance is still confused and requires further research. Finally, anxiety is a variable that may be useful as a measure of the *level* of experienced dissonance, and differences in susceptibility to anxiety could be related to individual tolerances for dissonance. But here again, this is a speculative comment; only additional research will help us determine any relationship between personality factors and dissonance arousal, tolerance, and reduction.

Situational Factors

The Brehm and Cohen review makes it abundantly clear that commitment plays a critical role in the arousal or induction of cognitive dissonance. According to their definition, commitment follows a *decision* among alternatives. The crucial variable in producing commitment is *choice* or *volition*, so that the person feels responsible for and, in general, bound to the decision or the act. When the act is at odds with his private beliefs, dissonance is created.

It seems evident that the experience of dissonance should be higher if the actor sees his decision as voluntary — as his own decision — than would be the case if he is forced or required to engage in behavior discrepant with his private beliefs. In the latter case, dissonance can be avoided or reduced very simply: "I am being forced to do this; I really didn't have any choice. Therefore, it doesn't change my own beliefs about the matter at all." The research provided and reviewed by Brehm and Cohen indicates that people do in fact experience more dissonance under the condition of commitment than they do when they can satisfactorily externalize the responsibility for their discrepant behavior. A reasonable modification of the "formula" given previously suggests the relationship of commitment to the amount of dissonance induced:

$$\text{Dissonance} \ = \ \frac{\text{Degree of}}{\text{Commitment}} \ \text{x} \ \frac{\text{Importance x Number of Consonant Cognitions}}{\text{Importance x Number of Dissonant Cognitions}}$$

We have a theoretical definition of commitment, but we still need to know how the concept has been defined operationally. Two techniques have received frequent experimental use. The first method of inducing commitment is to vary the degree of influence or persuasion utilized by the experimenter in getting the subject to engage in the attitude-discrepant behavior. For example, in order to produce a feeling of free choice and consequently high commitment, the experimenter might say to the subject, "I realize you are against issue X, but we are short of subjects and we really need someone to argue *for* issue X. Would you mind doing that?" Usually the experimenter takes care *not* to appear overfriendly or overly in need of the subject's help; in fact, the experimenter may behave in an especially brusque fashion in order to prevent the subject from reducing dissonance by justifying his attitude-discrepant behavior with a cognition such as "I really don't believe what I am about to say, but he needs help, and anything to help science."

The second technique commonly used to induce commitment is differential reward. Paying some subjects a large amount of money for behaving in a particular way presumably reduces their choice in engaging in the attitude-discrepant behavior, whereas paying other subjects a small amount for the same behavior presumably induces high commitment. In the latter case, it would seem that the subjects value their integrity more than their small payment and might say to themselves: "I am responsible for this reprehensible act, and this isn't enough payment to justify what I am doing."

An example of the use of this technique is the classic Festinger-Carlsmith study (1959) using forced compliance with differential reward. They first had college students perform a boring experimental task. A third of the subjects (the control group) was then asked how they felt about the task, and they frankly described it as an unpleasant one. The two other groups had one duty to perform before they rated the task: They were paid to assist the experimenter by introducing the next subject, who was waiting outside, to the task by describing it as interesting and enjoyable. The required behavior was obviously discrepant with the subjects' own cognitions about the pleasantness of the task. The members of one group were paid $1 for this attitude-discrepant behavior, and the others were paid $20.

Dissonance theory predicts that one way to reduce the dissonance aroused would be to change one's attitudes about the task to coincide with what he had just said about it — or decide that the task really wasn't so unpleasant. In addition, high reward for the behavior should lower the likelihood of attitude change because commitment to the expressed point of view is less than when one is paid very little.

The results of the experiment were that the group of subjects receiving $20 rated the original task neutrally; in fact, their ratings were not significantly different from those of the control group. The subjects who made the same discrepant statements but were paid only $1 rated the task as more pleasant and enjoyable than the other two groups did. These findings confirm the dissonance predictions that (1) making a statement discrepant with one's true evaluation tends to produce change in evaluation toward the position in the statement and that (2) the amount of change *decreases* as the amount of reward for making the statement *increases*.[1]

One consequence of adding the commitment variable as an important one in the production of a state of cognitive dissonance has been that a new question has been raised: Is it necessary for the person actually to *perform* the discrepant behavior once he has committed himself to it in order to produce attitude change, or is commitment alone sufficient to produce attitude change in the direction of the position to which the person is publicly committed but privately opposed? Brehm and Cohen report a number of experiments in which commitment alone was sufficient to produce some attitude change. The question has, therefore, become the relative *amount* of attitude change produced by commitment alone, commitment with subsequent dissonant behavior, and dissonant behavior alone (for example, improvisation of arguments against private attitude) without choice or commitment in performing this behavior. Specification of the conditions under which one of these techniques for inducing dissonance and subsequent attitude change is more effective than others has not yet been systematically undertaken but is another area for continued research.

At least two conclusions on the commitment variable have emerged. First, this addition to dissonance theory has made the theory more explicit and has been instrumental in generating further research. Second, the variable of commitment seems to separate clearly dissonance theory from a host of other currently popular cognitive consistency theories. It is clear that other consistency theories do not account for this variable and that it is a crucial one in dissonance theory in both extending it and indicating a limitation in terms of attitude change techniques.

---

[1] For two alternative interpretations of the findings of the Festinger and Carlsmith study (1959), see Bem's discussion of self-perception in Chapter 5 and the incentive theory interpretation by Elms and Janis in Chapter 9. In Chapter 10, Brehm answers Elms and Janis' criticisms.

**The Scope of
Research Generated by
the Theory: Factors in
Dissonance Arousal**

The following selection from the excellent review and summary by Brehm and Cohen (1962) condenses some of the major findings of research attempting to isolate the factors affecting the magnitude of induced dissonance. The extent of the list — and the fact that it is only a partial one — indicate the wide range of research stemming from just this one dissonance problem.

1. Dissonance arousal is greater the more attractive is the rejected alternative when the person chooses between attractive alternatives (college students chose between appliances and other consumer goods [Brehm, 1956]).

2. Dissonance arousal is greater the more negative are the characteristics of the chosen alternative (college students who decided to become engaged [Cohen in Brehm and Cohen, 1962]).

3. Dissonance arousal is greater the larger is the number of rejected alternatives when the person chooses between attractive alternatives (purchasers of cars in a Midwest city [Ehrlich *et al.*, 1957]).

4. Dissonance arousal is greater the more important are the relevant cognitions surrounding a decision (clerks in an office indicated their preferences for various jams [Deutsch, Krauss, and Rosenau, 1962]).

5. Dissonance arousal is greater the lower is the amount of positive inducement for commitment to the discrepant behavior:

    a. the smaller the financial incentive for commitment (college students who agreed to go without food for a long period of time [Brehm in Brehm and Cohen, 1962]).

    b. the less the justification for commitment (college students who wrote essays against their own positions on a salient issue [Cohen, Brehm, and Fleming, 1958]).

    c. the more negative the characteristics of the inducing agent (Army reservists who agreed to eat grasshoppers [Smith, 1961]).

6. Dissonance arousal is greater the more there is choice in commitment to the discrepant behavior (college students who delivered electric shocks to another person [Brock and Buss, 1962]).

7. Dissonance arousal is greater the less coercion that is applied in order to induce the discrepant behavior (nursery school children who gave up an attractive toy [Aronson and Carlsmith, 1963]).

8. Dissonance arousal is greater the less the person's ability or self-esteem would lead him to perform such a discrepant act (college students judged the homosexual arousal of others in an interpersonal assessment situation [Bramel, 1962]).

9. Dissonance arousal is greater the more the person has to actually engage in the negative behavior (junior high school students ate disliked foods [Brehm, 1960b]).

10. Dissonance arousal is greater the more negative information the person has about the discrepant situation to which he is committed (college students spent three hours copying tables of random numbers and learned that someone else, not themselves, was to be paid for the work [Brehm and Cohen, 1959a]).

Dissonance Reduction

Once dissonance has been aroused, theoretically, the person will be motivated to reduce it by using one or more of the various modes of dissonance reduction that may be available. In a discussion of dissonance reduction, two main questions should be considered. First, how may the person reduce his dissonance? Second, what determines the preferred or chosen mode of resolution?

To answer the first question, we shall outline three ways an individual may reduce the dissonance in a given situation: (1) revision of a dissonance producing *attitude,* (2) *selective exposure* to dissonant information, and (3) changing *behaviors* that produce dissonant cognitions.

Attitude Change

One of the most common forms dissonance research has taken requires that the subject find himself in a situation that contains dissonance for him because of some attitude he holds; that is, the subject's attitude toward some issue must be inconsistent with his behavior. A change in the attitude, as measured before and after performance of the behavior, is then said to be evidence for the psychological discomfort resulting from the inconsistency. Thus, the attitude change is theoretically motivated by and reduces the experience of dissonance. The discrepancy between a subject's attitudes and his behavior is often made salient by using either of two procedures termed "inadequate justification" and "effort expenditure."

The Festinger-Carlsmith study described previously, in which subjects were paid $1 or $20 for misrepresenting an experimental task by telling other subjects that it was enjoyable, is an illustration of the "inadequate justification" technique. Here it is assumed that a low reward is insufficient reason for the subject to express an attitude discrepant with one he privately holds; that this behavior is dissonant with his attitude; and that, because the behavior cannot be changed, the attitude will be changed. Subjects paid $20, on the other hand, had adequate justification for their behavior, and dissonance was thus not so strongly aroused.

The special significance of this design is in its implication that both high reward and strong coercion provide justification for attitude-discrepant behavior. Consequently, if one is interested in changing another's *attitude*, it is most effective to use as little reward or coercion as possible above some minimum amount in producing the necessary *behavior*. Note, however, that this behavior (or a commitment to behave in this way) must nevertheless occur.

The second experimental procedure for introducing a discrepancy between attitudes and behavior is "effort expenditure." This procedure focuses on the amount of effort the subject puts into an attitude-discrepant task. The more effort he expends (unpleasantness?), the more dissonance is aroused between the behavior on the task and the attitude toward the task. And one way to reduce the resulting discomfort is to change the attitude to fit more closely the behavior on the task (for example, to like the task more).

Yaryan and Festinger (1961) designed an experiment to examine this hypothesis. In order to show the effect of "preparatory effort" on one's belief in a future event, they asked subjects to prepare for an IQ test by studying an information sheet on which there were definitions essential to the test. The subjects were told that they were participants in a "techniques of study" experiment that was supposed to investigate the techniques, hunches, and hypotheses that students use to study for exams. The experimenter said that only half of them would later actually take the IQ test.

In the "high effort" condition, the subjects were asked to study the sheet and memorize the definitions; in the "low effort" condition, they were asked simply to glance over the definitions briefly and were told that they would have access to the sheet later if they were actually to take the test. After studying the material, the subjects gave their estimates of the probability that they were part of the group that would be taking the IQ test. The results showed that the high effort group considered themselves more likely to take the test.

The authors' interpretation of these results is that the more effort expended in preparation for a future event, the more dissonant is the cognition that the event may not occur. Thus, subjects in the high effort condition should believe more strongly in the likelihood of the occurrence of the event. This should be the case regardless of whether one is apprehensive about the event (considers it unpleasant) or whether one looks forward to it.

Selective Exposure

If a person holds two cognitions that are inconsistent with each other, it is theorized that he will try to find ways to reduce the feeling of dissonance caused by them. Searching for new cognitions that support the favored side of the dissonant pair would be one possibility; avoiding new cognitions that would increase the dissonance would be another. In situations in which a person has some control over the kind of information to which he is exposed, according to the principle of selective exposure, he will (1) seek out dissonance reducing information and/or (2) actively avoid dissonance increasing information.

One of the earliest dissonance studies is related to this hypothesis. Ehrlich, Guttman, Schonbach, and Mills (1957) looked at the selective reading of automobile advertisements by people who had just purchased a new car and by others who owned older cars. The researchers guessed that someone who had recently made an important decision in favor of one make of automobile would be more likely to read material favoring that make than would people who had either bought another make or not made a recent decision in favor of any automobile. They also expected new car owners to avoid reading materials that favored a brand other than the one they chose.

The first prediction, that owners of new cars read advertisements of their own car more often than of cars they considered but did not buy and more often than other cars not involved in the choice, was supported by the evidence. However, this experiment as well as several others, such as Mills, Aronson, and Robinson (1959), Rosen (1961), and Adams (1961), did not yield evidence confirming the proposition that dissonant information will be avoided in proportion to the amount of dissonance produced. It seems, then, that people tend to seek out dissonance *reducing* information, but they do not necessarily *avoid* dissonance *increasing* information.

Perhaps this rather consistent finding, which conflicts with a direct prediction of the theory, can suggest a direction in which attempts to modify the theory might proceed. We know that people seek consonant information but can also tolerate dissonant information. In fact, there is some more recent evidence (Feather, 1963) that not only do smokers not avoid information linking lung cancer and smoking but, if anything, show a slight preference for it. This finding has been replicated in an unpublished work by Brock in 1965. Canon (1964) has shown that even though information increases dissonance, it may also be *useful* to the individual. The utility of information may often be more important than the dissonance it arouses, in which case it will be carefully studied. Canon's data also suggest that people may expose themselves to dissonant information largely because it is dissonant — they can in this way develop counterarguments to refute the dissonant position (Weick, 1965, p. 1268).

An expansion of the basic dissonance idea in order to incorporate these findings could use the concept of "information processing." When people develop arguments and attitudes, they seem to require a certain amount of information on both sides of the question in order to feel justified in holding them. This means an individual may purposefully introduce dissonant cognitions. Dissonant and consonant information may be *processed* differently by the individual, but to assume that the latter is sought for the comfortable feeling it provides and that the former is unpleasant and therefore to be avoided, denied, or distorted is far too simple for a theory of human behavior.

Behavioral Changes

If behaving in a certain way produces cognitions that are inconsistent with some attitude, dissonance theory predicts that either the attitudes or the behavior will change. In order to demonstrate this concept experimentally, Weick (1964) devised a situation in which the subject could reduce dissonance only by changing the level of a behavior; other ways of reducing dissonance were blocked. Weick was able to show significant attitude change *and* behavioral change in the form of enhancement of and working harder at an experimental task in which subjects were provided insufficient justification for engaging in that task.

In this experiment, the subjects were first assembled in a group. The experimenter then came into the room and in a rather discouraged manner informed the subjects that he had just been told by the head of the psychology department that he would not be allowed to offer class credit to participants in the experiment as originally promised because he was not a member of the psychology department staff. The experimenter then said rather brusquely that anyone who wanted to leave could at that time but that they might as well stay and participate in the experiment. (A few subjects did get up and leave at this point.) The subjects who stayed then worked at a concept attainment task. The startling finding was that these subjects worked harder at the task and liked it better than did subjects in control groups, who initially thought that they would get experimental credit. (Actually, at the end of the experiment, all subjects were informed of the ruse and were given equal credit for participating.)

The surprising aspect of this outcome is that Weick was able to demonstrate an increase in productivity with a reduction in the reward offered — an outcome exactly opposite to what traditional incentive theory would predict. This outcome may be seen by comparing the experimental and control conditions. In the experimental group, the subjects thought they were *not* going to receive class credit, and they were staying for an experimenter who was anything but warm-hearted. The latter aspect hopefully eliminated the dissonance reducing cognition that one is really staying to help out a warm, deserving person. The experimental subjects worked harder and performed better than those who received the expected reward of class credit. The manipulation, moreover, produced behavioral change in the form of increased productivity — not merely attitudinal change.

Choosing between Various
Modes of Dissonance Reduction

Three ways of reducing dissonance have just been discussed, and these are by no means exhaustive. Changing the importance of relevant cognitions, or the importance of the entire set of cognitions, selective recall of dissonant information, perceptual distortion, and denial of commitment or volition are all possibilities. What, then, determines which of these alternatives will be used by a given individual in preference to others?

We mentioned earlier that Festinger's original conception was that an individual would prefer to reduce dissonance by making the least effortful change he could make. The cognition least resistant to change would be selected, in other words. Research on this hypothesis has raised a number of questions indicating that the picture may be more complicated; indeed, the principle may eventually need to be replaced by a better one.

Dissonance theory itself is not equipped to predict which means of reducing dissonance will be chosen. Dissonance theorists, however, have made attempts in this direction. For example, Weick (1964) has conducted research leading him to believe that people sometimes choose the method of dissonance reduction that affords the most *stable* resolution. If one has two inconsistent attitudes about some issue, it might be easiest simply to change one's attitudes on one side of that issue and thus reduce dissonance. But if one *behaves* in a way that is consistent with one attitude but not the other (thus producing a behavioral commitment to the first), then one's position is solidified, less resistant to change, and more stable. Weick's research on behavioral change reinforces this notion; he feels that behavior can be used to *validate* a cognitive realignment.

Other research has "sharpened the kinds of issues that must be resolved to gain greater accuracy in predicting how dissonance will be reduced" (Weick, 1965, p. 1266). Weick includes these: (1) Are attitudes easier to change than behavior? (2) Do people not under experimental constraints typically use more than one mode of dissonance reduction simultaneously? (3) Are denial mechanisms more likely to be used than acceptance mechanisms? (4) Is dissonance reduced in the least effortful manner or by the method that yields the greatest gain?

McGuire reviews the work of such people as Abelson, McGuire, Newcomb, Rosenberg, and Tannenbaum on the question of alternative modes of dissonance reduction and concludes that "despite (or because of) all this work, the issue remains conceptually confused and cries for further, less haphazard study" (McGuire, 1966b, p. 27).

Summary of the Dependent
Variables in Dissonance Reduction

To complement our summary of research on dissonance arousal, the following outline, again from Brehm and Cohen (1962), indicates the range of experimental contexts used to investigate this segment of the theory.

1. Attitude change: Changes in opinion (acceptance of a compulsory religious requirement or abolition of all intercollegiate athletics at Yale University)

2. Attitude change: Changes in evaluation

   a. liking for people (for example, one's fiancee)

   b. attraction to groups (for example, a sexual discussion group)

   c. preference for objects (for example, toys, appliances)

   d. evaluation of activities (for example, a boring and time consuming task)

   e. food preferences (for example, jam, grasshoppers, disliked vegetables)

   f. sensory characteristics (for example, preference for colors, judgment of weights)

   g. subjective experiences (for example, pain, hunger, thirst)

3. Exposure to information (selective exposure to and avoidance of information on child rearing practices, car advertisements, probabilities of winning or losing in a gambling situation)

4. Recall of information (selective recall of ratings about oneself or about one's favorite TV personalities)

5. Perceptual distortion (projection of one's own experience of homosexual arousal onto another person)

6. Change in overt behavior (job productivity, drinking water, conforming to a group norm)

Dissonance Theory
in the Context of Other
Psychological Theories

Festinger's theory can be considered the third major phase in the development of consistency theories in general. Consistency theories focus on those aspects of man's behavior, thoughts, attitudes, and beliefs that are organized in meaningful and sensible ways. These theories are concerned with man's apparent need to believe himself rational, even if he has to distort or ignore reality to preserve this belief. They reinforce the psychoanalytic notion of rationalization, which holds that man strives to understand and justify painful experiences and to make them sensible and rational but sometimes employs completely irrational methods to achieve this end.

Zajonc (1960a) has provided an excellent historical review of the development of consistency theories, from Heider's balance theory, to Osgood and Tannenbaum's principle of congruity, to Festinger's theory of cognitive dissonance. Zajonc's review will be briefly sketched here.

Balance Theory

In 1946, Heider formulated a system for looking at one particular set of relationships — those involving a person (P) who is the focus of analysis, some other person (O), and one impersonal entity (X), which could be a physical object, an idea, an event, or the like. These three elements form a triad, among which are three possible relationships: the relation between P and O, between P and X, and between O and X. Heider's inquiry was to discover how relations among P, O, and X are organized in P's cognitive structure and whether there exist recurrent and systematic tendencies in the way these relations are experienced.

P's cognitive structure representing these relations is either what Heider called balanced or unbalanced. In particular, he proposed that a balanced state exists if (1) all three relations are positive or (2) two are negative and one is positive. All other configurations would be unbalanced, unstable, and likely to change to a more balanced state. For example, if one person likes another (P likes O) and also likes a certain activity (P likes X), but O does not like X, there is only one negative relation, and the system is unbalanced. If P decides to dislike O or to dislike X, balance would be restored. Similarly, if O decides to like X, the system would again be in balance.

Heider's contribution was a significant one and has stimulated much of the thought on the subject of consistency. However, there are some shortcomings. The theory does not concern cognitive structures including more than three elements. In addition, it does not specify the rules governing which elements would change in the case of an unbalanced structure; nor does it allow for P's beliefs about himself, which could conceivably be negative — for example, P could have very low self-esteem. Third, the theory does not allow for degrees of liking; according to this theory, a relation is either positive or negative.

The first of these objections was dealt with by Cartwright and Harary (1956), who constructed a more general definition of balance by using digraph theory. Their formulation covers any number of cognitive elements and also treats balance as a matter of degree, ranging from 0 to 1.

The balance notion is, of course, testable, but its apparent simplicity is misleading. It is easy to demonstrate that certain "balanced" situations are preferred to their "unbalanced" counterparts, but it is equally easy to think of examples that do not seem to fit. For example, when two attractions exist but are very dissimilar in nature and origin, do the predictions of balance theory still hold? Zajonc recalls an inquiry that Festinger once offered in a jocular mood: Would it follow from balance theory that, because he likes chicken and chickens like chicken feed, he must also like chicken feed or experience the tension of imbalance (Zajonc, 1960a, p.285)?

The Principle of Congruity

Osgood and Tannenbaum (1955) advanced the principle of congruity, which is a special case of balance. It deals specifically with the *direction* of attitude change.

> The authors assume that "judgmental frames of reference tend toward maximal simplicity." Thus, since extreme "black-and-white," "all-or-nothing" judgments are simpler than refined ones, valuations tend to move toward extremes or, . . . there is "a continuing pressure toward polarization." Together with the notion of maximization of simplicity is the assumption of identity as being less complex than the discrimination of fine differences. Therefore, related "concepts" will tend to be evaluated in a similar manner. Given these assumptions, the principle of congruity holds that when change in evaluation or attitude occurs it always occurs in the direction of increased congruity with the prevailing frame of reference (Zajonc, 1960a, pp. 286-287).

Typically, a person (*P*) has attitudes, either positive or negative, toward both a *source* (*S*) and an *object* (*O*). Moreover, person *S* is said to make assertions, either positive or negative, about the object *O*. Thus, for example, if one originally has positive attitudes about *S* and *O*, and *S* makes a positive assertion about *O*, the assertion is *congruent*. If *S* makes a negative assertion, then, as was the case with balance theory, the single negative element is *incongruent*. Congruity theory would predict that *P* will discredit either the source or the object but not both. The one chosen will depend on which of the two is more polarized − that is, extreme − in his attitude system.

The great advantage of the congruity principle over earlier attempts is in its precision. Congruity theorists can make predictions of the extent and direction of attitude change − predictions that their studies confirmed fairly well. Refined measurements have been made using Osgood's (1952) method of the "semantic differential" that are significant improvements over the positive-negative dichotomy to which balance theory is limited.

Dissonance Theory

Festinger has used the same basic assumptions as those in the consistency theories just mentioned, but his dissonance principle has been found useful in a wider range of situations. Of the three formulations, dissonance theory has been associated with the largest systematic program of research. This theory has organized a diverse body of empirical knowledge by means of a limited number of fairly reasonable assumptions.

Before assailing a theory so firmly entrenched as this one with the criticisms that come in the next section, perhaps it is wise — and only fair — at this point to compliment its special achievements. Weick (1965), in a critical review of the theory, calls attention to several issues in social psychology that have, intentionally or not, come into sharper focus as a result of work related to dissonance theory.

First, dissonance theory has emphasized that "rewards" are not always attractive. More accurately, inadequate extrinsic rewards do not always produce cessation of activities or dislike of them. "Instead, low rewards seem to prod individuals to look more closely at what they are doing and to discover satisfying features that had gone unnoticed" (Weick, 1965, p. 1271). Moreover, increasing reward may increase the feeling of coercion as well, thus producing a more stubborn unwillingness to perform the task.

> What these findings suggest is that high rewards have their drawbacks. Frequently, they constrain actions. Furthermore, when extrinsic rewards are diminished, persons may substitute their *own* rewards which are often more appropriate and satisfying. It seems clear that any social psychological research should take careful note of the fact that *cognitions* about rewards exert a significant effect on their *impact* (Weick, 1965, p. 1272, italics added).

Dissonance theory has been successful in clarifying another issue in social psychology — that of the discrepancy between public and private beliefs. Attention has been directed to the finding that these discrepancies generate more tension than was suspected. In addition, evidence has been collected to support the idea that private beliefs may change so that they furnish more support for the public actions. It was generally assumed before than an individual could maintain discrepancies with few costs and no changes.

In their efforts to find theories to oppose dissonance theory, persons have found that few exist. This is not because dissonance theory is necessarily robust, but rather because there just are not many useful theories of social behavior available. The interest generated by dissonance theory may be due more to the lack of theories than to its unique characteristics and predictive power (Weick, 1965, p. 1271).

Criticisms of the Theory and Its Evidence

Several facts associated with the theory of cognitive dissonance cannot be disputed and provide reasons for giving it so much attention. One of these facts is that a great deal of research on the theory has been done in the last 10 years, most of which confirms the theory's predictions. Another is that many researchers have used the theory to explain a wide array of events and phenomena, and the explanations usually seem reasonable. These facts suggest, more than anything else, that the theory has been surprisingly fashionable, although this trend is beginning to decline.

Chapanis and Chapanis (1964) provided one of the first extended criticisms of dissonance theory and also offered a reason for its popularity. In their words, the theory is engagingly simple:

> its magic . . . seems to lie in the ease with which imponderably complex social situations are reduced to simple statements, most often just two such statements. This having been done, a simple inspection for rational consistency is enough to predict whether or not change will occur. Such uncomplicated rationality seems especially welcome after having been told for years that our attitudes and behavior are strongly dependent on motivational, emotional, affective, and perceptual processes (p. 2).

Theoretical Problems with the Theory

This engaging simplicity of dissonance theory is a problem that theorists have been hard-pressed to solve. In any situation, including the laboratory setting, an individual will entertain an impossibly large number of cognitions. Even if we could know what all of these are, how do we decide which pairs or sets are dissonant? To say that dissonance is culturally determined merely bypasses the difficulty; the responsibility for specifying the dissonant aspects of a situation must eventually fall on the personal judgment of the observer. This responsibility gives the researcher the tempting possibility of creating situations that have predictable (intuitive) outcomes, then generating the cognitions to which it would be reasonable to attribute dissonance, and finally offering the results as support for the theory.

Given these considerations, it is surprising to realize that no special effort has been made to determine whether a subject has *experienced* the tension called dissonance; or whether the "salient" cognitions were actually salient to him; or the extent to which contaminating cognitions were present. It would not seem unreasonable to *ask* the subject after an experiment if he saw the problem the way the experimenter did, even though this procedure admittedly calls attention to a certain vagueness in the theory.

A related problem is that of "confounding" the relationships between cognitions. The more complex a social setting, the greater the number of inter-related cognitions. One can *assume* that a particular pair of this large set of cognitions will arouse dissonance and will in turn change some dependent variable. But it is inevitable that other pairs will be dissonant, either more or less so, and, because all the other possible pairs cannot be tested, they are commonly ignored. Thus, the experimental "effect" is attributed, say, to the dissonance created by cognitions *a* and *b*. Yet in fact, some other pair, *a* and *e*, or *e* and *f*, might be responsible for the effect — in other words, they might be confounding the main effects of *a* and *b*. There is no way to control this problem completely, but Chapanis and Chapanis feel that it will be minimized if dissonance researchers will restrict themselves to less complex social situations. In those experiments where discrepant internal cognitions are said to follow the presentation of relatively simple contradictory statements, syllogisms, or opinions, the results are more consistent and clear-cut.

Weick (1965, p. 1263) cites the work of Adams and Jacobsen (1964) as an example of an "uncomplicated" dissonance study, one not so "needlessly complex" as many dissonance experiments. These researchers explored what happened to the quality and quantity of output on a proofreading task when there was a marked discrepancy between a person's input and the salary he received. Here it is relatively easy to isolate the cognitions that will be most salient for the subject and to infer the amount of dissonance he will experience in the situation.

But even though this study involves relationships between dissonance and expenditure of effort, "a problem that seems easier to simplify than problems of attitude change, decision-making, or interpersonal perception," Weick himself later offers an alternative set of cognitions that may be operating in the Adams and Jacobsen experiment. In their study,

> a person takes a test of proofreading ability, fails it, and then is hired "reluctantly" by an employer to be a professional proofreader. This manipulation is intended to create a discrepancy between what a person contributes to a job and what he receives. [The subject] may not be bothered as much by this discrepancy as by the discrepancy between the

initial test data and his beliefs about his capabilities. He may believe that he is qualified to detect typographical errors only to discover that tests show he is not. An easy way to resolve the discrepancy between self-concept and test data is to discredit the test. If this occurs, [the experimenter] has created dissonance, but not where he intended (Weick, 1965, pp. 1264-1265).

The ambiguity in the locus of dissonance, or even of the "major" or "important" cognitions in a situation, is subject to interpretation. This ambiguity too often leads to more than one "reasonable" interpretation and thus to a misleading ability to "explain" nearly anything.

It is to this flaw that Bem (1967) refers when he argues that dissonance theory has attempted to bypass a functional analysis, which will eventually have to be performed to eliminate the ambiguity in the definition of dissonance. He offers a theoretical alternative to dissonance and explains much of the same data given in its support. The paper appears as Chapter 5 of this book.

Methodological Problems with Dissonance Research

The five years following the appearance of Festinger's first statement of the theory saw the rapid growth of experimental work testing its propositions. The empirical evidence supporting dissonance theory was impressive and, to many critics, convincing. It was at this point, however, that Chapanis and Chapanis (1964) discussed in a lengthy critique some aspects of dissonance research that, taken together, left them unconvinced about the theory's generality. Their controversial paper dealt largely with two major flaws in the methodology typically applied to dissonance research. The first was concerned with the extremely complex manipulations used to create a dissonant situation in the laboratory — that is, with "whether an experimenter really did what he said he did." The second involved what Chapanis and Chapanis considered technically questionable methods of treating the experimental data — "whether the experimenter really got the results he said he did."

To illustrate the first argument, let us look again at Yaryan and Festinger's (1961) study using the "effort expenditure" paradigm. The experiment was designed to show that high effort on a task (preparing to take an IQ test) would lead to a stronger belief that the event the task prepared for (the test) would occur. The high effort group was told to study their list carefully, whereas the low effort group merely glanced over the list without studying it. The former group thought it was more probable that they would take the test.

Yaryan and Festinger explain these results by *inferring* that the high effort subjects held the cognition that they had exerted "a great deal of effort" and that this cognition is inconsistent with not taking the test. There is no way to observe any *direct* evidence that the subjects actually held these cognitions or thought in these terms. Moreover, Chapanis and Chapanis offer an alternative explanation of the results that seems equally reasonable:

> in this experiment the variable of effort is confounded with the presence of other predictors for the event. All subjects had been told that this was an experiment on the techniques of study, but the only group which *did* any studying was the high-effort group. In addition, the studying that was done was highly relevant for the IQ test. Under the circumstances, it does not seem at all surprising that subjects in this group took these additional cues to mean that they were assigned to the complete experiment and to the IQ test. As it stands now, the Yaryan and Festinger experiment does not separate the effect of effort from that of additional cues (Chapanis and Chapanis, 1964, p. 9).

For such reasons, it is not at all clear that an experimenter always sets up the conditions or the controls that he thought he did.

Another study described earlier, that of Ehrlich *et al.* (1957) on the selective exposure of automobile buyers to information about different brands, was among those criticized for committing a different kind of error common to many dissonance experiments. A technique used many times in these studies is to discard the data from certain subjects because those data are "unreliable" or "inappropriate." In the Ehrlich *et al.* study, "as much as 82% of the original sample was discarded in certain categories!" (Chapanis and Chapanis, 1964, p. 15).

Under some conditions, this procedure is justifiable; however, under other conditions, it can lead to a definite bias in the results. The above example was criticized because the *reasons* for rejecting parts of the data were not made clear in the presentation of the study. But in some cases, selecting the data can *"violate the whole concept of controlled experimentation."* Chapanis and Chapanis outline the faulty reasoning used by some dissonance researchers:

> If some subjects do not follow the specific predictions in a particular experiment (for instance, if they fail to show any opinion change) then those subjects are probably reducing their dissonance through some other channel or else they had little dissonance to begin with. If either of these conditions holds it is legitimate to exclude these subjects from the analysis since they could not possibly be used to test the particular hypothesis in the experiment. An inspection of results is considered sufficient to determine whether subjects are, or are not, to be excluded. Unfortunately, this line of reasoning contains one fundamental flaw: *it does not allow the possibility that the null hypothesis may be correct.* The experimenter, in effect, is asserting that his dissonance prediction is correct and that subjects who do not conform to the prediction should be excluded from

the analysis. This is a foolproof method of guaranteeing positive results (Chapanis and Chapanis, 1964, p. 17).

Perhaps, then, experimenters do not always get the results they thought (or said) they did.

These criticisms, of course, do not apply equally to all of the experiments in the dissonance context — many of them are relatively unassailable. Chapanis and Chapanis call attention to only a segment of the evidence and ask that it not be taken so unequivocally as the evidence obtained with more care and logic.

One of the classic dissonance experiments (Festinger and Carlsmith, 1959), the forced compliance design using $1 and $20 conditions to produce attitude change, has been criticized by Rosenberg (1965) for containing a confounding influence he calls "evaluation apprehension." This is essentially a suspicion on the part of the subject that he is being evaluated by the experimenter. Rosenberg's replication of the former study obtained results directly opposite to those of Festinger and Carlsmith.

Rosenberg's study was, in turn, replicated and expanded by Linder, Cooper, and Jones (1967), and a variable accounting for the discrepancy between the two experiments was reportedly isolated. The entire issue is too lengthy to be included here, but is recommended to the reader as an excellent example of the use of experimentation to test the conflicting predictions of two theories.

Current Status and Some Predictions about the Future

The Role of Dissonance — The Beginning of a Theory?

Zajonc (1960a) has drawn an interesting parallel between dissonance as an explanatory principle and another principle that is important in the history of science. He suggests that the role of these two principles may be comparable and that making the comparison can help us understand their common context and bring both the faults and the contributions of the dissonance formulation into perspective.

For centuries, a number of related phenomena were accounted for by a commonly accepted principle. The principle was used to "explain" such facts as (1) pumps can lift a column of water by removing the air from the top of a tube; (2) two hemispheric vessels, placed together with the air removed from between them, are held to each other; and (3) a suction (force) can be established by drawing air from a vessel. Each of these phenomena involves the absence of air, and all were accounted for by the principle "Nature abhors a vacuum." The evidence for this principle was so overwhelming that it was seldom questioned.

Then people noticed an exception. Pumps can only draw water to a height of 34 feet. The principle had to be modified to deal with this observation. This state of affairs was satisfactory until Torricelli discovered that mercury can only be lifted 30 inches. It was becoming uncomfortable to employ a principle that had to include so many exceptions — it now read: "Nature abhors a vacuum but only below 34 feet when we deal with water and below 30 inches with mercury." Torricelli was therefore led to formulate the more general notion that it is atmospheric pressure that forces air into a vacuum and that this force can sustain the weight of 34 feet of water or 30 inches of mercury. This was a revolutionary concept, and its consequences had a drastic impact on physics.

Similarly, human nature is said to abhor dissonance. But there are many exceptions to the consistency principle — people enjoy watching a magician, whose task it is to produce dissonance. In a magical act, the obverse of what you see follows from what you know. People spend a good portion of their income on insurance, and many at the same time are willing to gamble at casinos. The first action is intended to protect against risks; the second implies an enjoyment of taking risks. The dissonance principle as it stands does not seem to be universally or unequivocally true, and yet it serves a useful function. Returning to Zajonc's parallel:

> . . . *horror vacui* served an important purpose besides explaining and orga-
> nizing some aspects of physical knowledge. Without it the discomfort of
> "exceptions to the rule" would never have been felt, and the important
> developments in theory might have been delayed considerably. If a
> formulation has then a virtue in being wrong, the theories of consistency
> do have this virtue. They do organize a large body of knowledge. Also,
> they point out exceptions, and thereby they demand a new formulation. It
> will not suffice simply to reformulate them so as to accommodate the
> exceptions. I doubt if Festinger would be satisfied with a modification of
> his dissonance principle which would read that dissonance, being psycho-
> logically uncomfortable, leads a person to actively avoid situations and
> information which would be likely to increase the dissonance, except
> when there is an opportunity to watch a magician.
>
> Also simply to disprove the theories by counterexamples would not in
> itself constitute an important contribution. We would merely lose
> explanations of phenomena which had been explained. And it is doubtful
> that the theories of consistency could be rejected simply *because* of
> counterexamples. Only a theory which accounts for all the data that the
> consistency principles now account for, for all the exceptions to those
> principles, and for all the phenomena which these principles should now
> but do not consider, is capable of replacing them. It is only a matter of
> time until such a development takes place (Zajonc, 1960a, p. 296).

On this optimistic note, let us look at a theoretical trend that may eventually assimilate the principle of dissonance and fit it into a more comprehensive framework.

Future Directions: Consistency Theory versus Complexity Theory

In Feldman's (1966) book entitled *Cognitive Consistency*, McGuire contributes an excellent account of "the place of consistency theory in the larger psychological scene." He, too, assumes that the theory will eventually come to be considered a part of some larger, more inclusive formulation. One possibility is that dissonance, or, more generally, consistency, will be fitted into psychological thinking as a *motive*, thereby joining the ever increasing number of new motives proposed by psychologists (for example, the achievement motive, the affiliation motive, and the approval motive). Another possibility is to consider consistency from a *functional* point of view:

> Attitudes have been analyzed as serving many functions: utility, expression, meaning, ego-defensiveness, etc. It seems likely that maintenance of consistency plays an important role in all of these functions; certainly, in the last two. We feel that an integration into the functional approach is another avenue by which consistency theories, to the mutual benefit of both kinds of approach, could be brought into heuristically provocative interaction with other approaches (McGuire, 1966b, p. 35).

A less cautious prediction, but one with which we tend to agree, is McGuire's extension of what he considers a new, corrective trend in psychology — one antithetical to the consistency approach but able to integrate some of its concepts. He cites Berlyne (1960), Fiske and Maddi (1961), and Fowler (1965) as representative of approaches he subsumes under the "unsatisfactory rubric of 'complexity theories.'" Contrasting the "classical" view of an organism as having a "penchant for stability, redundancy, familiarity, confirmation of expectance, avoidance of the new, the unpredictable," complexity theory's "romantic organism works on a quite different economy. It has a stimulus hunger, an exploratory drive, a need curiosity. It takes pleasure in the *unexpected*, at least in intermediate levels of unpredictability. It wants to experience everything; it shows alternation behavior; it finds novelty rewarding" (McGuire, 1966b, p. 37).

Complexity notions, although not logically contradictory to consistency theory, seem to have the reverse psychological flavor. McGuire feels that the two approaches are interrelated and that, in the swing he sees in psychology from a classical to a romantic phase, complexity theories may be expanded to encompass both points of view. Perhaps then several "principles" of social psychology can be integrated into a realistic theory. Nonetheless, one thing remains clear. Whatever the future directions of the theoretical work in this area, dissonance research has contributed a wealth of experimental data that will continue to support, challenge, and contradict the attempts of later workers to find a way of systematizing it.

5

Self-Perception: An Alternative Interpretation of Cognitive Dissonance Phenomena

Daryl J. Bem

Bem presents an alternative approach to some of the data that were thought to be explained by dissonance theory. Bem suggests that attitude change may derive not from a motivational drive to reduce dissonance, but from "interpersonal judgments in which the observer and the observed happen to be the same individual." In addition to presenting his theoretical alternative, Bem describes and re-examines — theoretically *and* experimentally — several key studies described in Chapter 4. The contrast helps both to clarify and to place in a broader perspective the basic principles proposed by the theory of cognitive dissonance.

Additional critiques of dissonance theory can be found in Zajonc (1960a), Chapanis and Chapanis (1964), and Feldman (1966).*

If a person holds two cognitions that are inconsistent with one another, he will experience the pressure of an aversive motivational state called cognitive dissonance, a pressure which he will seek to remove, among other ways, by altering one of the two "dissonant" cognitions. This proposition is the heart of Festinger's (1957) theory of cognitive dissonance, a theory which has received

*The paper following this editorial introduction is slightly abridged from D. J. Bem, Self-perception: An alternative interpretation of cognitive dissonance phenomena, *Psychological Review*, 1967, *74*, 183-200, by permission of the author and the publisher, the American Psychological Association.

This research was supported in part by Ford Foundation Grant 140055 to Carnegie Institute of Technology and in part by the Center for Research on Language and Language Behavior, University of Michigan, with funds from the Bureau of Higher Education Research, United States Office of Education. The author is grateful to George R. Madaras and Kenneth M. Peterson for aid in conducting the research and to Sandra L. Bem for critical comments on the manuscript.

more widespread attention from personality and social psychologists in the past 10 years than any other contemporary statement about human behavior.

The theory has had its critics, but no theoretical alternative to dissonance theory has been proposed which attempts both to embrace its major phenomena and to account for some of the secondary patterns of results which have appeared in the supporting experiments but which were not predicted by the theory. This article proposes such an alternative.

Like many theories in psychology, the theory of cognitive dissonance attempts to account for observed functional relations between current stimuli and responses by postulating some hypothetical process within the organism, in this case, an inferred process of the arousal and reduction of dissonance. Like many other contemporary personality and social psychological theories, dissonance theory is further characterized by an emphasis on the individual's current phenomenology; the explanatory account in the theory itself is ahistorical.

In contrast, the alternative formulation to be presented here eschews any reference to hypothetical internal processes and seeks, rather, to account for observed functional relations between current stimuli and responses in terms of the individual's past training history. Such an approach has been called "radical" behaviorism (see Scriven, 1956), a position most often associated with the name of B. F. Skinner. In analyzing a complex behavioral phenomenon, the radical behaviorist attempts to establish it as a special case of some previously substantiated functional relation discovered in the experimental analysis of simpler behaviors. His functional analysis is thus based on empirical generalization and, accordingly, is frankly inductive not only in its experimental execution, but in its formal presentation.

A functional analysis characteristically begins by inquiring into the ontogenetic origins of the observed dependent variable and attempts to ascertain the controlling or independent variables of which that behavior is a function. The present analysis of dissonance phenomena proceeds in the same way by noting first that the dependent variable in cognitive dissonance studies is, with very few exceptions, a subject's (S's) self-descriptive statement of an attitude or belief. Indeed, this is the dependent variable in nearly all of contemporary social psychology. But how are such self-descriptive behaviors acquired? What are their controlling variables? It is to these questions that the analysis turns first.

Self-Perception:
A Special Case
of Interpersonal Perception

Self-perception, an individual's ability to respond differentially to his own behavior and its controlling variables, is a product of social interaction

(Mead, 1934; Ryle, 1949; Skinner, 1957). Verbal statements that are self-descriptive are among the most common responses comprising self-perception, and the techniques employed by the community to teach its members to make such statements would not seem to differ fundamentally from the methods used to teach interpersonal perception in general. The community, however, does face severe limitations in training the individual to make statements describing internal events to which only he has direct access. Skinner (1953, 1957) has analyzed the limited resources available to the community for training its members thus to "know themselves," and he has described the inescapable inadequacies of the resulting knowledge.

Skinner suggests that some self-descriptions of internal stimuli can be learned through metaphor or stimulus generalization. The child, for example, can easily learn to describe "butterflies in the stomach" without explicit discrimination training. More often, however, a socializing community must teach the descriptive responses more directly. In training a child to describe pain, for example, the community, at some point, must teach him the correct response at the critical time when the appropriate private stimuli are impinging upon him. But the community itself must necessarily identify the "critical time" on the basis of observable stimuli or responses and implicitly assume that the private stimuli are, in fact, accompanying these public events.

This analysis suggests that many of the self-descriptive statements that appear to be exclusively under the discriminative control of private stimuli may, in fact, still be partially controlled by the same accompanying public events used by the training community to infer the individual's inner states. Private stimuli may play a smaller role than the individual himself suspects. For example, by manipulating the external cues of the situation, Schachter and Singer (1962) were able to evoke self-descriptions of emotional states as disparate as euphoria and anger from Ss in whom operationally identical states of physiological arousal had been induced. It appears that these Ss utilized internal stimuli only to make the gross discrimination that they were emotional, but that the more subtle discrimination of *which* emotion they were experiencing was under the control of external cues.

A similar division of control between internal and external stimuli appears to operate in the domain of attitude statements. In particular, it is suggested that self-descriptive attitude statements can be based on the individual's observations of his own overt behavior and the external stimulus conditions under which it occurs. A number of recent experimental studies provide support for this proposition.

Several studies have shown that an individual's belief and attitude statements can be manipulated by inducing him to role-play, deliver a persuasive communication, or engage in any behavior that would characteristically imply his endorsement of a particular set of beliefs (Brehm and Cohen, 1962; King and Janis, 1956; Scott, 1957, 1959a). A recent experimental analysis of these phenomena of "self-persuasion" demonstrates that an individual bases his subsequent beliefs and attitudes on such self-observed behaviors to the extent that these behaviors are emitted under circumstances that have in the past set the occasion for telling the truth (Bem, 1965, 1966). For example, in one of three studies reported in Bem (1965), Ss were first trained to tell the truth in the presence of a colored light and to tell lies in the presence of another. Later in the experimental session, Ss were required to state attitudes with which they disagreed; one of the two colored lights was illuminated as each attitude statement was made. It was found that Ss subsequently endorsed the attitude statements they had uttered in the presence of the "truth light" significantly more than attitude statements they had made in the presence of the "lie light"; the lights, in short, determined the degree to which Ss believed what they had heard themselves say. Furthermore, no S could report any awareness of the control exerted by his statements or the lights over his subsequent attitudes.

In another study, the same technique was employed to demonstrate that an individual can be induced to believe in "false confessions" he has made if there are external cues present that characteristically set the occasion for telling the truth (Bem, 1966). These several studies have also illustrated that the control over an individual's beliefs and attitudes exerted by his overt behavior is vitiated to the extent that cues are present implying that the behavior is deceitful or, more generally, is being emitted for immediate specific reinforcement. For example, just as a communicator is more persuasive to others if he is known to be receiving no payment for his communication, so too, it is found that he is more likely to believe himself under such circumstances (Bem, 1965). The effectiveness of self-persuasion can thus be altered by many of the techniques typically used to manipulate the credibility of any persuasive communicator.

The major implication of these findings is that, to the extent that internal stimuli are not controlling, an individual's attitude statements may be viewed as inferences from observations of his own overt behavior and its accompanying stimulus variables. As such, his statements are functionally similar to those that any outside observer could make about him. When the answer to the question, "Do you like brown bread?" is "I guess I do, I'm always eating it," it seems unnecessary to invoke a fount of privileged self-knowledge to account for the reply. In such a case the reply is functionally equivalent to one his wife might give for him: "I guess he does, he is always eating it." Only to the extent that "brown bread" elicits strongly conditioned internal responses might he have additional evidence, not currently available to his wife, on which to base his self-descriptive attitude statement.

The present analysis of dissonance phenomena, then, will rest upon the single empirical generalization that an individual's belief and attitude statements and the beliefs and attitudes that an outside observer would attribute to him are often functionally similar in that both sets of statements are partial "inferences" from the same evidence: the public behaviors and accompanying stimulus cues upon which the socializing community has relied in training him to make such self-descriptive statements in the first place.

Phenomena of Dissonance Theory

The major phenomena of dissonance theory have been classified into three main categories (Brehm and Cohen, 1962, p. 21): (1) forced-compliance studies; (2) free-choice studies; and (3) exposure-to-information studies. Within each category, this discussion will treat the major functional relation predicted and subject the data from a single dissonance experiment to detailed analysis. Two sets of secondary findings will also be discussed.

Because the literature of dissonance theory has now become so large that it would be impossible to discuss all the experimental paradigms that have been employed, the specific experiments selected for detailed analysis had to satisfy certain criteria. First, whenever possible, they had to be illustrative of several others in the same category so that the applicability of the self-perception analysis to studies not explicitly discussed would be apparent. Second, for each experiment there had to be at least one other study in the literature that had successfully replicated the same conceptual phenomenon employing different experimental procedures if possible. These first two criteria together attempt to ensure that the analysis avoids "explaining" phenomena that are artifactual, while at the same time not requiring that the particular study under analysis be invulnerable to methodological criticism. Finally, the studies selected are those which are best known and most widely reprinted or cited and which the dissonance theorists claim to be "entirely closed to the judgmental interpretation and rather unequivocally explainable by the dissonance formulation [Brehm and Cohen, 1962, p. 111]."

The Forced-Compliance Studies

The most frequently cited evidence for dissonance theory comes from an experimental procedure known as the forced-compliance paradigm. In these experiments, an individual is induced to engage in some behavior that would imply his endorsement of a particular set of beliefs or attitudes. Following his behavior, his "actual" attitude or belief is assessed to see if it is a function of the behavior in which he has engaged and of the manipulated stimulus conditions under which it was evoked. The best known and most widely quoted study of this type was conducted by Festinger and Carlsmith (1959). In their experiment, 60 undergraduates were randomly assigned to one of three experimental conditions. In the $1 condition, S was first required to perform long repetitive laboratory tasks in an individual experimental session. He was then hired by the experimenter as an "assistant" and paid $1 to tell a waiting fellow student (a stooge) that the tasks were enjoyable and interesting. In the $20 condition, each S was hired for $20 to do the same thing. Control Ss simply engaged in the repetitive tasks. After the experiment, each S indicated how much he had enjoyed the tasks. The results show that Ss paid $1 evaluated the tasks as significantly more enjoyable than did Ss who had been paid $20. The $20 Ss did not express attitudes significantly different from those expressed by the control Ss.

Dissonance theory interprets these findings by noting that all Ss initially hold the cognition that the tasks are dull and boring. In addition, however, the experimental Ss have the cognition that they have expressed favorable attitudes toward the tasks to a fellow student. These two cognitions are dissonant for Ss in the $1 condition because their overt behavior does not "follow from" their cognition about the task, nor does it follow from the small compensation they are receiving. To reduce the resulting dissonance pressure, they change their cognition about the task so that it is consistent with their overt behavior: they become more favorable toward the tasks. The Ss in the $20 condition, however, experience little or no dissonance because engaging in such behavior "follows from" the large compensation they are receiving. Hence, their final attitude ratings do not differ from those of the control group.

In contrast with this explanation, the present analysis views these results as a case of self-perception. Consider the viewpoint of an outside observer who hears the individual making favorable statements about the tasks to a fellow student, and who further knows that the individual was paid $1 ($20) to do so. This hypothetical observer is then asked to state the actual attitude of the individual he has heard. An outside observer would almost certainly judge a $20 communicator to be "manding" reinforcement (Skinner, 1957); that is, his behavior appears to be under the control of the reinforcement contingencies of the money and not at all under the discriminative control of the tasks he appears to be describing. The $20 communicator is not credible in that his statements cannot be used as a guide for inferring his actual attitudes. Hence, the observer could conclude that the individual found such repetitive tasks dull and boring in spite of what he had said. Although the behavior of a $1 communicator also has some mand properties, an outside observer would be more likely to judge him to be expressing his actual attitudes and, hence, would infer the communicator's attitude from the content of the communication itself. He would thus judge this individual to be favorable toward the tasks. If one now places the hypothetical observer and the communicator into the same skin, the findings obtained by Festinger and Carlsmith are the result. There is no aversive motivational pressure postulated; the dependent variable is viewed simply as a self-judgment based on the available evidence, evidence that includes the apparent controlling variables of the observed behavior.

If this analysis of the findings is correct, then it should be possible to replicate the inverse functional relation between amount of compensation and the final attitude statement by actually letting an outside observer try to infer the attitude of an S in the original study. Conceptually, this replicates the Festinger-Carlsmith experiment with the single exception that the observer and the observed are no longer the same individual.

An Interpersonal Replication of the Festinger-Carlsmith Experiment

Seventy-five college undergraduates participated in an experiment designed to "determine how accurately people can judge another person." Twenty-five Ss each served in a $1, a $20, or a control condition. All Ss listened to a tape recording which described a college sophomore named Bob Downing, who had participated in an experiment involving two motor tasks. The tasks were described in detail, but nonevaluatively; the alleged purpose of the experiment was also described. At this point, the control Ss were asked to evaluate Bob's attitudes toward the tasks. The experimental Ss were further told that Bob had accepted an offer of $1 ($20) to go into the waiting room tell the next S that the tasks were fun, and to be prepared to do this again in the future if they needed him. The Ss then listened to a brief conversation which they were told was an actual recording of Bob and the girl who was in the waiting room. Bob was heard to argue rather imaginatively that the tasks were fun and enjoyable, while the girl responded very little except for the comments that Festinger and Carlsmith's stooge was instructed to make. The recorded conversation was identical for both experimental conditions in order to remain true to the original study in which no differences in persuasiveness were found between the $1 and the $20 communications. In sum, the situation attempted to duplicate on tape the situation actually experienced by Festinger and Carlsmith's Ss.

All Ss estimated Bob's responses to the same set of questions employed in the original study. The key question required Ss to rate the tasks (or Bob's attitude toward them) on a scale from -5 to +5, where -5 means that the tasks were extremely dull and boring, +5 means they were extremely interesting and enjoyable, and 0 means they were neutral, neither interesting nor uninteresting.

Results

Table 1 shows the mean ratings for the key question given by Ss in all three conditions of both the original experiment and the present replication.

The results show that in both studies the $1 and control conditions are on different sides of the neutral point and are significantly different from one another at the .02 level of significance (t = 2.48 in the original study; t = 2.60 in the replication).[1] In both studies, the $1 condition produced significantly more favorable ratings toward the tasks than did the $20 condition ($t$ = 2.22, $p < .03$ in the original study; t = 3.52, $p < .001$ in the replication). In neither study is the $20 condition significantly different from the control condition; and, finally, in neither study were there any significant differences between conditions on the other questions asked of Ss about the experiment. Thus, the inverse relation between amount of compensation and the final attitude rating is clearly replicated; and, even though the present analysis does not require the attitude judgments themselves of the interpersonal observers to duplicate those of Ss in the original experiment, it is seen that the two sets of ratings are quite comparable on the 10-point scales.

Since the above replication was conducted, Jones (1966) has reported a study in which Ss' attitudes and observers' judgments were compared directly in

Table 1. Attitude Ratings and Interpersonal Estimates of Attitude Ratings toward the Tasks for Each Condition

	Experimental Condition		
Study	*Control*	*$1 Compensation*	*$20 Compensation*
Festinger-Carlsmith	- 0.45	+1.35	- 0.05
Interpersonal replication	- 1.56	+0.52	- 1.96

Note — For the Festinger-Carlsmith study, N = 20 in each condition; for the interpersonal replication study, N = 25 in each condition.

[1] All significance levels in this article are based on two-tailed tests.

the same experiment. Again, the observers' judgments not only replicated the inverse functional relation displayed by the attitude statements of Ss themselves, but the actual scale positions of observers and Ss were again similar.

These successful replications of the functional relation reported by Festinger and Carlsmith provide support for the self-perception analysis. The original Ss may be viewed as simply making self-judgments based on the same kinds of public evidence that the community originally employed in training them to infer the attitudes of any communicator, themselves included. It is not necessary to postulate an aversive motivational drive toward consistency.

These interpersonal replications are illustrative of others which have been reported elsewhere (Bem, 1965). It has been shown that the present analysis applies as well to forced-compliance experiments which utilize compensations much smaller than $20, to studies which manipulate variables other than the amount of compensation, and to studies which evoke different behaviors from S. Alternative dependent variables have also been considered. For example, Brehm and Cohen show that S's rating of how hungry he is can be manipulated by inducing him to volunteer to go without food for different amounts of compensation (1962, pp. 132-137), and a successful interpersonal replication of that experiment again supports the present self-perception analysis of these forced-compliance phenomena (Bem, 1965).

The merits of alternative formulations to an established theory are often sought in their ability to explicate functional relations about which the original theory must remain mute. Accordingly, the analysis now turns to a pattern of related findings which have not been adequately accommodated by dissonance theory: the observed relationships between the *amount* of behavior evoked from S in a forced-compliance setting and his final attitude statements.

A number of forced-compliance experiments have demonstrated that the differential effects of the stimulus manipulations on attitude statements can be obtained even before any of the behavior to which the individual has committed himself is actually emitted (Brehm and Cohen, 1962, pp. 115-116). That is, the behavior of volunteering to emit the behavior is sufficient to control the individual's subsequent self-judgment of attitude. (The self-perception interpretation of this effect has also been confirmed by an interpersonal replication [Bem, 1965].) In fact, in an experiment in which Ss volunteered to write essays against their initial opinions, Rabbie, Brehm, and Cohen (1959) report that the mean of attitude ratings obtained before the essays were actually written was not significantly different from the mean of attitude ratings obtained after the essays were written. But the variance across Ss was much greater in the latter case. That is, actually writing the essays increases *and* decreases the initial effect of volunteering. In addition, there was a negative relationship between the number of arguments S wrote and the degree to which his final attitude statement agreed with the position advocated in the essay. On the other hand, Cohen, Brehm, and Fleming (1958) report a positive relationship between "original arguments" and amount of attitude change, but this relationship appeared in only one of the experimental conditions. Unpublished data from the Festinger-Carlsmith experiment show a negative correlation in one condition between attitude ratings and "number and variety" of arguments and a positive correlation in the other (reported by Brehm and Cohen, 1962, p. 119). Finally, when Ss themselves rate the quality of their persuasive communications, the confusion is further compounded. Brehm and Cohen conclude that "the role of discrepant verbal behavior in the arousal and reduction of dissonance remains unclear [p. 121]." How might the self-perception analysis treat these effects?

If an outside observer begins with the discrimination that a communicator is credible, then the more arguments put forth, the more persuasive the speaker might well become, *if* nothing intervenes to change the observer's judgment of the communicator's credibility. If, however, the observer discriminates the communicator as manding reinforcement, then it seems likely that the more insistent the speaker becomes in pushing his point of view, the more it appears to the observer that he "doth protest too much," and the less likely it is that the speaker's statements will be taken to express his "actual" attitudes.

Now consider the self-observer. If Ss in the dissonance experiments begin with the discrimination that they are not manding (Ss in the low compensation conditions, for example), then the more arguments they put forth, the more self-persuasive they might become. For any given S, however, presenting a communication counter to his initial position might itself provide him with the cues that he is manding and hence destroy the initial effect of volunteering under nonmand conditions; he will become less self-persuasive as he continues. This analysis, then, leads one to expect the increased variability in postessay as compared to pre-essay measures of attitude. It is equally clear, however, that to confirm this analysis, the hypothesized discrimination of credibility must be brought under experimental control rather than being left under the control of the unique past histories of individual Ss. To do this, the Festinger-Carlsmith experiment is again used as an illustrative example.

An Extended Interpersonal Replication of the Festinger-Carlsmith Experiment

Festinger and Carlsmith found that within the $1 condition, the greater the number and variety of arguments stated by S about the tasks, the more favorable his final evaluation was of them. Within the $20 condition, however, the greater the number and variety of arguments, the less favorable his final rating. The following study thus seeks to replicate this pattern of results with interpersonal observers.

Method

In the earlier replication, the persuasive communication heard by Ss was identical for both conditions. All Ss heard the speaker present a fairly imaginative and lengthy set of reasons as to why he had enjoyed the tasks. For the present extension, a second communication was designed, which was somewhat shorter and contained comparatively unimaginative arguments. The replication was then rerun on an additional 50 Ss assigned either to a $1 or a $20 condition. The Ss were again asked to estimate the actual attitude of the speaker. Thus, except for the length and variety of arguments in the communication, this replication is identical with the earlier one. The total design, then, contains four experimental groups: $1-long communication, $1-short communication, $20-long communication, and $20-short communication.

If the present analysis is correct, then within the $1 condition, where the communicator is more likely to be perceived as credible, the long communication should lead interpersonal observers to infer that the communicator enjoyed the tasks more than the short communication would. Within the $20 condition, however, the long communication should be *less* persuasive than the short one; the longer the speaker carries on, the harder he appears to be trying to earn his $20. He "doth protest too much." Thus, an interaction effect is predicted between the two variables of communication length and amount of compensation. It will be noted that this is equivalent to saying that the "dissonance" effect, the inverse functional relation between compensation and attitude change, is itself a function of communication length. The shorter the communication, the smaller the inverse relationship should become, perhaps even reversing itself at very short communication lengths.

Results

Tables 2 and 3 display the results and their analysis, respectively. It will be recalled that scores can range from -5 to +5, the higher the score, the more favorable the communicator is judged to be toward the tasks.

It is seen that the interpersonal interpretation of self-perception is supported by these results. By employing attitude estimates of outside observers, the study

Table 2.   Interpersonal Estimates of Attitude Ratings toward the Tasks

Experimental Condition	Long Communication	Short Communication
$1 compensation	+0.52	- 1.04
$20 compensation	- 1.96	- 0.64

Note − N = 25 in each cell

Table 3.   Summary of Analysis of Variance of Interpersonal Estimates of Attitude Ratings toward the Tasks

Source of Variation	Sum of Squares	df	Mean Square	F
Long versus short	0.360	1	0.360	0.05
$1 versus $20	27.040	1	27.040	4.07*
Interaction	51.840	1	51.840	7.80**
Within cells	637.920	96	6.645	

*$p < .05$.
**$p < .01$.

has replicated Festinger and Carlsmith's positive correlation between number of arguments and attitude change within the $1 condition and the negative correlation between these two variables within the $20 condition. The main effect of compensation seen in Tables 2 and 3 is, of course, the primary "dissonance" effect reported earlier. As also noted earlier, however, the "dissonance" effect is itself a function of communication length, and the main effect is due entirely to the inverse relation appearing in the conditions employing the long communication, the communication designed to duplicate those found in the original Festinger-Carlsmith experiment.

In sum, it is suggested that the interpersonal model of self-perception provides a viable alternative to the theory of cognitive dissonance in accounting for the attitudinal phenomena that have emerged from the forced-compliance experiments.

The Free-Choice Studies

In the second major category of data on dissonance theory, an S is permitted to make a selection from a set of objects or courses of action. The dependent variable is his subsequent attitude rating of the chosen and rejected alternatives.

Dissonance theory reasons that any unfavorable aspects of the chosen alternative and any favorable aspects of the rejected alternatives provide cognitions that are dissonant with the cognition that the individual has chosen as he did. To reduce the resulting dissonance pressure, the individual exaggerates the favorable features of the chosen alternative and plays down its unfavorable aspects. This leads him to enhance his rating of the chosen alternative. Similar reasoning predicts that he will lower his rating of the rejected alternatives. These predictions are confirmed in a number of studies, (see Brehm and Cohen, 1962, p. 303; see also Festinger, 1964).

A number of secondary predictions concerning parameters of the choice have also been confirmed. In an experiment by Brehm and Cohen (1959b), school children were permitted to select a toy from either two or four alternatives. Some children chose from qualitatively similar toys; others chose from qualitatively dissimilar alternatives. The children's postchoice ratings of the toys on a set of rating scales were then compared to initial ratings obtained a week before the experiment. The main displacement effect appeared as predicted: Chosen toys were displaced in the more favorable direction; rejected toys were generally displaced in the unfavorable direction. In addition, however, the displacement effect was larger when the choice was made from the larger number of alternatives. This is so, according to dissonance theory, because "the greater the number of alternatives from which one must choose, the more one must give up and consequently the greater the magnitude of dissonance [p. 373]." Similarly, the displacement effect was larger when the choice was made from dissimilar rather than similar alternatives because "what one has to give up relative to what one gains increases [p. 373]," again increasing the magnitude of the dissonance experienced.

To interpret these findings within the framework of self-perception, consider an observer trying to estimate a child's ratings of toys; the observer has not seen the child engage in any behavior with the toys. Now compare this observer with one who has just seen the child select one of the toys as a gift for himself. This comparison parallels, respectively, the prechoice and the postchoice ratings made by the children themselves. It seems likely that the latter observer would displace the estimated ratings of the chosen and rejected alternatives further from one another simply because he has some behavioral evidence upon which to base differential ratings of these toys. This is the effect displayed in the children's final ratings.

The positive relation between the number of alternatives and the displacement effect can be similarly analyzed. If an observer had seen the selected toy "win out" over more competing alternatives, it seems reasonable that he might increase the estimated displacement between the "exceptional" toy and the group of rejected alternatives. Finally, the fact that the displacement effect is larger when the alternatives are dissimilar would appear to be an instance of simple stimulus generalization. That is, to the extent that the chosen and rejected alternatives are similar to one another, they will be rated closer together on a scale by any rater, outside observer, or the child himself.

In sum, if one regards the children as observers of their own choice behavior and their subsequent ratings as inferences from that behavior, the dissonance findings appear to follow. The following demonstration illustrates the point.

An Interpersonal Replication of the Toy Study

Twenty-four college students served as control Ss by estimating how an 11-year-old boy might rate several different toys. These toys were selected from the list reported by Brehm and Cohen (1959b) and were rated on the same rating scales. The toys to be rated in the subsequent experiment were then selected on the basis of these ratings according to the same criteria of selection employed by the original investigators.

For the experiment itself, 96 college students were given a sheet of paper with the following information: "In a psychology experiment, an 11-year-old boy was asked to rate how well he liked toys that are typically popular with this age group. He was then permitted to select one of these toys to keep for himself. We are interested in how well college students can estimate his ratings." Each sheet also informed S which toy the child had chosen and from which alternatives he was permitted to choose. He then made his estimates of the child's ratings. The Ss were randomly assigned to one of four conditions corresponding to the combinations of number of alternatives (two or four) and similarity of alternatives (similar or dissimilar).

Results

Table 4 lists the toys employed, the control group means, and the displacements from those means of the corresponding experimental group means for the chosen and rejected alternatives in each condition. Scores can range from 0 to 5, where a higher number indicates greater liking for the toy; a positive displacement indicates increased liking for the toy. To facilitate comparisons among conditions, the toy rated as most popular by the control group, the swimming snorkel, was employed as the "chosen" toy in all experimental conditions. In addition, it will be noted that it was possible to match closely the combined mean ratings of the rejected alternatives in the four-alternative

Table 4. Mean Displacement in Toy Ratings from Control Group Means for Chosen and Rejected Alternatives in Each Condition

Experimental Condition		Similar Alternatives			Dissimilar Alternatives		
		Toy	Control	Displacement	Toy	Control	Displacement
Two alternatives	Chosen	Swimming snorkel	3.45	+.35	Swimming snorkel	3.45	+.22
	Rejected	Swimming mask	3.44	−.39	Archery set	2.79	−.42
Four alternatives	Chosen	Swimming snorkel	3.45	+.69	Swimming snorkel	3.45	+.99
	Rejected	Swimming mask			Archery set		
		Swimming fins	2.54	−.01	Bowling game	2.58	−.26
		Life jacket			Ship model		

Note − N = 24 in the control and each experimental condition.

conditions; unfortunately this could not be done for the two-alternative conditions.

It is seen in Table 4 that the chosen alternative was rated higher and the rejected alternatives were rated lower than the corresponding control group means in every condition. In both of the two-alternative conditions, the total displacement effect is significant at the .01 level (t = 3.66 and 2.81 for the similar and dissimilar conditions, respectively); for both of the four-alternative conditions, it is significant at the .001 level (t = 5.26 and 9.18, respectively). Some of the downward displacement of the rejected alternatives in the two-alternative conditions can be attributed to regression effects since the initial means of these alternatives are above the grand mean, but this problem has been avoided in the four-alternative conditions by combining the ratings of the three rejected alternatives; in this case the predicted displacement effect is opposite in direction to that due to regression, as is the upward displacement of the chosen alternative in all four conditions. Thus, the main displacement effect is clearly replicated by interpersonal judgments.

Similarity of alternatives.   From simple considerations of stimulus generalization, it was predicted that the displacement effect should be greater in the dissimilar than in the similar conditions. Because of the differential effects of regression, mentioned above, however, the analysis must be confined to the four-alternative conditions where it was possible to match the control group means of the rejected alternatives. Within this condition, the mean total displacement is .70 in the similar condition and 1.25 in the dissimilar condition, a difference significant at the .05 level (t = 2.22). The hypothesis is confirmed insofar as it is possible to test it with these data.

Number of alternatives. The present experiment is attempting to replicate the positive relation found between the displacement and the number of alternatives. Again, the displacements of the rejected alternatives in the two-alternative conditions cannot be legitimately incorporated into the comparison. The present analysis, therefore, is confined to the upward displacement of the chosen alternative. For the four-alternative conditions, the mean upward displacement of the swimming snorkel is seen to be .84; for the two-alternative conditions, it is .28. This difference is significant at the .01 level ($t = 3.29$). The dissonance findings are again replicated by interpersonal observers.

Although it would have been desirable to test the predictions unconfounded by the noncomparability of the two-alternative base lines, this would have required departing from the toys employed in the original experiment. More importantly, however, this would still not have yielded a more direct comparison between the replication and the original experiment because the results reported by Brehm and Cohen are themselves confounded by uncorrected regression effects. The present replication actually provides clearer evidence for the predicted effects than the original study.

It is suggested that this same kind of analysis can be applied to the other studies in this category of dissonance experiments. Once again, it seems unnecessary to invoke a motivational construct to account for the data.

Exposure-to-Information Studies

The third category of dissonance studies includes two general paradigms: experiments in which an individual is involuntarily exposed to information that is discrepant with information he already possesses, and studies that examine an individual's willingness to expose himself voluntarily to dissonant information.

An experiment of the first type in which male Ss received information discrepant with their "self-images" was conducted by Bramel (1962). Each S was first led to view himself favorably or unfavorably on a number of personality characteristics and then given information that implied that he was sexually aroused by homoerotic pictures. This information was in the form of numerical readings from a meter which was supposedly measuring S's sexual arousal to the stimulus pictures; actually, all Ss received the same meter readings. The dependent variable of the study was S's prediction of the meter readings that were obtained from his "partner," another male S who was participating in the experiment concurrently.

Bramel reasons from dissonance theory that the arousal information would be quite dissonant for Ss who had been led to view themselves favorably. In order to reduce this dissonance, these Ss would "project" or attribute a higher amount of homosexual arousal to their partners than would Ss in the Unfavorable condition, who would find the information less dissonant with their self-image. The results are consistent with this prediction. The data show that the higher S's measured self-esteem, the more arousal he attributed to his partner.

This study may be reanalyzed by considering the nature of the task given S. He is asked to make a comparative judgment of another person along a numerical scale. His only standard of reference is his own meter reading. In addition, he knows that high meter readings are to be associated with a negative attribute, and he can again use himself as the reference for a standard of "good" and "bad." It would appear to follow that the more an S judges himself as "good," the higher an arousal number, relative to his own, he would assign to another person on whom he has no additional data, precisely the relationship reported by Bramel.[2]

This straightforward "psychophysical" interpretation is further supported by the observed relationship between S's prediction of his partner's arousal and his overall evaluation of the partner which he had made prior to receiving the experimental manipulation. A simple "halo effect" is evident: Ss attribute high readings to partners toward whom they had generally unfavorable attitudes; they attribute moderate readings to moderately esteemed partners; and, with one exception, they attribute low readings to highly esteemed partners. This monotonic relation is violated at only one point: Ss who have high self-esteem appear to use their own meter reading as a lower bound of "goodness" and simply assign a similar level of arousal to partners whom they also regard favorably. This finding, too, is consistent with the judgmental interpretation of Bramel's data.

A number of other experiments examine the effects of giving Ss information that is dissonant with their self-images. Unfortunately, the more remarkable effects (e.g., Aronson and Carlsmith, 1962) are apparently difficult to reproduce, and it is still possible that the original findings are artifactual. (See McGuire, 1966a, for a review.)

Throughout this discussion, it has been argued that the data under analysis could be accounted for without postulating an aversive motivational drive. The second kind of exposure-to-information studies may be viewed as a direct test for the existence of such a drive. If cognitive dissonance is, in fact, an aversive state, then a person should avoid exposure to sources of dissonant information and seek out nondissonant sources. Compared with the theoretical chain of

[2]Bramel briefly considers a similar interpretation, but rejects it in favor of the dissonance interpretation.

reasoning behind the other studies discussed, this deduction from dissonance theory is by far the most direct, the easiest to test, and the most crucial for justifying a motivational construct like dissonance. The available evidence, however, is not supportive. In an extensive review of the relevant studies, most of which were conducted by investigators whose theoretical orientation would lead them to look for selective exposure to nondissonant information, Freedman and Sears (1965) conclude that "clearly experimental evidence does not demonstrate that there is a general psychological tendency to avoid non-supportive and to seek out supportive information."

There is, of course, nothing within the behaviorist's functional framework that would rule out a motivational phenomenon. For example, it is not implausible to suppose that punishment is often contingent upon being inconsistent, illogical, or just plain wrong in our highly verbal culture. This would be particularly true for the college students who typically serve as Ss in cognitive dissonance experiments. Accordingly, evidence demonstrating that it is aversive for such Ss to maintain incompatible responses in their verbal repertoires might well be forthcoming. Such a phenomenon is appropriately labeled motivational, but it would be the consequence of a particularly common cultural practice and would not, it is suggested, justify the reification of a new internal drive that is assumed to be an inherent characteristic of behaving organisms. In any case, the assumption of any motivational process to account for the data reviewed in this discussion would seem gratuitous.

Some Metatheoretical Considerations

In the opening remarks, some contrasts were noted between the conceptual approach typified by dissonance theory and the behavioral approach represented here by the functional analysis of self-perception. It was pointed out that the behaviorist's goal is to account for observed relations between current stimuli and responses in terms of an individual's past training history and a small number of basic functional relations discovered in the experimental analysis of simpler behaviors. The behaviorist's functional analysis of complex behaviors like dissonance phenomena was thus seen to be based on empirical general-ization, a feature which infuses it with an inductive flavor and spirit.

In contrast, the dissonance theorists clearly prefer the "deductive" nature of their theory and explicitly derogate the "weakness of an empirical generalization as compared with a true theoretical explanation [Lawrence and Festinger, 1962, p. 17]." This criticism of the behaviorist's functional analysis, namely, that it has no deductive fertility or predictive power, is often expressed.

The radical behaviorist, so the criticism goes, will not venture a specific prediction without knowing the complete reinforcement history of the organism. He cannot provide a "true theoretical explanation."

It is suggested here that a functional analysis appears to have limited predictive power only because it makes explicit the kinds of knowledge about the past and present controlling variables that any theorist must have if he is to predict behavior accurately. How, for example, do the dissonance theorists conclude that dissonance is present in a particular case? That is, how do they decide when one cognition does not "follow from" another? According to Festinger, "the vagueness in the conceptual definition of dissonance — namely, two elements are dissonant if, considered alone, the obverse of one follows from the other — lies in the words 'follows from.' . . . One element may follow from another because of logic, because of cultural mores, because of things one has experienced and learned, and perhaps in other senses too [1957, p. 278]." Five years later, Brehm and Cohen note that "the 'follows from' relationship can sometimes be determined empirically but is limited by our abilities to specify and measure cognitions and the relationships among them . . . the 'follows from' relationship is not always clear and specifiable [1962, pp. 11-12]."

In actual practice, however, the dissonance theorists do not experience difficulty in inferring the existence of dissonance from their stimulus operations. But this is so precisely because in that inference the dissonance theorists sneak through the back door the very knowledge they claim to do without. It is in that inference that they implicitly make use of the fact that they have been raised by the same socializing community as their Ss. The dissonance theorists can thus infer that a $1 compensation will produce more dissonance than a $20 compensation, just as it has been *our* common history with these same Ss that permits *us* to speculate that the difference in compensation represents a difference in the mand properties of the induced behavior. Interpersonal observers are successful in replicating dissonance phenomena for the same reason. Dissonance theorists and radical behaviorists need the same kinds of knowledge. Only the behaviorists, however, take as their explicit obligation the necessity for accounting for both their own and their Ss' differential response to such controlling variables.

In sum, it is concluded that the greater "deductive fertility" of dissonance theory is largely illusory. In the process of adequately explicating the phrase "follows from" in their fundamental statement, the dissonance theorists will necessarily have to perform the explicit functional analysis they had hoped to finesse. It remains our conviction that the appeal to hypothetical internal states of the organism for causal explanations of behavior is often heuristically undesirable. Such diversion appears only to retard and deflect the thrust of the analysis that is ultimately required.

6

A Structural Theory of Attitude Dynamics

Milton J. Rosenberg

Most of the balance theory or consistency theory approaches to attitude change consider consistency between two or more attitudes. In the following paper, attitude change is investigated from the point of view of consistency *within a single attitude*. As was indicated in the introductory chapter, theorists generally agree that attitudes have three basic elements — affective (evaluation of the object), cognitive (information or beliefs about the object), and "action tendency" (tendency to respond behaviorally toward the object). Rosenberg's thesis is that inconsistency between the affective and cognitive elements of a given attitude leads to change in one or the other of the elements of that attitude.

Many investigators have shown that a change in the cognitive element can lead to changes in the affective element. New information about a person, for example, may lead to a change in one's liking for the person. Almost no studies, however, have considered whether beliefs about an object can change as a function of change in the evaluation of the object. It is this question that concerns Rosenberg.*

*The paper following this editorial introduction is excerpted from M.J. Rosenberg, A structural theory of attitude dynamics, *Public Opinion Quarterly*, 1960, *24*, 319-340, by permission of the author and the publisher.

Common insight suggests that when stable feelings and beliefs refer to the same object they tend toward congruence with one another. This paper reports a structural theory of attitude dynamics which has been developed through elaboration and extension of this insight. The theory is "structural" because it is not so much concerned with conditions and variables influencing the erection or reorganization of attitudes as with the problem of what attitudes *are* and the related problem of what happens "inside" them as they undergo change.

In support of the theory, a few experimental studies are briefly reviewed and one recent experiment is presented in greater detail. The last section of this report examines the theory for its bearing upon some problems in attitude measurement and persuasion.

Theory and Data

Most, though by no means all, definitions of the attitude concept have been restricted to the notion of emotional "einstellung": when some object or class of objects regularly and dependably elicits an affective evaluative set that can be characterized as either "pro" or "con," "positive" or "negative," the individual is said to hold an attitude.

The theory outlined here flows from the contention that typically such stable affective sets are integrated with other psychological processes and that a more useful approach to attitude is one in which these processes are somehow represented. (Among the writers who have discussed this point are Chein [1948], Katz and Stotland [1959], Krech and Crutchfield [1948], Peak [1955], and Tolman [1951].) One convenient way to do this is to conceive of an attitude as consisting of a *cognitive* as well as an affective component. Of the many possible kinds of cognitions about attitude objects one variety is here singled out as requiring representation in the minimum definition of the attitude concept: these are beliefs about the relations between the attitude object and other "objects" of affective significance to the individual. Thus a physician's negative attitude toward Federal medical insurance involves not only the fact of his affectively colored opposition but also the fact that he believes that Federal medical insurance, if instituted, would lead to "socialism" and "debasement of medical standards," which for him are negatively evaluated conditions, and that it would tend also to defeat, or reduce the likelihood of, such positively valued conditions as "professional freedom" and "maintenance of my income."

Attitude Structure

As employed by behavioral scientists the word "structure" usually denotes some constellation of component events or processes so related to one another that the irreversible alteration of the quality or magnitude of a particular component will set in motion comparable changes in the other components. If the structure of an attitude is simply conceptualized in terms of two major components, the affective and the cognitive, confirmation of this conceptualization can be obtained by demonstrating that these components co-vary in close relation to each other. Evidence of such co-variation may be sought either with regard to stable attitudes or with regard to attitudes undergoing change.

The first-mentioned case is exemplified by a group of studies which show that within a population of persons varying in their attitudinal affects toward some social object there exist correlate and consistent variations in *beliefs* about that object (Cartwright, 1949; Smith, 1949; Woodruff and DiVesta, 1948). A similar study was conducted by the author (1956) in which the attitudinal affects of a large number of subjects were measured with regard to two separate social issues. One month later these same subjects took a "test of cognitive structure" requiring them to rate a group of "values" both for the degree of positive or negative reward each represented and also for the extent to which each value was believed to be fostered or defeated through the influence of each of the two attitude objects, respectively. From these judgments it was possible to compute an over-all "index of cognitive structure." By testing the relationship between this index and the independent measure of attitudinal affect it was shown that stable positive affect toward an attitude object is associated with beliefs relating that object to the attainment of positive values and the blocking of negative values, while stable negative affect toward an attitude object is associated with beliefs relating it to the attainment of negative values and the blocking of positive values. It was also confirmed that moderate attitudinal affects, as compared to extreme ones, are associated with beliefs that relate the attitude object to less important values, or if to important values then with less confidence as to the existence of clear-cut instrumental relationships between the attitude object and the values in question. Data from this study also indicated that variation in attitudinal affect is separately correlated with at least two aspects of the person's set of attitudinal cognitions. The first of these is the over-all believed potency of the attitude object for achieving or blocking the realization of his values; the second is the over-all felt importance of those values.

In general terms what emerged from this study was the conclusion that stable patterns of feeling toward social objects are accompanied by, or organized in close relationship with, stable beliefs consistent with those affects. The major key to such consistency appears to be that the individual tends to relate positive attitude objects to goal attainment and negative attitude objects to frustration of his goal orientations.

Attitude Change

The conception of attitude as an affective-cognitive structure has utility not only because it fits correlational findings such as those reported above but also because it suggests a way of theorizing about attitude change. The author's approach to the formulation of a structural theory of attitude change is founded on the following basic propositions:

1. When the affective and cognitive components of an attitude are mutually consistent, the attitude is in a stable state.

2. When these components are mutually inconsistent, to a degree that exceeds the individual's "tolerance limit" for such inconsistency, the attitude is in an unstable state.

3. In such an unstable state the attitude will undergo reorganizing activity until one of three possible outcomes is achieved. These outcomes are: (a) rejection of the communications, or other forces, that engendered the original inconsistency between affect and cognition and thus rendered the attitude unstable, i.e. restoration of the original stable and consistent attitude; (b) "fragmentation" of the attitude through the isolation from each other of the mutually inconsistent affective and cognitive components; (c) accommodation to the original inconsistency-producing change so that a new attitude, consistent with that change, is now stabilized, i.e. attitude change.

In broad terms it is possible to specify some of the conditions under which each of these three outcomes is most likely to occur. Thus on the assumption that an individual's attitudes (defined as his consistent and persisting affective-cognitive structures) usually enable effective regulation of his adaptive behavior and are thus of value to him, it would be predicted that he will attempt to preserve them intact. From this it follows that *if possible* an individual will ultimately reject influences which have caused a temporary alteration in either the affective or cognitive component of one of his attitudes.

Frequently, however, the potency of the force leading to the alteration of one of the major components of an attitude is so great, or so persistent, as to make it *impossible* of rejection. When this is the case, fragmentation of the attitude is likely to result if, by virtue of the needs or "objective realities" that maintain it, the component persisting from the original attitude structure is unalterable. However, when this component is capable of alteration, it would be expected to give way, and general reorganization leading to the erection of a new attitude (i.e. attitude change) will result.

Restricting our concern to the case in which attitude change *does* occur, it may be asked: What are the specific lawful relationships between its occurrence and such variables as the content and organization of the change-inducing communication, the individual's level of tolerance for affective-cognitive inconsistency, and the relation of the attitude to other attitudes held by the same individual? No answer to such questions will be attempted here except to indicate that a large part of the available experimental literature on attitude change may be interpreted as indicating some of the parameters and parameter values that are associated with the attitude-change outcome in situations where inconsistency between attitude components has been produced.[1]

The validity of a theoretical perspective, however, is not established by the claim that data collected for other purposes can be fitted to it; rather it is necessary to show that hypotheses derived from it are directly supported by available experimental evidence. For the purposes of this report, then, it seems desirable to elaborate not upon details and extensions of the propositions given above but rather upon the main attitude-change hypothesis resident in that set of propositions. In its simplest form this hypothesis is that *the production of inconsistency between the affective and cognitive portions of an attitude will culminate in a general attitude reorganization (through which the affective-cognitive inconsistency is reduced or eliminated) when (1) the inconsistency exceeds the individual's present tolerance limit and (2) the force producing it cannot be ignored or avoided.* In the remainder of this paper these two qualifying conditions are assumed, though not necessarily restated, whenever this hypothesis or data bearing upon it are discussed.

Two different predictions can be derived from this hypothesis. The first is simply that if a person somehow undergoes an "irreversible" change in his beliefs about an attitude object his affect toward that object will show corresponding change. The second prediction is the converse: if a person somehow undergoes an "irreversible" change in his *affect* toward an object his beliefs about that object will show corresponding change.

At present there is much clearer and stronger evidence available for the former prediction than for the latter one. Some of this evidence is based upon the impression of applied workers in the persuasion professions that if an audience member's beliefs about the value-serving and value-blocking powers of an "object" (such as a consumer product, a social policy, or a political candidate) can be reorganized, his feelings toward that object, and ultimately his behavior toward it, will undergo corresponding change. In addition to this kind of evidence there are scores of experimental studies in which communications designed to change cognitions about attitude objects are directed at subjects. A result found in the majority of these studies is that such communications, if

[1]For a useful review of this literature see Hovland (1954).

potent enough, do produce further change effects in evaluative (affective) responses. Most of these studies, however, do not provide for a precise check of whether, and to what extent, the communications designed to alter cognitions actually do so. Recently, however, a number of methods for the measurement of the cognitive aspects of attitude structures have become available. The test of cognitive structure used in the aforementioned correlational study by the author is one of these. It has since been employed in attitude change studies by Carlson (1956) and Peak (1959). While neither of these experiments was intended as a test of the present theoretical formulation, both were concerned with the prediction that change in beliefs about an attitude object will generate change in feelings toward that object.

In Carlson's study subjects were tested on two separate occasions for their affective and cognitive responses toward the social object "Negroes being allowed to move into white neighborhoods." Intervening between the two testing sessions was a manipulation designed to produce changes in the "perceived instrumentality" aspect of a number of the subject's beliefs about the attitude object. Thus the typical anti-desegregation subject who at first believed that housing desegregation would *lower* the worth of property (a negative instrumental relation between the attitude object and the value "worth of property") was exposed to a special manipulation intended to transform his belief to one in which desegregation would be seen as *raising* the worth of property.

Comparison of the premanipulation and postmanipulation cognitive structure tests showed that the typical subject *did* alter his beliefs about the separate relationships of the attitude object to each of a number of separate values. Furthermore, it was found that, along with the production of such changes in the cognitive component of the person's attitude, consistent change, of roughly corresponding magnitude, was also obtained in his *affective* response toward the attitude object. Thus these data lend support to the first of the two predictions stated above; they confirm the hypothesis that the production of inconsistency in an attitude structure through modification of its cognitive component does eventuate in correlated consistency-restoring modification of its affective component.

In the study by Peak an attempt was made to produce a temporary alteration in the strength or pertinence of a general value ("making good grades") seen by her subjects to be instrumentally served by such attitude objects as the use of discussion techniques in college courses. It was shown that when attitudinal cognition changes, in the sense that the goal seen as served by the attitude object increases in its importance to the person, the affective response toward that object undergoes corresponding change.

While it does not deal with the sort of large-scale affective-cognitive inconsistency that Carlson is concerned with, this study too seems to demonstrate that change in the cognitive portion of an attitude tends to generate consistent change in its affective portion. A further value is that it shows that affect modification will be fostered not only by changes in the "instrumentality" aspect of cognitions about attitude objects but also by changes in the felt importance of the goals believed to be attained through the attitude object's instrumental powers.

However, to demonstrate, as our basic hypothesis asserts, that affective-cognitive inconsistency (rather than mere cognitive reorganization) is an underlying condition for attitude change, the reverse prediction must also be confirmed: it must be shown that the production of an irreversible change in an attitude's affective component will generate corresponding change in its cognitive component.

This prediction, unlike its opposite, does not receive unequivocal confirmation in the available experimental literature. Nevertheless, some of the attitude change techniques that have been reported, particularly those involving direct approval or disapproval from peer groups or prestigeful figures, might be interpreted as producing direct modification of affective responses. A similar impression is created when nonexperimental examples of "emotional" persuasion techniques are examined. But in either the experimental or nonexperimental case it is likely that such influence procedures also tend to directly modify some attitudinal cognitions.

A specific aim in two recent studies by the author was to develop and investigate the effects of a "pure" experimental manipulation of attitudinal affect, one which did not directly act upon the cognitive content of the attitude being modified. The intention was to test experimentally the second of the two predictions drawn from the main hypothesis given above. The manipulation used in these studies involved posthypnotic suggestion of affect change. The second of these studies will be described in detail both for its bearing upon the main hypothesis and also to provide some idea of the style of experimentation by which the theory is being more fully developed.

An Experiment Involving Direct and Sustained Alteration of Attitudinal Affect

In the first study involving hypnotic manipulation of attitudinal affect eleven experimental and eleven control subjects were tested on two separate occasions for their affective and cognitive responses toward various attitude objects. Between the two testing sessions the experimental subjects (all of whom were capable of achieving deep hypnosis) were placed in hypnosis and then given the suggestion that upon awakening their affective reactions toward two separate attitude objects would be changed (from positive to negative, or vice versa) and that they would have no memory of the suggestion's having been made until the presentation of an amnesia-removing signal. It was assumed that such post-hypnotic suggestion would foster strong and "irreversible" affect change for as long as posthypnotic amnesia was maintained. In a control group which received no affect manipulation the affective and cognitive responses toward attitude objects remained stable from the first to the second test administrations. In the experimental group significant change occurred not only in the subjects' affects toward the attitude objects but also in their *beliefs* about the relationships between each of those objects and various "values" deemed important by the subjects. Additional control data ruled out the possibility that these changes could have been due to any general tendency toward response instability rather than to the effects of the affect manipulation.

By using a second control procedure in which subjects "role-played" the occurrence of affect change, and by interviewing conducted both before and after removal of the experimental subjects' posthypnotic amnesias, it was found that the affect and belief changes achieved by the experimental subjects were experienced by them as legitimate and veridical; the subjects really felt and *believed* differently about the attitude objects on which they had received the posthypnotic suggestions of affect change. Aspects of this study have been reported in a number of publications (Rosenberg, 1957; Rosenberg and Gardner, 1958), and it will not be further described or discussed here except to note that its replication and extension were the main purposes of the study described below.

In this second study[2] the hypnotic manipulation of attitudinal affect was kept in force for a full week rather than for a period of one or two hours, as was the case in the earlier study. Eight new experimental subjects were used in this experiment and were tested for both their affective and cognitive responses to three different attitude objects on six different occasions. The first of these occasions came three days before the delivery of a posthypnotic suggestion of affect change with regard to one of the three attitude objects. In all cases the subject's original affect toward this object ("the abandonment of the United States policy of giving economic aid to foreign nations") was originally negative

[2]This experiment was carried out under Contract 609 (27) with the Group Psychology Branch of the Office of Naval Research. Thanks are due to Charles W. Gardner, Carl I. Hovland, and Irving L. Janis for their useful advice and to Sheldon Feldman, who conducted the testing with all subjects.

and was hypnotically manipulated in the positive direction in a way that involved no reference to any of his beliefs about the attitude object's relationships with any of his values. Specifically each subject was told in hypnosis:

> After you awake, and continuing until our next meeting, you will feel very strongly opposed to the United States policy of giving economic aid to foreign nations. The mere idea of the United States giving economic aid to foreign nations will make you feel very displeased and disgusted. Until your next meeting with me you will continue to feel very strong and thorough opposition to the United States policy of economic aid to foreign nations. You will have no memory whatsoever of this suggestion's having been made . . . until the amnesia is removed by my giving you the signal at our next session.

Following the delivery of the posthypnotic suggestion the subject was awakened from hypnosis and the measures of affect and cognition were readministered. Two days later, and two days after that, these tests were again administered. Exactly one week after the hypnotic session the subject's amnesia for that session was removed and the experiment fully explained to him. Up to this point in the sequence all subjects had been led to believe that the hypnotic session and the testing sessions (the former conducted by the author and the latter by an associate) had no connection with each other, that they represented different and unrelated experiments.

However, toward the end of the first week, two subjects did gradually develop vague and uncertain suspicions that some sort of hypnotic manipulation might have been used. But both insisted that they had no memory of any such event, that they were merely "reasoning" from the fact that they had undergone sudden and intense changes in their feelings and beliefs on the foreign aid issue. Three days after amnesia removal, and seven days after that, the measures of affect and cognition were again administered to all subjects. Before presenting the data that bear on the prediction that the production of strong affect change generates corresponding change in associated cognitions it will be necessary to describe the separate measures of affect and cognition by which these data were obtained. These measures were similar to those used in the author's two earlier studies described above.

The measure of affect consisted of three scales covering a 16-point range from "extremely in favor" to "extremely opposed." One of these scales dealt with the issue on which the subjects received the hypnotic affect manipulation. The other two scales dealt with issues that were not subjected to any manipulation and thus served as control areas against which changes on the manipulated issue could be compared.

The measure of the cognitive component involved thirty-two so-called "value cards." Sample value items are "all human beings having equal rights," "people being well educated," "making one's own decisions," "attaining economic security." In taking this test the subject first judges each of the thirty-two values in terms of its importance to him, using a scale with a range of 21 points. The scale runs from −10 (which stands for "gives me maximum dissatisfaction") to +10 (which stands for "gives me maximum satisfaction"). He then judges each of these same values in terms of whether, and to what extent, he thinks it will be attained or blocked as a consequence of the attitude object. On this task he uses an 11-point scale running from −5 (which stands for "extreme blocking") through 0 (which stands for "neither blocked nor attained") to +5 (which stands for "extreme attainment"). Thus at the end of the testing procedure there are available for each value term the subject's judgment of its importance as a positive or negative state and his judgment of how that value's realization will be affected by the attitude object. These two judgments are algebraically multiplied for each value term respectively. In turn the thirty-two products are algebraically summed. The resulting quantity is taken as an index of the over-all import of the cognitive structure associated with the attitude object. In effect this index expresses, in a single number, the extent to which the subject sees the attitude object as serving the attainment or blocking of his values. This index was separately obtained for each of the three attitude objects (the one subjected to affect manipulation and the two not subjected to such manipulation) from the data collected during each of the six separate testing sessions.

To test the prediction that the production of a large and irreversible affect change will generate comparable changes in beliefs about the attitude object, affect-change scores and cognition-change scores were computed for the three separate attitude objects. These scores referred to the differences between the index obtained from the subject's premanipulation test performance and each of the five postmanipulation test performances respectively. By application of the Randomization Test for Matched Pairs[3] it was possible to determine whether the subject's affect-change and cognition-change scores for the manipulated attitude object were significantly greater than the means of their change scores for the two nonmanipulated attitude objects.

As shown in Table 1, until the amnesia removal the subjects showed significant change not only in their affective responses toward "abandoning the United States policy of economic aid to foreign nations" but also in their beliefs about how such abandonment will affect the realization of their values. When the test records are examined it is found that these statistically significant

[3] See S. Siegel, *Non-parametric Statistics for the Behavioral Sciences* (1956).

Table 1. Probabilities of the Differences between the Change Scores for the
Manipulated and Nonmanipulated Attitudes*

Testing Sessions from Which Change Scores Are Computed†	Affect Change	Cognitive Change
Session 1 − Session 2	.008	.024
Session 1 − Session 3	.008	.024
Session 1 − Session 4	.008	.008
Session 1 − Session 5	N.S.	.056
Session 1 − Session 6	N.S.	.064

*All probabilities are two-tailed and are obtained through application of the Randomization Test for Matched Pairs. All significant differences are in the direction: manipulated attitude > mean of nonmanipulated attitudes.

†The first testing session occurred three days before hypnotic manipulation of affect toward "foreign aid"; the second testing session came immediately after the manipulation; and the third and fourth sessions came three and five days, respectively, after the manipulation. The fifth and sixth sessions came ten days and seventeen days after the manipulation (i.e. three days and ten days after "amnesia removal"). The same tests were used in each of the six sessions − the affective scales dealing with the foreign aid issue and with the two unmanipulated issues, and the cognitive structure measures for each of those issues.

N.S. = not significant.

differences are based upon large-scale shifts in both affect and cognition. Thus a typical subject changes his affective evaluation from extreme opposition to abandonment of foreign aid to extreme approval. At the same time he changes many of his related beliefs. For example, whereas before the affect manipulation he believes that abandoning foreign aid would defeat such positive goals (for him) as "the avoidance of economic depression" and would serve such negative goals as "the open expression of disagreement between people" he now sees the abandonment of foreign aid as *fostering* the former goal and *defeating* the latter.

Nor is this the only kind of change observed in the subject's cognitions about the attitude object. He also alters his evaluation of some of the value terms, sometimes even to the extent of changing positive values to negative ones or negative values to positive ones. In the latter case beliefs about the relationship between the attitude object and such transformed values are usually left unaltered, thus reversing their import.

It should not be concluded, however, that *all* the beliefs expressed by the typical subject are consistent with the altered attitudinal affect. Usually some of his original beliefs persist within the new structure and are inconsistent with its over-all import, though typically the intensity with which these beliefs are held is reduced after the affect manipulation. But in the light of the theoretical propositions advanced above it is not assumed that total and perfect consistency need obtain in a stable attitude structure; all that is assumed is that in such a stable structure affective-cognitive inconsistency, if present at all, is at a level below the individual's tolerance limit. At any rate, examination of the postmanipulation attitude structures of the subjects reveals, in most cases, an impressive degree of cognitive reorganization in the direction consistent with the altered affect.

As in the first study involving affect manipulation, interview procedures revealed that the subjects' changes in affect and cognition were *experienced* by them rather than merely "role-played." Indeed, the findings reported in the last two rows of the table provide a special kind of evidence to this effect in connection with the subjects' cognitive changes. These findings refer to data obtained after the posthypnotic amnesia was removed and the nature of the experiment was fully explained to each subject. While the removal of amnesia for the affect manipulation is followed by a return to the initial affective response, enough of the cognitive changes persist to make for a significant difference between the cognition-change scores on the manipulated issue and the mean of the cognition-change scores on the two nonmanipulated issues.

Since after amnesia removal the subjects' affective responses reverted to their original scale positions it might be contended that the significant persistence of some of the cognitive changes calls into question our conception of attitude as an internally consistent affective-cognitive structure. Examination of the subjects' test performances reveals, however, that while a number of altered beliefs do persist, a still larger number are changed back to their original form. Thus, after amnesia removal, in seven out of the eight cases the over-all index of cognitive structure has a negative sign and is thus consistent with the restored negative affect.

Many other aspects of this study, including data drawn from a group of unhypnotized control subjects, have not been covered in this account but will be detailed in a later report. But the data that have been reported or reviewed in this paper seem to provide strong confirmation for the general hypothesis that the production of affective-cognitive inconsistency within a previously stable attitude makes for attitude change. The confirmation of this hypothesis argues for the validity of the more general set of theoretical propositions from which it was derived.

Some Additional
Theoretical Considerations

While it has been demonstrated that, under certain specified conditions, affective-cognitive inconsistency does lead to attitude change, it has not been demonstrated that attitude change is *always* due to the production of such inconsistency. Indeed, such a conclusion would be possible only by studying the underlying structural modifications involved in all phenotypically classified forms of attitude change. Nevertheless, it is the author's contention that commitment to an inconsistency-reduction analysis of the attitude-change process will prove heuristically useful in developing experimental programs looking toward the construction of an adequately detailed theory of attitude dynamics.

A number of additional matters of theory require clarification. One of these is the possible objection that the type of attitude-change sequence demonstrated in the affect-manipulation experiments is an uncommon, and thus unimportant, case. In this connection a point made earlier needs to be repeated: hypnotic suggestion was employed as an experimental analogue of a broad class of nonhypnotic experiences which seem to produce affect modification in everyday settings. It can be argued that whenever the expression of an old affective response is followed by negative reinforcement, or whenever the imitative or trial-and-error "rehearsal" of a new affective response is followed by positive reinforcement, affect change similar to that observed in the present experiment is fostered. Such reinforcement need not come only from external agencies. As the individual's inner needs and conflicts are altered through the vicissitudes of experience or of "growth," the expression of old affects may come to heighten frustration and tension while the expression of new affects may operate to reduce needs and resolve conflicts. Thus attitudinal affects may undergo transformation under control by reinforcements issuing from "within" the person (from changes in his hierarchy of motives and conflicts) rather than from other persons. By this point, much of the present analysis may be tied to the kind of "psychodynamic" approach to attitude that is exemplified in the contributions of Frenkel-Brunswik and her colleagues (Adorno *et al.*, 1950), Katz, Sarnoff, and McClintock (1956), and Smith, Bruner, and White (1956).

Another possible objection is that the reduction in this paper of all forms of attitude change to two underlying structural sequences has the status of an "ideal" typology. It must be acknowledged that in many instances attitude change does not begin with the manipulation of either the cognitive or the affective component but, rather, both may undergo manipulation at the same time. It should be clear, however, that from the present point of view the production of change in either major component will increase the likelihood of change in the other component. Furthermore, close analysis of attitude-change techniques and communications will probably indicate that they usually are specifically directed more toward one than toward the other of the two major components.

A third objection might be that this theoretical approach has said little or nothing about a number of variables usually assumed to be important in attitude-dynamic processes. Among these are such variables as the person's "cognitive style" and his orientation toward the sources of communication directed at him. Similarly, little attention has been given here to the ways in which such communications differ from one another. A general response to this objection is that the pertinence of such variables lies in the fact that they, together with many others, control and determine whether, and to what extent, a specific attitude in a specific individual can be rendered inconsistent to a degree that is discomforting and motivating to him. Some of these variables would be involved also in determining whether intolerable affective-cognitive inconsistency, once aroused, would be reduced through true attitude change or through either "fragmentation" of the attitude structure or ultimate rejection of the forces which aroused the initial inconsistency.

A further qualification should be noted. The present conceptualization of attitude as a stable and consistent structure of affective and cognitive components may seem to be contradicted by two particular lines of evidence. The first is that subjects tested for their affects and beliefs toward an "attitude object" sometimes reveal apparent patterns of moderate or even extreme inconsistency. On this basis Scott (1959b), in a useful discussion, has questioned the generality of formulations such as the present one. However, the kinds of data on which this objection is based are usually collected without regard for the obvious fact that just because a subject chooses a non-neutral point on an attitudinal affect scale it cannot be assumed that he actually *holds* that attitude. Frequently his scale choice or, for that matter, his response to an evaluation-eliciting interview question does not reflect a real attitudinal affect but rather is due to loose and unreliable reference to an associated object toward which he may have some affect. Just as often such pseudo-affective responses may be forced by the wording of the questions or by the subject's anticipations of the experimenter's or interviewer's own affective preferences. In the light of these considerations it can be argued that the presence of gross and extreme inconsistency between a subject's affective and cognitive responses to a given "attitude object" (except when he has just been exposed to potent inducements to change) is presumptive evidence that he does not really *have* an attitude toward that object. In such a case it would be expected that retesting at a later date would yield evidence of significant instability on measures of both "affect" and "cognition."

A more impressive line of counterevidence is that many persons are aware of holding a few strong and stable affects for which they cannot offer any impressive cognitive support. Depth psychological data of both the clinical and experimental varieties suggest, however, that "cognitionless" affects, such as phobias or certain kinds of intense feelings toward other persons, are embedded in structures composed of "unconscious" beliefs (or better, "percepts"). The inability to verbalize such percepts may be based on the fact that they were acquired preverbally or that they were derived and developed through symbol-substitution processes for which no consensual vocabulary is available; or such beliefs may involve various kinds of "magical-irrational" relationships that individuals are trained to disavow as they acquire the "ego habits" of realistic adjustment. Confirming this extended conjecture is the clear fact that, whether through the routines of psychoanalytic free association, hypnotic exploration, or dream investigation, ostensibly cognitionless affects are regularly found to be rich in associated cognitive material.

Summary

If people seek congruence between their beliefs about and feelings toward objects, then attitudes can be changed by modifying either the beliefs or feelings associated with them. The incongruity thereby aroused may, in the former case, result in the feeling changing to become consistent with the altered beliefs; in the latter case, the beliefs may change to become consistent with the altered feeling. The first type of change has already been demonstrated in research studies. Experimental verification of the second type would lend support to the theoretical proposition that the disruption of structural consistency is one condition under which attitude change may occur. To test for the second type, changes in feeling toward objects were induced during hypnosis, and in the posthypnotic sessions changes in belief were measured. Subjects' attitudes shifted from prehypnotic opposition to an object to approval of that object, in accord with the shift in affect induced by hypnosis, thereby confirming the theory.

7

The Principle of Congruity in the Prediction of Attitude Change

Charles E. Osgood

Percy H. Tannenbaum

Osgood and Tannenbaum attempt to quantify the attitude change that occurs when inconsistency between attitudes exists. As indicated in the introductory chapter, the authors consider a special case of consistency or inconsistency — that which exists when a source makes an assertion about an object (for example, "This university president condemns fraternities"). In this example, Osgood and Tannenbaum are interested in the relationship between a person's attitudes toward a source (university president) and an object (fraternities) as they are affected by the positive or negative nature of the assertion (condemns) made by the source about the object.

Two novel features of this approach are worth noting. First, Osgood and Tannenbaum take into account "incredulity" — that is, the possibility that a person will disbelieve that a source has made a particular assertion about a particular object. For example, many would find it incredible for the President of the United States to speak positively about "organized crime." If an assertion is seen as incredible, it does not lead to attitude change. Second, Osgood and Tannenbaum take into account the effect that making an assertion has on the relative change in a person's attitudes toward the source and the object; that is, because the assertion is directed toward an object, these theorists suggest that the attitude toward the object will be under more pressure to change than will be the attitude toward the source of the assertion.

Osgood and Tannenbaum's paper presents both a statement of their theory and some research conducted to test some of their predictions.*

The theoretical model presented in this paper attempts to cover those variables believed to be most significant with respect to the direction of change to be expected in any given situation. These variables are (1) existing attitude toward the source of a message, (2) existing attitude toward the concept evaluated by the source, and (3) the nature of the evaluating assertion which relates source and concept in the message. Predictions generated by the theory about the directions and relative amounts of attitude change apply to both sources and the concepts they evaluate.

Underlying Notions

Our work on attitude theory and measurement is an outgrowth of continuing research on experimental semantics, particularly the development of objective methods for measuring meaning (Osgood, 1952, 1953). From this viewpoint, the *meaning* of a concept is its location in a space defined by some number of factors or dimensions, and *attitude* toward a concept is its projection onto one of these dimensions defined as "evaluative." In the factor analytic work we have done so far, the first and most heavily loaded factor is always one clearly identifiable as evaluative by the labels of the scales it represents, e.g., good-bad, fair-unfair, valuable-worthless, pleasant-unpleasant, and the like. This conception of attitude as a dimension or factor in total meaning has a number of implications, including those explored in the present paper. It implies, for example, that people having the same attitude toward a concept, such as *Negro*, may be sharply differentiated in terms of other dimensions of the semantic space (e.g., some perceiving *Negro* as powerful and active, others as weak and passive).[1]

Attitudes toward the various objects of judgment associated in messages must be measured in the same units if comparative statements about attitude

[1]A study in progress exhibits precisely this phenomenon with respect to the concept *Negro*. Similar findings are evident with respect to *the Church* and *capital punishment*.

*The paper following this editorial introduction is slightly abridged from C. E. Osgood and P. H. Tannenbaum, The principle of congruity in the prediction of attitude change, *Psychological Review*, 1955, *62*, 42-55, by permission of the senior author and the publisher, the American Psychological Association.

change are to be made. There have been attempts to devise *generalized attitude scales* in the history of this field (Remmers, 1934; Remmers and Silance, 1934), but if one is to judge by the criterion of acceptance and use, they have not been outstandingly successful. In applying the *semantic differential* (a label that has come to be applied to our measuring instrument), various objects of judgment, sources and concepts, are rated against a standard set of descriptive scales. To the extent that location on the evaluative dimension of the semantic differential is a reliable and valid index of attitude (as determined by correlation with other criteria), it is then necessarily a generalized attitude scale. We have some evidence for validity[2] and more is being obtained; reliability of the differential, particularly the evaluative dimension, is reasonably high, running in the .80's and .90's in available data.

Another underlying notion about human thinking we have been exploring is that *judgmental frames of reference tend toward maximal simplicity*. Since extreme, "all-or-nothing" judgments are simpler than finely discriminated judgments of degree, this implies a continuing pressure toward polarization along the evaluative dimension (i.e., movement of concepts toward either entirely good or entirely bad allocations). We have evidence that extreme judgments have shorter latencies than more discriminative judgments (Osgood, 1953), and that extreme judgments are characteristic of less intelligent, less mature, less well educated, or more emotionally oriented individuals (Stagner and Osgood, 1941). Furthermore, since assumption of identity is a simpler process than maintenance of distinction, this also implies a continuing pressure toward elimination of differences among concepts which are localized in the same direction of the evaluative framework. We have evidence that in the judging of emotionally polarized concepts all scales of judgment tend to rotate toward the evaluative, e.g., their correlations with good-bad tend to increase and therefore the relative loading on the evaluative factor tends to increase (Osgood, 1953).

The most "simple-minded" evaluative frame of reference is therefore one in which a tight cluster of highly polarized and undifferentiated good concepts is diametrically opposed in meaning to an equally tight and polarized cluster of undifferentiated bad concepts. The same underlying pressure toward simplicity operates on any new or neutral concept to shift it one way or the other. For example, there is the tendency in American thinking, about which Pandit Nehru complains, requiring that India be either "for us or agin' us." This is, of course, the condition referred to by the general semanticists (e.g., Johnson, 1949), as a

---

[2]For example, the correlations between scores on the evaluative scales of the semantic differential and scores on the Thurstone scales on attitude toward *the Church, Negro*, and *capital punishment* are .74, .82, and .81, respectively.

"two-valued orientation," and it is unfortunately characteristic of lay thinking in any period of conflict and emotional stress. The more sophisticated thinker, according to this view, should show less tendency to polarize, more differentiation among concepts, and thus greater relative use of factors other than the evaluative.

The Principle of Congruity

The principle of congruity in human thinking can be stated quite succinctly: *changes in evaluation are always in the direction of increased congruity with the existing frame of reference.* To make any use of this principle in specific situations, however, it is necessary to elaborate along the following lines: When does the issue of congruity arise? What directions of attitude change are congruent? How much stress is generated by incongruity and how is it distributed among the objects of judgment?

The Issue of Congruity

Each individual has potential attitudes toward a near infinity of objects. It is possible to have varying attitudes toward diverse concepts without any felt incongruity or any pressure toward attitude change, as long as no association among these objects of judgment is made. As anthropologists well know, members of a culture may entertain logically incompatible attitudes toward objects in their culture (e.g., ancestor worship and fear of the dead) without any stress, as long as the incompatibles are not brought into association. The issue of congruity arises whenever a message is received which relates two or more objects of judgment via an assertion.

The simplest assertion is merely a *descriptive statement*: "Chinese cooking is good," "Jefferson was right," "This neurotic modern art." To the extent that the evaluative location of a particular qualifier differs from that of the thing qualified, there is generated some pressure toward congruity. Similar pressure is generated by ordinary *statements of classification*: "Senator McCarthy is a Catholic," "Tom is an ex-con," "Cigarettes contain nicotine." To the extent that the evaluative locations of instance and class are different, some pressure toward congruity exists. A more complex situation is that in which *a source makes an assertion about a concept*: "University President Bans Research on Krebiozen"; "Communists like strong labor unions." This is the most commonly studied situation and one for which we have some empirical data against which to test our hypotheses. Assertions may be explicit linguistic statements of evaluation or implicit behavioral, situational statements. A newsphoto of Mrs. Roosevelt smiling and shaking hands with a little colored boy is just as effective in setting up pressures toward congruity as a verbal statement on her part.

Directions of Congruence and Incongruence

To predict the direction of attitude change from this general principle it is necessary to take into account simultaneously the existing attitudes toward each of the objects of judgment prior to reception of the message and the nature of the assertion which is embodied in the message. Attitudes can be specified as favorable (+), neutral (0), and unfavorable (−). Assertions can be specified as positive or associative (+) or negative or disassociative (−). They may also, of course, include evaluative loading (e.g., when X denounces Y, we have both a disassociative assertion and negative evaluation of Y). When attitudes toward both objects of judgment are polar, the nature of the assertion determines congruence or incongruence. For *Eisenhower* (+) to come out in favor of *freedom of the press* (+) is, of course, congruent with the existing frame of reference of most people in this country, but for *The Daily Worker* (−) to speak in favor of *freedom of the press* (+) is attitudinally incongruent. In this simplest of states in which human thinking operates, sources we like should always sponsor ideas we like and denounce ideas we are against, and vice versa.

When the existing attitude toward one of the objects of judgment is neutral and the other polar, we must speak of what directions *would be* congruent. If, for example, a favorable source like *Eisenhower* were to make a favorable assertion about the *minister from Siam* (a neutral notion to most of us), it would be congruent *if* the latter were also favorable − hence pressure is generated toward attitude change in this direction. If *Pravda* (−) sponsors *gradual disarmament* (0), the pressure is such as to make the relatively neutral notion of disarmament less favorable; similarly, if a *professor* (0) as a source favors *premarital sexual relations* (−) as making for better marriages, it is the *professor* that becomes less favorable (this is not unlike the "guilt by association" technique). Conversely, for our neutral *professor* (0) to speak out against *moral depravity* (−) must have the effect of raising his esteem (this is the familiar "I am against sin" technique).

When both objects of judgment are neutral, there is no question of congruity between them, and movement is determined solely by the nature of the assertion, i.e., this becomes a case of simple qualification or classification. If *Mr. Jones* denounces *Mr. Smith*, neither of whom is known, there is presumably some negative pressure on *Mr. Smith* by virtue of the sheer devaluation of "being denounced." Since the evaluation applies to the concept and not the source, the effect should be chiefly upon the concept. We shall find evidence for such an "assertion effect" in the available data.

We may now make a general statement governing the direction of congruence which will hold for any object of judgment, source or concept, and any type of assertion.

1. *Whenever one object of judgment is associated with another by an assertion, its congruent position along the evaluative dimension is always equal in degree of polarization to the other object of judgment and in either the same (positive assertion) or opposite (negative assertion) evaluative direction.*

Figure 1 provides some graphic illustrations. In example 1, we have a positive assertion (indicated by the + on the bar connecting source and concept) associating two equally favorable objects of judgment; in this situation maximum congruity already exists. In all the other illustrations given, the existing positions are not those of maximum congruence, and those positions which would be maximally congruent for each object of judgment are shown by dashed circles. In situation 3, for example, a congruent source would be at -2 and a congruent concept would be at +3, given the favorable assertion between two items of opposite sign.

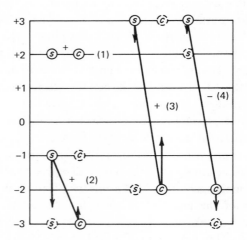

Figure 1. Graphic examples of four situations in which a source (s) makes an assertion (+ or —) about a concept (c). Positions of maximum congruity are indicated by dashed circles; predicted changes in attitude are indicated by arrows. See discussion in text.

Magnitude and Distribution
of Pressure toward Congruity

Knowing the existing locations of maximum congruence under the given conditions (by applying Principle 1), it becomes possible to state the amount and direction of application of total available pressure toward congruity.

2. *The total available pressure toward congruity for a given object of judgment associated with another by an assertion is equal to the difference, in attitude scale units, between its existing location and its location of maximum congruence along the evaluative dimension; the sign of this pressure is positive (+) when the location of congruence is more favorable than the existing location and negative (−) when the location of congruence is less favorable than the existing location.*

For example 2 in Figure 1, the total pressure toward congruity available for the source is -2 units and for the concept is +2 units. As can be seen by inspection of these examples, the total pressures toward congruity for both objects associated by an assertion are always equal in magnitude, although they may be the same or different in sign. The upper figures in each cell of Table 2 give the total pressures and directions of application for all possible relations among sources and concepts and both types of assertions. These computations are based upon the assumption of a 7-step scale with three degrees of polarization possible in each evaluative direction; they may be treated as general index numbers.

The third principle with which we shall operate incorporates the empirical generalization that intense attitudes are more resistant to change than weakly held ones (cf., Birch, 1945; Klapper, 1949; Tannenbaum, 1953), but does so in a way which generates more detailed predictions.

3. *In terms of producing attitude change, the total pressure toward congruity is distributed between the objects of judgment associated by an assertion in inverse proportion to their separate degrees of polarization.*

In other words, relatively less polarized objects of judgment, when associated with relatively more polarized objects of judgment, absorb proportionately greater amounts of the pressure toward congruity, and consequently change more.

In example 1 in Figure 1, there is no pressure and hence no change. In the other examples solid arrows indicate the direction and magnitude of predicted change. In example 2, the source must absorb twice as much pressure as the more polarized concept, and in a negative rather than a positive direction (e.g., *Bulgaria* -1 sponsors *hate campaign* -3). The unexpected prediction here, that the even more unfavorable concept, *hate campaign*, actually becomes a little less unfavorable under these conditions, derives directly from the theoretical model and will be discussed later.

The numbers in Table 1 represent the prediction of attitude change toward the concept for all combinations of original attitude toward source and concept when the assertion is positive.

Table 1. Predicted Attitude Change for Concept as a Function of Original Locations of Both Source and Concept — Positive Assertion (Uncorrected for Incredulity)

Original Attitude toward Source	Original Attitude toward Concept						
	+3	+2	+1	0	−1	−2	−3
+3	0.0	+0.6	+1.5	+3.0	+3.0	+3.0	+3.0
+2	−0.4	0.0	+0.7	+2.0	+2.0	+2.0	+2.0
+1	−0.5	−0.3	0.0	+1.0	+1.0	+1.0	+1.0
0	−1.0	0.0	−0.0	0.0	0.0	0.0	0.0
−1	−1.0	−1.0	−1.0	−1.0	0.0	+0.3	+0.5
−2	−2.0	−2.0	−2.0	−2.0	−0.7	0.0	+0.4
−3	−3.0	−3.0	−3.0	−3.0	−1.5	−0.6	0.0

Note that for all *incongruous relations* the predicted change is constant for a given original attitude toward a source (upper right and lower left corners of matrix) — a highly favorable source favoring a negative concept produces just as much attitude change when that concept is -3 as when it is -1. This prediction assumes complete credulity of the message on the part of the receiver, a condition that exists only rarely, in all probability, for incongruous messages. Certainly, when presented with the incongruous message, *Eisenhower* sponsors *communism*, in an experimental situation, very few subjects are going to give it full credence. If we are going to make predictions, it is apparent that the variable of credulity must be taken into account.

4. *The amount of incredulity produced when one object of judgment is associated with another by an assertion is a positively accelerated function of the amount of incongruity which exists and operates to decrease attitude change, completely eliminating change when maximal.*

Since incongruity exists only when similarly evaluated concepts are associated by negative assertions or when oppositely evaluated concepts are associated by positive assertions, the correction for incredulity is limited to the upper right and lower left corners of the matrix in Table 1. Within these situations, the *amount* of this correction is assumed to increase with the degree of incongruity, e.g., with the total pressure toward congruity available. It is assumed that no incongruity, and hence no incredulity, can exist where one of the objects of judgment is neutral, e.g., *Eisenhower* may come out either for or against a neutral concept like *St. Lawrence Waterway* without the issue of incredulity arising. It is realized, of course, that factors other than those discussed here may affect incredulity.

Figure 2 provides graphic illustration of the corrections made for incredulity. The original curves, level for the neutral point and beyond, derive from the upper right corner of Table 1 and represent three degrees of favorable original attitude toward the source (OJ_1). The dashed lines represent postulated incredulity, positively accelerated functions of total pressure toward congruity. The shape of this function is, of course, based on pure hunch and will probably have to be modified; it simply seems reasonable that a person's tendency to reject a message will be relatively much less for slightly incongruous relations (e.g., *Eisenhower* +3 praises *Bulgarians* -1) than for grossly incongruous ones (e.g., *Eisenhower* +3 praises *communism* -3). The light solid curves represent the result of subtracting incredulity functions from predicted attitude changes. The corrected values are given in Table 2. The same corrections, with appropriate regard to sign, apply to the lower left corner of Table 1 and are made in Table 2.

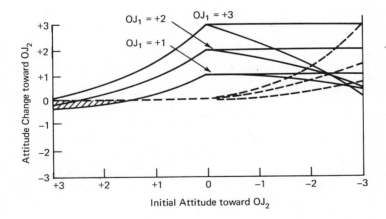

Figure 2. Predicted change in attitude toward OJ_2 and correction for incredulity (postulated incredulity indicated by dashed lines). *OJ* refers to the object of judgment — that is, the source of the concept. In this case, OJ_1 refers to the source, and OJ_2 refers to the concept about which the source has made an assertion.

Incredulity, to the extent it is present, will not only operate to "damp" changes in attitude but should also appear in expressions of disbelief and

Table 2. Total Pressure toward Congruity (Upper Numbers) and Predicted Changes in Attitude (Lower Numbers) as Corrected for Incredulity* (Positive Assertion)†

Initial Location of OJ_2	Initial Location of OJ_1							
	+3	+2	+1	0	−1	−2	−3	M
+3	0	+1	+2	+3	+4	+5	+6	
	0.0	+0.6	+1.5	+3.0	+2.6	+1.5	0.0	+1.3
+2	−1	0	+1	+2	+3	+4	+5	
	−0.4	0.0	+0.7	+2.0	+1.8	+1.3	+0.5	+0.8
+1	−2	−1	0	+1	+2	+3	+4	
	−0.5	−0.3	0.0	+1.0	+0.9	+0.7	+0.4	+0.3
0	−3	−2	−1	0	+1	+2	+3	
	0.0	0.0	0.0	0.0	0.0	0.0	0.0	0.0
−1	−4	−3	−2	−1	0	+1	+2	
	−0.4	−0.7	−0.9	−1.0	0.0	+0.3	+0.5	−0.3
−2	−5	−4	−3	−2	−1	0	+1	
	−0.5	−1.3	−1.8	−2.0	−0.7	0.0	+0.4	−0.8
−3	−6	−5	−4	−3	−2	−1	0	
	0.0	−1.5	−2.6	−3.0	−1.5	−0.6	0.0	−1.3
/ M /	0.3	0.6	1.1	1.7	1.1	0.6	0.3	

*The OJ whose change is being predicted, either source or concept, is always OJ_1 and the other is OJ_2.

†When dealing with negative assertions, reverse the sign of OJ_2 and look in that row.

rationalization. This makes it possible to ascertain the incredulity function independent of attitude change. A proposed experiment along these lines might be as follows: If subjects are presented with a number of messages and told that some are valid and others faked, we would expect the frequency of "fake" judgments to be some increasing function of the measured amount of incongruity (e.g., in terms of locations of original attitudes toward the associated objects of judgment). It is the shape of this function in which we would be particularly interested. If the same subjects were then assured that certain of the "fake" messages were actually valid, we would expect to record rationalizations and other attempts to interpret the message without modifying the evaluative frame of reference; e.g., told that *Russia* is actually sponsoring a *peace conference,* the subject is likely to rationalize this event as some subterfuge on the part of the Soviets in the Cold War. Use of the same messages on another group of subjects in a standard pre- and postmessage attitude change design should serve to test the prediction that attitude change for incongruous assertions is damped in proportion to the degree of incredulity produced.

This independence of credulity as a variable also means that it should be possible to approximate the attitude change values in Table 1 (uncorrected) under special conditions where credulity is made more probable. For example, if *Eisenhower* were actually to invite important *Communist party officers* to a friendly dinner at the White House, the effects on devaluating *Eisenhower* and vice versa should be extreme. The greater effectiveness of "event" as compared to "word" propaganda follows directly.

The lower numbers in each cell in Table 2 represent the predicted magnitudes and directions of attitude change for all combinations of original attitude — for *sources* or *concepts* and for either positive assertions or negative assertions (see instructions in table footnotes). Let us take illustration 2 in Figure 1 as an example: the original attitudes in this case are -1 (source) and -3 (concept), so we will be concerned with the cell defined by these values. Looking first for *source change* (e.g., *source* as OJ_1), we find a total pressure toward congruity of -2 (upper figure in cell) and a predicted attitude change of -1.5; looking then for *concept change* (e.g., *concept* as OJ_1), we find a total pressure of +2 and a predicted attitude change of +0.5. If this were the message *Bulgaria* praises *communism*, we might expect a considerable increase in unfavorableness toward *Bulgaria* and a slight decrease in unfavorableness toward *communism*. The reader may check the other illustrations against Table 2 if he wishes.

Predictions about attitude change are assumed to hold for any situation in which one object of judgment is associated with another by an assertion. In the special source-concept situation, we must take one additional factor into account — the fact that the *assertion itself*, whether positive or negative, typically applies to the concept rather than to the source. When X praises Y, the favorable effect of "praise" applies chiefly to Y; when X denounces Y, similarly, the unfavorable effect of "denounce" applies chiefly to Y. In other words, we must add to the equation predicting attitude change for concepts a constant $(\pm A)$ whose sign is always the same as that of the assertion. In the data we have available, the existence of such an assertion constant applying to the concept but not the source is clearly evident.

A Test of the Congruity Principle[3]

On the basis of a pretest of 36 potential objects of judgment, three source-concept pairs were selected which met the criteria of (1) approximately

[3]This experiment is described in detail in Tannenbaum (1953).

equal numbers of subjects holding favorable, neutral, and unfavorable original attitudes toward them, and (2) lack of correlation between attitude toward the source and the concept making up each pair. The three source-concept pairs finally selected were: *labor leaders* with *legalized gambling, Chicago Tribune* with *abstract art*, and *Senator Robert Taft* with *accelerated college programs*. Another group of 405 college students was given a *before-test*, in which the 6 experimental concepts along with 4 "filler" concepts were judged against a form of the semantic differential including 6 scales highly loaded on the evaluative factor. The sum of ratings on these six 7-step scales constituted the attitude score for each concept, these scores ranging from 6 (most unfavorable) to 42 (most favorable). Five weeks later the same subjects were given highly realistic newspaper stories including positive or negative assertions involving the experimental source-concept pairs. Immediately afterward the subjects were given the *after-test* again judging the same concepts against the semantic differential.

Original attitudes toward each source and concept were determined from the before-test scores, subjects being distributed into nine cells, s_+c_+, s_+c_0, s_+c_-, s_0c_+, etc. Attitude change amounts, for both source and concept, were obtained by subtracting the before-test score from the after-test score for each subject, a positive value thereby indicating increased favorableness.

Table 3 compares predicted attitude change scores (upper number in each cell) with obtained attitude change scores (lower number in each cell) for both sources and concepts and for both positive and negative assertions. The predicted values represent the algebraic mean of the attitude change scores in appropriate cells of Table 2 (e.g., the value for s_+c_+ with a positive assertion equals the average for the nine cells in the upper left corner); the obtained values represent the total attitude change scores, summed algebraically, for 45 subjects (15 subjects on each of 3 stories) on 6 evaluative scales. The reason for the gross difference in absolute magnitudes of predicted and obtained scores is therefore that the former are expressed in scale units and the latter in group totals. The general correspondence between predicted and obtained directions of attitude change is apparent from inspection of Table 3. In every case predicted positive changes (+) and predicted negative changes (−) show corresponding signs in the obtained data, and predicted lack of change (0) generally yields obtained changes of small magnitude.

The predictions obviously hold better for source changes than for concept changes, and it will be recalled that it was also predicted that *an assertion constant* ($\pm A$) would apply to the concept but not the source. This would mean that for comparable situations (e.g., s_+c_0 vs. s_0c_+, s_0c_- vs. s_-c_0, etc.) concept changes should be more in the favorable direction than source changes for

Table 3. Predicted (Upper Values in Cells) and Obtained (Lower Values in Cells) Changes in Attitude

Original Attitude toward Source	Positive Assertions			Negative Assertions		
	Original Attitude toward Concept			Original Attitude toward Concept		
	+	0	−	+	0	−
	Source Changes					
+	+ 0.2	0.0	−1.1	−1.1	0.0	+0.2
	+ 25	+ 16	− 42	− 45	+ 1	+ 34
0	+ 2.0	0.0	−2.0	−2.0	0.0	+2.0
	+150	+ 25	− 94	− 68	+ 17	+ 96
−	+ 1.1	0.0	−0.2	−0.2	0.0	+1.1
	+ 49	+ 13	− 7	− 33	− 3	+ 34
	Concept Changes					
+	+ 0.2	+ 2.0	+ 1.1	−1.1	− 2.0	−0.2
	+ 51	+245	+107	− 88	−180	− 39
0	0.0	0.0	0.0	0.0	0.0	0.0
	+ 39	+ 80	+ 48	− 72	− 79	− 34
−	−1.1	−2.0	−0.2	+0.2	+ 2.0	+1.1
	− 24	− 52	− 10	+ 19	+ 22	+ 16

positive assertions and more in the negative direction for negative assertions. Table 4 provides a test of this prediction. As can be seen, when comparable conditions for source and concept changes are arranged, the differences in magnitudes of attitude change are regularly positive for positive assertions (concept changes more toward favorable direction) and regularly negative for negative assertions (concept changes more toward unfavorable direction). With 17 of the 18 values in the predicted direction, this is obviously significant.

A rough estimate of the size of this constant can be obtained from the average difference between source and concept changes for comparable situations: it turns out to be $A = \pm 46$ in total change score or $A = .17$ in units of the 7-step attitude scale employed. In other words, under the general conditions of this experiment, the assertion constant applied to concept changes equals about $1/6$ of a scale unit.

Table 4. Effects of Assertion Itself (A)

Source	Concept	Difference (A)
Positive Assertions (Predicted That A is +)		
$s_+ c_+$ + 25	$s_+ c_+$ + 51	+ 26
$s_0 c_+$ + 150	$s_+ c_0$ + 245	+ 95
$s_- c_+$ + 49	$s_+ c_-$ + 107	+ 58
$s_+ c_0$ + 16	$s_0 c_+$ + 39	+ 23
$s_0 c_0$ + 25	$s_0 c_0$ + 80	+ 55
$s_- c$ + 13	$s_0 c_-$ + 48	+ 35
$s_+ c_-$ − 42	$s_- c_+$ − 24	+ 18
$s_0 c_-$ − 94	$s_- c_0$ − 52	+ 42
$s_- c_-$ − 7	$s_- c_-$ − 10	− 3
Negative Assertions (Predicted That A is −)		
$s_+ c_+$ − 45	$s_+ c_+$ − 88	− 43
$s_0 c_+$ − 68	$s_+ c_0$ − 180	− 112
$s_- c_+$ − 33	$s_+ c_-$ − 39	− 6
$s_+ c_0$ + 1	$s_0 c_+$ − 72	− 73
$s_0 c_0$ + 17	$s_0 c_0$ − 79	− 96
$s_- c_0$ − 3	$s_0 c_-$ − 34	− 31
$s_+ c_-$ + 34	$s_- c_+$ + 19	− 15
$s_0 c_-$ + 96	$s_- c_0$ + 22	− 74
$s_- c_-$ + 34	$s_- c_-$ + 16	− 18

That the magnitudes of attitude changes as well as their directions tend to follow predictions is also evident by inspection of Table 3. This can be seen more clearly in the correlation plot between predicted changes and obtained changes given as Figure 3. The predicted values are here treated as categorical and the obtained as continuous, and the latter have been corrected for the assertion constant by adding 46 to concept changes with negative assertions and subtracting 46 from concept changes with positive assertions. The correlation between predicted and obtained changes in attitude is high (r = .91).

A number of corollaries derive from the congruity principle, some of which can be tested against Tannenbaum's data and others of which cannot. They are as follows.

1. *Shifts in evaluation always tend toward equalization of the degrees of polarization of the objects of judgment associated by an assertion.* If two

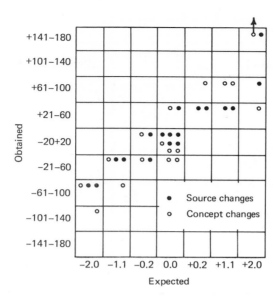

Figure 3. Correlation plot between predicted and obtained attitude changes
after corrections for incredulity and for constant effect of assertion.

unequally polarized concepts are associated, the less polarized one becomes
more so and the more polarized less so; if a neutral concept is associated with a
polarized one, it always becomes more polarized. In Tannenbaum's data this
means that the less polarized object of judgment (neutral) should always change
more than the more polarized object of judgment (plus or minus); this holds for
all relevant conditions except one (s_0c_+, negative assertion), and even here when
correction for the assertion constant is made. The comparisons shown in
Table 5, where concept changes have been corrected for the assertion constant,
clearly substantiate this prediction — in every case the neutral member shows a
large shift and the polar member a small shift.

2. *When the total pressure toward congruity is constant, it is easier to make
an object of judgment more polarized than less so.* That this prediction follows
from the theory can be seen in Table 2 by comparing magnitudes of attitude
change within the same row or column (for a given location of source or
concept) when the total pressure is the same in amount but opposite in sign —
amount of attitude change is always larger in the same direction as the sign of
the row or column. This cannot be checked in Tannenbaum's data because he
does not differentiate between degrees of original attitude in the same direction.

Table 5. Comparison of Attitude Changes for Neutral and Polar Objects of Judgment

Situation	Change for Neutral	Change for Polar
	Positive Assertions	
$s_0\,c_+$	+ 150 (*s*)	− 7 (*c*)
$s_+\,c_0$	+ 199 (*c*)	+ 16 (*s*)
$s_-\,c_0$	− 98 (*c*)	+ 13 (*s*)
$s_0\,c_-$	− 94 (*s*)	+ 2 (*c*)
	Negative Assertions	
$s_0\,c_+$	− 68 (*s*)	− 26 (*c*)
$s_+\,c_0$	− 134 (*c*)	+ 1 (*s*)
$s_-\,c_0$	+ 48 (*c*)	− 3 (*s*)
$s_0\,c_-$	+ 96 (*s*)	+ 12 (*c*)

It would be expected, however, from our general notion that evaluative frames of reference tend toward maximum simplicity.

3. *Attitude change toward an object of judgment is an inverse function of intensity of original attitude toward that object.* That weakly held attitudes are more susceptible to change is a widely held notion, but it is only valid, according to present theory, for the *average* of all degrees of attitude toward the other object with which a given one is associated *regardless of sign* (the absolute means, $|M|$, given at the bottom of Table 2) or for maximally polarized attitudes toward the other object (+3 and -3 rows in Table 2). The "law" definitely does not hold for other degrees of attitude toward the second object of judgment, as can be seen by inspection of this table. The data in Table 6 compare predicted values (absolute means at bottom of Table 2) with those obtained by Tannenbaum, both being expressed in attitude scale units in this case. The close correspondence in trend is apparent, and the obtained trend is statistically significant. The difference in absolute magnitude presumably represents the limited effect of a single message upon attitude change. The theoretical model as developed so far takes account of neither learning via successive messages nor of intensity of assertions.

4. *Attitude change for a given object of judgment in the direction of the assertion is an approximately linear function of the favorableness of the original attitude toward the other object of judgment with which it is associated.* The more favorable the attitude toward a source, the greater the effect of a positive

Table 6. Attitude Change toward an Object of Judgment as a Function of
Original Attitude toward That Object Itself

	Original Attitude toward Object of Judgment		
	+	0	−
Predicted	0.6	1.7	0.6
Obtained (source)	0.2	0.5	0.2
Obtained (concept)	0.3	0.7	0.2

assertion on raising attitude toward the concept and the greater the effect of a
negative assertion upon lowering attitude toward the concept. Strongly
unfavorable sources have just the opposite effects. The same statements hold for
changes in attitude toward sources when original attitudes toward concepts are
varied. Table 7 compares predicted and obtained values. Again, the generally
lower levels of obtained changes as compared with predicted changes are
presumably due to the limited effects of a single message. Changes in attitude
have been corrected for the assertion constant, here as in Table 6. The obtained
functions are in the direction predicted, and their trend is statistically
significant.

Table 7. Attitude Change toward One Object of Judgment as a Function of
Original Attitude toward the Other Object of Judgment

Assertions	Original Attitude toward Object of Judgment		
	+	0	−
Positive			
Predicted	+0.8	0.0	−0.8
Obtained (source)	+0.3	0.0	−0.2
Obtained (concept)	+0.3	0.0	−0.3
Negative		0.0	
Predicted	−0.8	0.0	+0.8
Obtained (source)	−0.2	0.0	+0.2
Obtained (concept)	−0.2	−0.1	+0.2

5. *Whenever a congruent assertion associates two differently polarized
objects of judgment, and neither of them is neutral, the more polarized boject of
judgment becomes less so.* This deduction includes the rather paradoxical

situations noted earlier in this paper in which, for example, a highly favorable source comes out in favor of somewhat less favorable concept and becomes slightly less favorable itself in doing so, according to theory. The locations in Table 2 where this prediction arises are italicized. Here we are forced to predict, for example: when *Eisenhower* +3 praises *golfing* +1, he loses a little prestige while giving a big boost to the concept; when *Eisenhower* +3 denounces *comic books* -1, he may make the latter considerably more unfavorable, but he loses a little ground himself in the exchange. It is as if a highly favorable source should only favor equally good things or be against extremely bad things and a highly unsavory concept should be only sponsored by equally unsavory sources or condemned by highly noble sources.

If such an effect could be demonstrated, it would be convincing evidence for the whole theory. Tannenbaum's study provides only a partial test for this phenomenon in that the experimental situation probably lacked the necessary sensitivity to get at the very minimal changes predicted. However, of 38 cases that met the necessary conditions, 21 (55.3 percent) showed relatively small changes in the predicted direction, 15 (39.5 percent) showed no change, and only 2 (5.3 percent) changed in the opposite direction.

Summary

This paper describes a general theory of attitude change which takes into account original attitude toward the source of a message, original attitude toward the concept evaluated by the source, and the nature of the evaluative assertion. Predicted changes in attitude toward both source and concept are based upon the combined operation of a principle of congruity, a principle of susceptibility as a function of polarization, and a principle of resistance due to incredulity for incongruous messages. Comparison of predictions with data obtained in a recent experiment provides a test of the theory. No attempt has been made to integrate this particular theoretical model with more general psychological theory, and we feel no urge at this time to attempt such detailed translations. We are, of course, aware that there are many variables other than those considered here which contribute to attitude change.

8

An Overview of Persuasibility Research

Irving L. Janis
Carl I. Hovland

The following selection by Janis and Hovland represents the learning theory approach to the study of attitude change. The rationale for attaching a "learning" label to the approach is that such theorists treat attitude change as a learning process — a response (the attitude, as evidenced through statements, behavior, and so on) to a stimulus (the object of the attitude) is extinguished, and a new response (attitude) replaces it. The style of these theorists is indicated by their use of such concepts as "communication stimuli" and "communication effects or responses." Communication stimuli include the information or message that a person receives about an object of an attitude, as well as who sends the message, the medium used, the conditions under which it is sent, and so on. Research and theory attempt to delineate the effects of various communication stimuli on attitudinal responses.

Janis and Hovland move beyond a strict consideration of stimulus and response and speculate about variables that qualify the S-R relationship. These theorists consider some of the ways in which personal characteristics of recipients of messages may differentially affect the communication stimulus-communication response relationship. For example, they suggest that some people may be predisposed to be more persuasible than others about particular topics or to be more easily persuaded by

139

information presented by particular media. The major portion of this paper is devoted to introducing various constructs used to account for individual differences in persuasibility.*

Definition of Persuasibility

By "persuasibility factor" is meant any variable attribute within a population that is correlated with *consistent individual differences* in responsiveness to one or more classes of influential communications. The meaning of the key terms in this definition will become somewhat clearer if we consider a brief schematic analysis of the communication process involved in successful persuasion.

Whenever an individual is influenced to change his beliefs, decisions, or general attitudes, certain identifiable external events occur which constitute the *communication stimuli*, and certain changes in the behavior of the person take place which constitute the *communication effects*. Communication stimuli include not only what is said, but also all of the intentional and unintentional cues which influence a member of the audience, including information as to who is saying it, why he is saying it, and how other people are reacting to it. The observable communication effects could be said to subsume all perceptible changes in the recipient's verbal and nonverbal behavior, including not only changes in private opinions or judgments but also a variety of learning effects (e.g. increased knowledge about the communicator's position) and superficial conformist behavior (e.g. public expression of agreement with the conclusion despite private rejection of it). However, our main interest centers upon those changes in observable behavior which are regarded as components of "genuine" changes in opinions or in verbalizable attitudes. This requires observational methods which enable us to discern, in addition to the individual's public responses, those indications of his private thoughts, feelings, and evaluations that are used to judge whether the recipient has "internalized" the communicator's message or is merely giving what he considers to be a socially acceptable response.

We use the term "attitude change" when there are clear-cut indications that the recipient has internalized a valuational message, as evidenced by the fact that

*The paper following this editorial introduction is excerpted from I. L. Janis and C. I. Hovland, An overview of persuasibility research, in C. I. Hovland and I. L. Janis (Eds.), *Personality and persuasibility* (New Haven, Conn.: Yale Univ. Press, 1959), pp. 1-16, by permission of the senior author and the publisher.

the person's perceptions, affects, and overt actions, as well as his verbalized judgments, are discernibly changed. When there is evidence of a genuine change in a *verbalized belief or value judgment*, we use the term "opinion change," which usually constitutes one component of attitude change. Almost all experiments on the effects of persuasive communications have been limited to investigating changes in opinion. The reason, of course, is that such changes can readily be assessed in a highly reliable way, whereas other components of verbalizable attitudes, although of considerable theoretical interest, are much more difficult to measure.

Neither "opinion change" nor "attitude change" is used to refer to those instances of surface conformity in which the person *pretends* to adopt a point of view that he does not really believe. Thus, the area of opinion change with which we are concerned includes studies dealing with what has been referred to as "internalization" and "identification," but excludes those dealing with "compliance" (cf. Kelman, 1959).

Figure 1 gives a schematic outline of the major factors that enter into attitude change. The observable communication stimuli and the observable effects are represented as the two end-points of the communication process. These are the antecedent and consequent events that are observable; they constitute the empirical anchorage for two main types of constructs which are needed in order to account for the inter-relationships between the communication stimuli and observable effects: *predispositional factors* and *internal mediating processes*. Predispositional factors are used to account for *individual differences in observable effects when all communication stimuli are held constant*. Constructs referring to internal, or mediating, processes are used in order to account for the differential effects of different stimuli on a given person or group of persons. In other words, internal-processes constructs have been formulated primarily to account for the different effects attributable to *different types of communications* acting on the *same people*; whereas, predispositional constructs are needed to account for the different effects observed in *different people* who have been exposed to the *same communications*.

Hovland, Janis, and Kelley (1953) have reviewed and analyzed the experimental evidence on the effects of low vs. high credibility sources, strong vs. weak fear-arousing appeals, one-sided vs. two-sided presentation of arguments, and other such variations in communication stimuli. From such studies it has been possible to formulate a number of generalizations concerning the conditions under which the probability of opinion change will be increased or decreased for the *average* person or for the *large majority* of persons in any audience. Such propositions form the basis for inferences concerning the

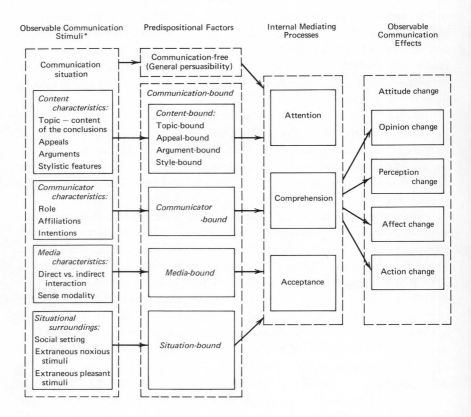

Figure 1. Major factors in attitude change produced by means of social communication*

mediating processes responsible for the differential effectiveness of different communication stimuli.

Mediating processes can be classified in terms of three aspects of responsiveness to verbal messages (see Hovland, Lumsdaine, and Sheffield, 1949; and Hovland, Janis, and Kelley, 1953). The first set of mediating responses includes those which arouse the *attention* of the recipient to the verbal content of the

*The categories and subcategories are not necessarily exhaustive, but are intended to highlight the main types of stimulus variables that play a role in producing changes in verbalizable attitudes.

communication. The second set involves *comprehension* or decoding of verbal stimuli, including concept formation and the perceptual processes that determine the meaning the message will have for the respondent. Attention and comprehension determine what the recipient will *learn* concerning the content of the communicator's message; other processes, involving changes in motivation, are assumed to determine whether or not he will accept or adopt what he learns. Thus, there is a third set of mediating responses, referred to as *acceptance*. Much less is known about this set of responses, and it has become the main focus for present-day research on opinion change.

Two major classes of predispositions can be distinguished. One type, called "topic-bound," includes all of those factors which affect a person's readiness to accept or reject a given point of view on a particular topic. The other main type, called "topic-free," is relatively independent of the subject matter of the communication. In the discussion which follows, we shall first make some comments about the nature of topic-bound predispositions and about the more general class of "content-bound" factors, including those referred to as "appeal-bound," "argument-bound," and "style-bound." Then we shall attempt to extend the analysis of predispositional factors by making further distinctions, calling attention to a number of content-free factors that are nevertheless bound to other properties of the communication stimuli. These various types of "communication-bound" factors will be contrasted with the unbound or "communication-free" factors to which our research efforts have primarily been directed.

Topic-Bound Predispositions

Topic-bound factors have been extensively studied by social psychologists and sociologists over the years, and many propositions have been investigated concerning the motives, value structures, group affiliations, and ideological commitments which predispose a person to accept a pro or con attitude on various issues. The well-known studies of authoritarian personalities by Adorno and others (1950) have provided a major impetus toward understanding attitude change on specific issues, such as racial prejudice, in relation to unconscious motives and defense mechanisms. Some findings which bear directly on topic-bound predispositions have been reported by Bettelheim and Janowitz (1950): Anti-Semitic propaganda (in the form of two fascist pamphlets) was most likely to be approved by men who either had already acquired an intolerant ideology toward Jews or who had acquired a tolerant ideology but were insecure personalities with much undischarged hostility. Another pioneering study in this field is that of Smith, Bruner, and White (1956); these authors conducted a small series of intensive case studies for the purpose of determining the personality functions served by holding certain flexible and inflexible opinions about Soviet Russia and communism. Many other studies have been made concerning the personality correlates of readiness to accept favorable or unfavorable communications about specific types of ethnic, national, and political groups (Hartley, 1946; Sarnoff, 1951).

Some recent studies of topic-bound predispositions deal with relatively general factors that are not limited to the modification of attitudes toward only one type of social group. For instance, Weiss and Fine (1955, 1956) investigated the personality factors which make for high readiness to accept a message advocating a strict, punitive stand toward social deviants. The findings suggest that persons who have high aggression needs combined with strong extrapunitive tendencies will be prone to adopt a strict, punitive attitude toward anyone who violates social norms. In order to test this hypothesis in its most general form, it would be necessary to use many different communications to determine whether the specified personality attributes are correlated with attitude change whenever a punitive stand is advocated toward any type of social deviant. If the hypothesis is confirmed, we shall be able to speak of a very general type of topic-bound predisposition.

This example highlights the fact that the difference between topic-bound and topic-free is not necessarily the same as the dimension of specificity-generality. Some topic-bound predispositions may be very narrowly confined to those communications expressing a favorable or unfavorable judgment toward a specific trait of a particular person (e.g. the members of an organization, after having been embarrassed by the gauche manners of their highly respected leader, would be disposed to reject only those favorable statements about him which pertain to a limited aspect of his social behavior). Other topic-bound predispositions may be extremely general (e.g. certain types of persons may be inclined to accept any comments which express optimism about the future). A topic-bound predisposition, however, is always limited to one class of com-munications (a narrow or a broad class) which is defined by one or another characteristic of the *content of the conclusion*.

Similar restrictions hold for some of the topic-free factors. For example, Hovland, Janis, and Kelley (1953) point out that many topic-free factors may prove to be bound to specific characteristics of the communication:

> Some of the hypotheses concerning topic-free predispositions deal with factors which predict a person's responsiveness only to those persuasive communications that employ certain types of argumentation. Investiga-tions of topic-free predispositions ultimately may reveal some that are associated primarily with the nature of the communicator, others that are associated with the social setting in which the communication takes place, and perhaps still others that are so broad in scope that they are relatively independent of any specific variables in the communication situation.

Thus, for any communication, we assume that there are likely to be several different types of personality predispositions, topic-bound and topic-free, whose joint effects determine individual differences in responsiveness. The essential point is that, by also taking account of topic-free factors, it should be possible to improve predictions concerning the degree to which members of the audience will be influenced by persuasive communications. Such factors have generally been neglected in analyses of audience predispositions (p. 176).

In the discussion which follows, we shall attempt to trace the implications of the distinction — which we now believe to be extremely important — between topic-free factors that are bound in some nontopic way and those that are completely unbound. A suggested list of bound predispositions is provided in the second column of Figure 1. We shall briefly consider those topic-free factors which are bound to other features of the communication situation before turning to a detailed examination of the unbound, or communication-free, factors.

Content-Bound Factors

The content of a communication includes appeals, arguments, and various stylistic features, as well as the main theme or conclusion which defines its topic. The effectiveness of each of these content characteristics is partly dependent upon certain predispositional factors which we designate as "content-bound."

Appeal-bound factors. In the content of many communications one finds appeals which explicitly promise social approval or threaten social disapproval from a given reference group (see Newcomb, 1943). Responsiveness to these social incentives partly depends upon the degree to which the person is motivated to be affiliated with the reference group (see Kelley and Volkart, 1952). Personality differences may also give rise to differences in responsiveness to special appeals concerning group consensus and related social incentives (Samelson, 1957). Different types of personalities may be expected to have different thresholds for the arousal of guilt, shame, fear, and other emotions which can be aroused by special appeals. For example, Janis and Feshbach (1954) have found that certain personality factors are related to individual differences in responsiveness to fear-arousing appeals. Experimental studies by Katz, McClintock, and Sarnoff (1956, 1957) indicate that the relative effectiveness of rational appeals, and of self-insight procedures designed to counteract social prejudices, depends partly upon whether the recipient rates low, medium, or high on various measures of ego defensiveness.

Argument-bound factors. Many variables have been investigated which involve stimulus differences in the arrangement of arguments and in the logical relationship between arguments and conclusions. Cohen (1957) presents evidence indicating that predispositional factors play a role in determining the extent to which an individual will be affected by the order in which information is presented. Individuals with low cognitive-need scores were differentially influenced by variations in order of presentation while those with high scores were not. One would also expect that individual differences would affect the degree to which a person will be influenced by such variations as the following: (1) The use of strictly rational or logical types of argument vs. propagandistic devices of overgeneralization, innuendo, *non sequitur,* and irrelevant *ad hominem* comments. (2) Explicitly stating the conclusion that follows from a set of arguments vs. leaving the conclusion implicit. (A comparison of effects for subjects with high and low intelligence is presented in Hovland and Mandell, 1952.)

Style-bound factors.   Differences in social class and educational background probably account for some of the individual differences in responsiveness to variations in style — for example, a literary style as against a "folksy" approach. Other variations in treatment that may be differentially effective are technical jargon vs. simple language; slang vs. "pure" prose; long, complex sentences vs. short, declarative sentences. Flesch (1946) and other communication researchers have presented evidence concerning individual differences in responsiveness to such stylistic features.

Communicator-Bound Factors

The effectiveness of a communication depends on the recipient's evaluation of the speaker (see, e.g., Hovland and Weiss, 1951–52). The phase of the problem which has been most extensively studied is that concerned with the authoritativeness of the communicator. That personality differences in the recipients are associated with the extent to which particular communicators are effective is clearly shown in a study by Berkowitz and Lundy (1957). Their college-student subjects who were more influenced by authority figures tended to have both higher self-confidence and stronger authoritarian tendencies (high F-scale scores) than those who were more influenced by peers.

The affiliation of the communicator is also an important factor, in interaction, of course, with the group membership of the recipient. Thus the communicator who is perceived as belonging to a group with which the recipient is also affiliated will be more effective on the average than a communicator who is perceived either as an outsider or as a member of a rival group (Kelley and Volkart, 1952; Kelley and Thibault, 1954). When, for example, a speaker's affiliation with a political, social, religious, or trade organization becomes salient to the audience, persons who are members of the same organization will be most likely to be influenced by the speaker's communication.

Finally, the intent of the communicator is perceived differently by different members of the audience, with a consequent influence on the speaker's effectiveness. A number of studies have shown that the fairness and impartiality of the communicator is viewed quite differently by individuals with varying stands on an ideological issue, and this in turn is related to the amount of opinion change effected. For a discussion of this problem see Hovland, Harvey, and Sherif (1957).

Media-Bound Factors

It seems probable that some persons will be more responsive to communications in situations of direct social interaction, whereas others may be more readily influenced by newspapers, magazines, radio programs, television, movies, and mass media in general. (See the discussion by Lazarsfeld, Berelson, and Gaudet, 1944, concerning the psychological differences between propaganda emanating from mass media and from informal social contacts.) Other media characteristics that may evoke differential sensitivities involve variations in the sense modalities employed: e.g. some people may be more responsive to visual than to auditory media. There is some evidence that individuals with less education may be more influenced by aural presentations (e.g. by radio and lectures) than by printed media (see summary of studies by Klapper, 1949). However, few systematic studies have been made as yet on the relation between predispositions and media characteristics.

Situation-Bound Factors

While no systematic studies can be cited, there are indications that some persons tend to be more influenced when socially facilitative cues accompany the presentation of a persuasive communication (e.g. presence of others, applause). The experiments by Asch (1952) and other investigators contain some indirect implications bearing on individual differences in responsiveness to an expression of consensus on the part of others in the audience. Research by Razran (1940) and an unpublished study by Janis, Kaye, and Kirschener indicate that some people are affected by the pleasantness or unpleasantness of the situation in which a communication is received. For example, the effectiveness of persuasive messages was found to be enhanced if they were expressed at a time when the subjects were eating a snack. We might expect to find some personality factors associated with low vs. high sensitivity to extraneous stimulation of this type.

Just as in the case of topic-bound factors, each of the above content-bound, communicator-bound, media-bound, and situation-bound factors may include some predispositions that are very narrow in scope (e.g. applicable only to communications which emanate from one particular communicator) and other predispositions that are broadly applicable to a large class of communications (e.g. to all communications emanating from purported authorities or experts). It is the predispositions at the latter end of the specificity-generality continuum that are of major scientific interest, since they are the ones that increase our theoretical understanding of communication processes and help to improve predictions of the degree to which different persons will be responsive to social influence.

Predictive Value of Unbound Persuasibility Factors

Unbound persuasibility factors involve a person's general susceptibility to many different types of persuasion and social influence. We assume that these factors operate whenever a person is exposed to a persuasive communication and that they do not depend upon the presence or absence of any given type of content or on any other specifiable feature of the communication situation. Thus unbound factors are communication-free, and this differentiates them from even the most general of the bound factors.

One long-range product of research on bound and unbound persuasibility factors might be conceived of as a set of general formulae which could be used to predict, within a very narrow range of error, the degree to which any given person will be influenced by any given communication. The formulae would be multiple regression equations and would specify the personal attributes (X_1, X_2, X_3, ... X_n) that need to be assessed in order to make an accurate prediction concerning responsiveness to a given class of communications (Y_A). More than one regression equation would presumably be necessary in order to take account of the major bound personality factors; i.e. certain attributes might have high weight for one type of communication (Y_A) but low or zero weight for other types (Y_B, Y_C, Y_D, etc.). This way of looking at persuasibility research helps to clarify the essential difference between bound and unbound factors. Unbound factors would enter with a sizable weight into *every one* of the regression equations, irrespective of the type of communication for which predictions are being made (Y_A, Y_B, ... Y_Z). Bound factors, on the other hand, would have *varying* weights, ranging from zero in some regression equations to very high weights in others.

The concept of a set of multiple regression equations highlights the descriptive character of persuasibility factors. They are, in effect, individual traits whose consequences are directly measurable by observing changes in verbal behavior and in overt nonverbal behavior. They enable us to estimate the probability that a given individual will change his opinions or attitudes in response to a given class of communications. The unbound predispositions are communication-free factors which permit estimates concerning the probability of change in response to any communication, i.e. they purport to apply universally to all communications.

It should be noted, incidentally, that a given attribute (e.g. degree of motivation to conform to the demands of others) might turn out to be partly bound as well as unbound. That is to say, the attribute may be a communication-free factor because it enters into every regression formula with a substantial weight but, at the same time, it might be partly bound in that the weight may be much higher in a regression equation that applies to one particular class of communications (e.g. those which contain arguments and incentives appealing directly to the recipient's social conformity motives).

It should also be borne in mind that a seemingly unbound factor might actually be bound in a rather subtle or unexpected way. During the early stages of research, a given persuasibility factor may seem to be unbound, since it consistently enables better-than-chance predictions for a wide variety of communications differing in topic, communicator characteristics, media characteristics, and so forth. Subsequent research, however, might reveal that the factor is bound to some very broad category (e.g. it may apply to one-way mass-media situations but not to direct interpersonal relationships in which two-way communication takes place). Although more limited in its scope than had at first been apparent, the factor might, nevertheless, remain a valuable predictive attribute for an extremely wide range of communication situations. This example again points to the need for regarding "bound" and "unbound" as end-points of a continuum rather than as a dichotomy, since there may be wide variation in "degree of boundedness."

Some bound factors may apply to such small or trivial classes of communications that they are of little value for predictive or theoretical purposes, whereas other bound factors may pertain to extensive and socially significant classes of communication. Certain bound factors may conceivably turn out to be almost as broad in scope as the unbound ones and may permit the formulation of some general laws of persuasibility with relatively few limiting conditions. Thus, the quest to discover unbound persuasibility factors need not be regarded as having failed in its scientific purposes when the investigator discovers instead a set of bound factors. If they are sufficiently broad in scope, they may help to formulate general propositions concerning the type of person who will be influenced by various kinds of social communications.

9

Counter-Norm Attitudes Induced by Consonant versus Dissonant Conditions of Role-Playing

Alan C. Elms
Irving L. Janis

This study is an example of the learning theory approach to attitude change in which the values of "incentives" are of primary interest. In this case, the incentives are of two kinds — the financial reward given for the role-playing performance and the sponsorship of the role-playing (the Soviet Union was assumed to be an unfavorable sponsor, or negative incentive, whereas the U.S. Government was assumed to be a favorable sponsor, or positive incentive).

Elms and Janis use role-playing as a procedure to study the influence of incentives on attitude change. Previous research has shown that role-playing often results in attitude change. Role-playing usually consists of a person assuming a role that is not a part of his usual repertoire of behaviors and acting as he would if he were occupying the particular role in a specified situation. For example, a student and a teacher might switch roles, and the teacher might play the role of "a student seeking advice from a professor." What often happens is that the person's attitudes begin to change in a direction consonant with the role he is playing — the teacher playing the student role may begin to "see the student's side" of a problem.

Counter-norm attitudes are attitudes that deviate to some extent from the usual norms of a given group.

The illustrative value of this study is augmented by the researchers' attempt to investigate phenomena for which learning theory and dissonance

theory make *different* predictions about ways in which just
rewards for role-playing influence the amount of attitude change. E
conclude that their findings bear out predictions from incenti
contradict predictions from dissonance theory. In Chapter 10
disagrees with their conclusion and offers an alternative interpre
findings.*

"Dissonance" Theory versus "Incentive" Theory Predictions

change

Social scientists have long taken account of the strong social pressures that
are exerted on men and women to live up to the demands of prescribed norms
whenever they enter a new occupational role, advance to a more responsible
position in an organizational hierarchy, or acquire a new social status in the
community. It has been observed that many people, when complying to role
demands, express the prescribed attitudes and values even though they do not
privately accept them. Less frequently observed has been the transformation
from outer to inner compliance that seems to be a central feature of role
adaptation — a gradual change whereby the person comes to accept privately the
beliefs and value judgments that he has expressed publicly while playing the
expected social role. During the past decade, a number of experimental studies
have begun to present systematic evidence concerning the effects of role-playing
on attitude change. Janis and King (1954; King and Janis, 1956) found that
when college students were induced to improvise a talk, in order to fulfill the
demands of a public-speaking task which required them to express opinions that
differed from their private beliefs, they showed more opinion change than an
equivalent control group exposed to the same informational content. Kelman
(1953) found a similar increase in opinion change when school children were
given a mild incentive to write essays in support of an arbitrarily assigned
position; but he observed no such gain in an equivalent group of children put

*The paper following this editorial introduction is reprinted from A. C. Elms and
I. L. Janis, Counter-norm attitudes induced by consonant versus dissonant conditions of
role-playing, *Journal of Experimental Research in Personality*, 1965, *1*, 50-60, by permission of the senior author and the publisher, Academic Press.

This experiment was conducted under the auspices of the Yale Studies in Attitude and
Communication, which is directed by I. L. Janis and supported by a grant from the
Rockefeller Foundation. The authors wish to express their thanks to Dean Robert Evans of
Quinnipiac College for his helpful cooperation, which enabled us to conduct the experiment
with students at that college.

under strong pressure to conform with the role-playing task, many of whom showed signs of constriction, resentment, and negativism.

In these experiments, and in most of the subsequent research on the gain in attitude change produced by role-playing (e.g., Carlson, 1956; Culbertson, 1957; Festinger and Carlsmith, 1959; Harvey and Beverly, 1961; Janis and Gilmore, 1965; Scott, 1959), the beliefs and judgments investigated were relatively innocuous ones about which most communities tolerate a wide range of divergent positions, and consequently there was little likelihood that the induced changes would be regarded by Ss as violating the norms of any of their reference groups. One of the purposes of the present experiment was to extend the systematic investigation of the role-playing phenomenon to counter-norm attitudes by asking U.S. college students to argue in favor of a pro-Soviet Union proposal that entails deviating to some extent from the usual norms of most American groups and the national society at large.

The present study was not designed merely to see if the role-playing phenomenon could be replicated with a counter-norm attitude. Our main purpose was to test opposing predictions from two theories of attitude change, both of which have testable consequences concerning the ways in which justifications and rewards for the role-playing performance will influence the amount of attitude change. One of the rival theories in question, known as "dissonance" theory, predicts that when very weak incentives are used to induce someone to play the role of an advocate of an unaccepted position (e.g., unfavorable sponsorship and low financial reward), the amount of dissonance will be greater than if strong incentives are used, and hence the person will show more attitude change (Brehm and Cohen, 1962; Festinger, 1957). As will be seen shortly, exactly the opposite prediction follows from an "incentive" theory of attitude change.

Festinger (1957, p. 112) gives the following explanation of the role-playing effects observed in the Janis and King experiments:

> These studies lend support to the idea that attitude or opinion change is facilitated if a person finds himself in a situation where, by showing compliant behavior, he is engaged in actions which are dissonant with his private opinions. The changes in private opinion which ensue are the end result of a process of attempting to reduce or eliminate this dissonance.

"Dissonance" theory postulates that the amount of attitude change is proportional to the total magnitude of dissonance, which, in turn, is an inverse function of the number and importance of the pressures, rewards, and justifications used to induce the person to present arguments in favor of attitudes and beliefs that differ from his own.

Brehm, Cohen, and their collaborators claim that "dissonance" theory is supported by a number of their experimental studies in which groups of role-players given high justification or large monetary payment for their role-playing performance showed less attitude change than equivalent groups given low justification or small payment (see Brehm and Cohen, 1962, pp. 73-78 and pp. 252-258). But the validity of the evidence from these studies has been seriously called into question (Chapanis and Chapanis, 1964; Rosenberg, 1965), and two recent attempts to replicate their research have failed to support their findings and conclusions (Janis and Gilmore, 1965; Rosenberg, 1965).

A carefully executed experiment by Festinger and Carlsmith (1959) appears to give clear-cut support to the dissonance theory prediction that a small monetary reward ($1) for role-playing will elicit more opinion change than a large monetary reward ($20), but there are ambiguities in this study which make it plausible to consider alternative interpretations of the findings. For example, E told Ss that he, as a research investigator affiliated with the university's Psychology Department, was interested in obtaining knowledge about human behavior; he then gave each S an hour-long series of monotonous tasks designed to induce negative attitudes about the experiment, explaining immediately afterward that he had a hidden purpose which involved a deliberate deception. Then, with "some confusion and uncertainty . . . [and] with a degree of embarrassment," E asked each of the male Ss (who up until that point had been required to serve in this experiment as part of his course work) to take on the job of a laboratory assistant, which involved playing the role of a "stooge" to help carry out the deception with a young woman who was alleged to be the next S. Under these somewhat ambiguous and even negative circumstances, the extraordinarily large reward of twenty dollars might have functioned as a *negative* incentive and reduced the amount of attitude change by unintentionally generating some degree of suspicion (about being exploited by E) or some degree of guilt (about being paid handsomely to lie to a fellow student).

Unfortunately, the Es have provided no information as to how the Ss perceived the large versus small reward, and consequently there is no way of knowing whether E's explanation operated primarily as a positive or negative incentive. If the latter type of incentive were to predominate, an alternative interpretation of the Festinger and Carlsmith findings could be constructed on the basis of "incentive" theory. This theory postulates that attitude change is a process involving conflict between positive and negative incentives (Janis, 1959) and explains role-playing effects in terms of "self-persuasion" from focusing predominantly on the positive incentives supporting the hitherto rejected position (see Hovland, Janis, and Kelley, 1953, pp. 223-237).

Janis and Gilmore (1965) point out that this alternative theoretical approach specifies several conditions for inducing maximal attitude change via role playing that are quite different from those specified by dissonance theory:

> According to this "incentive" theory, when a person accepts the task of improvising arguments in favor of a point of view at variance with his own personal convictions, he becomes temporarily motivated to think up all the good positive arguments he can, and at the same time, suppresses thoughts about the negative arguments which are supposedly irrelevant to the assigned task. This "biased scanning" increases the salience of the positive arguments and therefore increases the chances of acceptance of the new attitude position. A gain in attitude change would not be expected, however, if resentment or other interfering affective reactions were aroused by *negative* incentives in the role playing situation. Among the obvious instances of negative incentives would be information that lowers the prestige of the sponsor or that leads to his being perceived as a manipulative person who is trying to influence people for his own personal aggrandizement or for other alien purposes. Any signs of exploitative intentions in the behavior of the sponsor would also be expected to operate as negative incentives, evoking responses that conflict with the positive incentive value of improvising arguments in support of the conclusion assigned by the sponsor.

One of the predictions from this theory, tested by Janis and Gilmore, is that role-playing will give rise to more attitude change under favorable rather than unfavorable sponsorship conditions, i.e., when the sponsor who induces S to engage in the role-playing task is perceived as being affiliated with an organization or cause that promotes public welfare rather than one that has commercial, exploitative, or other objectionable purposes. Confirmatory results were obtained when they compared two groups of role-players who wrote essays in favor of an unpopular educational policy (that of requiring all undergraduates in the United States to have additional courses in mathematics and science). Less personal approval of the role-played position was found under unfavorable sponsorship conditions (E presenting himself as a representative of a commercial company that was hiring Ss to help prepare advertising copy to promote the sale of science textbooks) than under favorable sponsorship conditions (E presenting himself as a representative of a public welfare organization that was hiring Ss to help prepare for a nationwide educational survey). These findings tend to support incentive theory and contradict dissonance theory since they show that overt role-playing was more effective when the sponsors' affiliations and goals were regarded by Ss as consonant with their own values than when they were regarded as being relatively dissonant. Additional findings from the same experiment showed that (1) under favorable sponsorship conditions, *overt* role-playing (actually writing an essay in which S improvises arguments in favor of an opposed point of view) was more effective in inducing attitude change than *nonovert* role-playing (merely agreeing to write such an essay without actually having the opportunity to do so); and (2) there were no significant differences between role-players who were paid $20 in advance and those paid $1 in advance for writing the essays (although the largest amount of attitude change occurred in the subgroup given the large amount of money under favorable sponsorship conditions). The latter finding fails to confirm the outcome of the Festinger and Carlsmith (1959) experiment in which exactly the same amounts of money were compared. Janis and Gilmore report observations indicating that the large financial reward of $20 elicited mixed feelings in the Ss and all of them expressed a great deal of puzzlement about the inordinately large sum they were being paid for their services.

Incentive theory predicts that the amount of attitude change induced by role-playing will *increase* if a large monetary reward generates positive feelings of satisfaction, but will *decrease* if the same large reward generates negative affects, which tend to interfere with the type of open-minded set needed to be influenced by one's own improvised arguments as they are being scanned during the role-playing performance. Janis and Gilmore point out that an interaction effect might therefore be expected on the basis of incentive theory: *With positive sponsorship, a large monetary reward will have a predominantly positive incentive effect and thus make for an increase in the amount of attitude change; whereas with negative sponsorship, a large reward will tend to induce guilt, suspicion, or other negative affects that would give rise to interfering responses during the role-playing performance and therefore lead to less attitude change.* They point out that their finding that the $1 versus $20 payment had no effect does not necessarily tend to disconfirm this hypothesis because the ambivalent reactions evoked by the overpayment in the high-reward condition could obscure any such interaction effect. Moreover, in the unfavorable condition used in their experiment, the purpose of the role-playing task, despite the commercial motives of the sponsors, might have been regarded as socially accepted, since it involved helping to develop a legitimate advertising campaign. On the basis of these considerations, Janis and Gilmore point out that, in order to test the interaction hypothesis, the effects of a small reward should be compared with the effects of a more *plausible* large reward, and, in addition, a favorable sponsorship condition for the role-playing task should be compared with a more objectionable condition in which a distrusted sponsor asks Ss to violate important social norms by deceiving their peers (as in the Festinger and Carlsmith experiment) or by helping a despised out-group to spread its propaganda.

With these considerations in mind, we designed the present experiment in a way that would enable us to investigate the same variables as in the Janis and Gilmore experiment, but with a role-playing task that requires Ss to advocate a counter-norm attitude under conditions that are appropriate for testing the above-stated interaction hypothesis derived from incentive theory. Accordingly, we selected as the unfavorable (high-dissonant) condition a role-playing situation that was defined as *helping the Soviet Union to prepare for a propaganda campaign to be directed to American students*, in contrast to the more favorable (low-dissonant) condition of *helping the United States government to prepare for a survey in order to take account of current attitudes among American students*. In both favorable and unfavorable sponsorship conditions we used a plausible large monetary reward in contrast to a small one and, as in the Janis and Gilmore experiment, we also compared the effects of overt role-playing with a control condition in which the same information was given. In the latter condition, Ss agreed to perform the role-playing task and were paid for it, but the attitude effects were assessed before any overt role-playing took place. Thus, the present experiment involved a three-dimensional factorial design to investigate the amount of attitude change as a function of (1) overt vs. nonovert role-playing: (2) favorable vs. unfavorable sponsorship of the role-playing task; and (3) large vs. small monetary reward for the role-playing performance.

Method

The experiment was conducted in a New England teacher's college with both male and female undergraduates, all of whom volunteered for the experiment following class announcements which promised payment to students who volunteered to participate in a new research project requiring less than 1 hour of time. The Ss were assigned, according to chance, to one of the eight experimental conditions within the three-dimensional factorial design. (The number of cases in each subgroup is shown in Table 1.)

All Ss were given an initial pretreatment questionnaire of ten items which asked them to express their personal attitude toward a new proposal that would involve sending American students to the Soviet Union to take their entire 4 years of college education in a Soviet university. They were assured that their answers would be kept anonymous.

After the initial questionnaire, all Ss were given the same instructions concerning the role-playing task, which was introduced in all conditions by the following standard background information:

"Negotiations have been under way for some time between the Soviet Union and our Government, involving a joint program to send qualified

U.S. students to study in the Soviet Union for 4 years. These American students would go through a complete 4-year course in a Russian university, where they would study the Soviet system of government and the history of Communism. Our Government is somewhat skeptical about the value of this training and will not agree to the program unless it can be shown that a significant number of eligible U.S. students favor the plan. The Soviet Government wishes to go ahead with the plan for obvious reasons. Although our State Department believes the program might have some serious disadvantages, in addition to any advantages, it is withholding final judgment until an accurate evaluation of student sentiment can be made."

In the *unfavorable sponsorship* condition, *S*s were informed by the interviewer (*E*) that he was a representative of a private attitude-research firm which had contracted to carry out this study for the Soviet Embassy (after the firm had checked with the U.S. State Department and obtained permission to do so). The *E* asserted that the Soviet government had hired his firm to collect the materials needed to produce a pamphlet which representatives of the Soviet Union would distribute to all U.S. college campuses, presenting arguments in favor of the proposed program that would be appealing and convincing to American students. The *S*s were then instructed to outline the most convincing arguments they could think of to use in the Soviet propaganda pamphlet aimed at students like themselves.

The *S*s in the *favorable-sponsorship* condition, after being given exactly the same background information (quoted above), were told that the interviewer's firm had a contract with the U.S. State Department to help find out the attitudes of American students toward the program. The *E* said that his firm was getting ready to conduct a large-scale survey of U.S. students, whose opinions would be assessed after asking them to examine a pamphlet containing arguments on *both sides* of the question, which would make them fully aware of the issues involved. The *S*s were then told that *E* had already gathered sufficient arguments *against* the program, and therefore he was now asking a few students to outline some arguments in *favor* of the program, to be inserted in the pamphlet.

Thus, the information presented in the unfavorable and favorable sponsorship conditions was identical, except for assertions about (1) the employer's being the Soviet Union vs. the U.S. State Department, and (2) the purpose of *S*'s role-playing performances being to help the Soviet Union conduct a propaganda campaign vs. helping the U.S. State Department obtain information about the attitudes of American students.

Anonymity was again assured for both conditions and, in order to make the financial reward plausible, all *S*s were told: "Please consider the arguments carefully and express them as clearly as possible, since our survey groups are small and the arguments you write down will almost certainly be included in the pamphlet." Within both sponsorship conditions, half the Ss were told that every participant would be paid a large amount of money ($10.00), which our pretesting results indicated would be regarded as a plausible large reward. The other half were offered a small reward ($0.50).

Before beginning the task, all Ss were paid the large or small reward in cash, *in advance*, and signed a receipt at E's request, after which they were assigned on a stratified random basis to the overt role-playing condition or the control condition. Those in the former condition were asked to write down their arguments and, after 2 minutes, E mentioned four general questions to consider, in order to stimulate their thinking about cogent arguments (e.g., "How would this program affect relations between the U.S. and the U.S.S.R., particularly with regard to world peace?"). After Ss had written for 5 minutes more, their outlines were collected and they were given the final (post-treatment) questionnaire. In the control (nonovert role-playing) condition, the same four "stimulating questions" were asked immediately after S agreed to perform the role-playing task. Then, instead of allowing the control S to write down his arguments, he was told that before beginning to think of arguments, there was one other thing to be done — to fill out another brief questionnaire.

The Ss in both the overt and nonovert role-playing conditions were given exactly the same rationale for the post-treatment questionnaire: Whereas the previous questionnaire had dealt with student opinion about study in Russia in general, the second questionnaire was to be used as part of an initial survey of student opinion concerning the specific "students-to-Russia" program, about which they had just been informed. The final questionnaire contained the same questions as the first one, except that the opening item made it clear that the students were to evaluate the new Soviet-sponsored proposal.[1] The other nine questions, which were worded in exactly the same way on both questionnaires, asked each S to indicate his personal desire to participate in the program, his expectations concerning its potentially favorable or unfavorable consequences, his judgments of its importance, and his anticipations of how it would be regarded by most other American students and by his parents.

---

[1]On the pretreatment questionnaire, the opening item was worded as follows: "Certain educators have proposed a program to send qualified American students to study in Russian Universities for a period of 4 years, beginning as freshmen and continuing through their complete undergraduate training there. If this program were permitted by the U.S. Government, would you favor or oppose the proposal?" On the final questionnaire, the opening item was modified in the following way, so as to provide the appropriate context for the post-treatment questions: "United States and Soviet governmental authorities are negotiating on a program to send qualified American students to Russian universities to study the Soviet system of government and the history of Communism for a period of 4 years. Would you favor or oppose this program?"

After completing the final questionnaire, each of the overt role-players was asked to rate the quality of the arguments he had written in his essay. Then, after all the data were collected from each *S*, *E* carefully went through a dehoaxing procedure, correcting the misinformation given earlier and explaining that the procedure was part of a psychological study completely unconnected with the Soviet Embassy or the State Department. The *S*s who had been given $10.00 returned the money and were paid the same standard amount as the controls ($1.50) for their participation.

Just before being dehoaxed, every *S* was asked several open-ended questions to find out whether he had accepted the various explanations *E* had given concerning the experimental procedures. The *S*s' answers (as well as their spontaneous comments following the "dehoaxing" information, at the very end of the session) indicated that the information *E* had presented was generally regarded as genuine and valid. The comments by *S*s in the favorable sponsorship condition indicated that they fully accepted *E*'s statement that the study was being done as part of an educational survey for the U.S. State Department. Similarly, none of the *S*s given the information about the unfavorable sponsorship expressed any disbelief about the alleged fact that the job was being done for the Soviet Union. Some of their answers, in fact, indicated that they perceived the purpose as being even more malignant than *E* had asserted. One *S*, for example, said he believed the real purpose was to try to pick up new recruits for the Communist Party and to help the Soviet Union in ways that would be just within the law.

The *S*s in the unfavorable sponsorship condition, all of whom eventually complied, showed considerable hesitation, tension, and other manifestations of dissonance or conflict about writing an essay to help the Soviet Embassy conduct a propaganda campaign. Signs of disturbance were noted in their overt behavior at the time the purpose of the study was being described as well as in their written answers to the open-ended questions asked at the end of the session. For example, when we made completely blind ratings of the attitudes expressed in their responses to questions about how they thought their essays would be used, we found that none of the 36 *S*s in the unfavorable sponsorship condition expressed any personal approval whatsoever; seven of them took pains to make it clear that they felt strong opposition or resentment, as compared with only one *S* in the favorable sponsorship condition. Moreover, at the beginning of the session, a number of additional *S*s in the unfavorable sponsorship-low payment group showed open reluctance to participate in the study. Several asked if they should take part even if they did not approve of the program or raised other questions that delayed their decision about whether or not to accept the job.

At the end of the session, when E told the truth about the purpose of the study, three Ss in the unfavorable sponsorship condition who had been paid $10.00 were disinclined to return any of the money, arguing that they had agreed to do the job because of the high pay. No such difficulties were encountered among the Ss who had been given the large payment in the favorable sponsorship condition. Another distinctive reaction, which was observed in most Ss in the unfavorable sponsorship condition, was the marked relief displayed when they were given the dehoaxing information.

Although the behavioral signs and the written answers to the post-treatment questions indicate that the high-dissonance condition succeeded in generating a relatively high degree of disturbance and conflict about engaging in the role-playing task, the amount of dissonance was nevertheless not so great as to interfere with the research by leading to a high incidence of outright refusals to participate in the study. Only one man (in the unfavorable sponsorship-low payment condition) refused to write the essay, and hence the differential loss of Ss was negligible among the various treatments to be considered.[2]

Results and Discussion

The appropriateness of regarding the role-played position as a counter-norm attitude is indicated by results from the pretreatment questionnaire, which revealed that the Ss generally shared the widespread negative attitude of U.S. citizens toward Soviet institutions. The majority of students expressed strong opposition to the proposed educational policy of having American students receive their entire college education in the Soviet Union and asserted that their peers and their parents would also be opposed. There were no significant differences among any of the subgroups on the pretreatment attitude measures ($p > .20$, two-tailed, for every pair of means).

The attitude changes induced by the various conditions of role-playing were assessed by scoring the changes on each of the ten items in the attitude scale in terms of 0, +1 or -1, depending on whether the responses remained unchanged or shifted in the direction of favoring or opposing the Soviet-sponsored proposal. A net attitude-change score was computed for each S, and represented the total number of questions on which he changed positively from the "before" to the "after" questionnaire, minus the total number of those on which he changed

[2]Two other Ss who wrote the essay were eliminated from the tabulations of the results because they expressed some vague suspicions that the large ($10.00) payment might entail something more than E had asserted. One of the Ss was in the favorable sponsorship condition and the other in the unfavorable sponsorship condition of the overt role-playing treatment.

negatively. (This measure was selected in advance because in our prior research on attitude change we have noted that a total score based on the presence or absence of change on each item generally entails less error variance than a score that summates the *amount* of change shown on every item.) The *mean* net attitude-change score for each condition is shown in Table 1.

Table 1.   Mean Net Attitude-Change Scores*

Sponsorship of Role-Playing Task	Control Groups: No Overt Role-Playing			Experimental Groups: Overt Role-Playing		
	Small Payment, $0.50	Large Payment, $10.00	Total	Small Payment, $0.50	Large Payment, $10.00	Total
Favorable: U.S. Gov't. N	0	5	10	18	16	34
M	+ 0.2	+0.8	+ 0.5	+0.9	+ 2.4	+1.7
Unfavorable: Soviet Union N	5	5	10	17	19	36
M	−2.0	+1.6	−0.2	+0.6	−0.1	+0.3

*Positive scores indicate change in counter-norm direction.

It will be noted that the largest amount of attitude change occurred in the *overt* role-playing group that was exposed to the *least* dissonant condition, i.e., favorable sponsorship with large monetary reward. The mean net change of +2.4 shown by this group was found to differ significantly at beyond the 5% confidence level from each of the other groups of overt role-players (when t tests were computed in two different ways, one basing the standard error of the mean differences solely on the two distributions being compared and the other using an over-all error estimate obtained from an overall 2x2x2 analysis of variance). These findings indicate that overt role-playing is most effective when the inducements for performing the task are consonant with the Ss' personal values. The outcome clearly contradicts the dissonance-theory prediction and supports the incentive-theory prediction.

Further support for the same conclusion was obtained from the over-all analysis of variance of attitude change scores, which showed a significant triple interaction effect ($F = 7.88$, $df = 1/82$, $p < .01$ for favorable vs. unfavorable sponsorship x low vs. high payment x overt vs. nonovert role-playing). A separate analysis of variance for the four groups of overt role-players showed a significant main effect for the sponsorship variable ($F = 5.00$, $df = 1/66$, $p < .05$) and a near-significant interaction of the sponsorship variable with the financial reward variable ($F = 3.66$, $df = 1/66$, $p < .07$).

In order to obtain some additional information about the effects of different amounts of monetary payment, we added two more groups of overt role-players to the experiment, one receiving favorable sponsorship (N = 18) and the other unfavorable sponsorship (N = 17), both of which were paid $1.50 in advance. The mean net attitude-change scores for these two additional groups were approximately zero (-0.1 and +0.2, respectively) and differed hardly at all from the near-zero means obtained from the corresponding two groups that had been paid $0.50. The findings indicate that a small reward of either $0.50 or $1.50 had essentially the same effect (and yielded essentially the same differences in attitude-change scores from a large reward of $10.00). This conclusion is supported by the data from a 2x3 analysis of variance for overt role-players, in which one variable was favorable vs. unfavorable sponsorship and the other was the three different amounts of financial reward. The results of this analysis of variance show a near-significant main effect for the sponsorship variable (F = 2.60, df = 1/99, p = .11) and a significant interaction of sponsorship with amount of financial reward (F = 3.22, df = 2/99, p < .05). It will be noted that this outcome is essentially the same as that obtained from the 2x2 analysis of variance (which gave corresponding p values of < .05 and < .07).

The above findings indicate that when the role-playing performance was carried out under *favorable* sponsorship conditions, the *large* financial reward produced *more* attitude change than the smaller financial rewards; but when the same type of performance was carried out under unfavorable sponsorship conditions, the large reward did not have a facilitating effect. This differential outcome, which is in line with predictions from "incentive" theory, is limited to the overt role-players. The four means for the control Ss who did not engage in role-playing (shown on the left-hand side of Table 1) do not duplicate the pattern found in the four experimental groups of overt role-players (shown on the right-hand side of Table 1). In contrast to the significant second-order difference noted among the overt role-playing groups, the corresponding second-order difference among the control groups is in the opposite direction, but it is nonsignificant (F = 2.12, df = 1/16, p > .15) and is attributable largely to the very low attitude change scores in the group of controls given the most dissonant treatment (unfavorable sponsorship with small reward, which had a mean net change of -2.0).

Interviews conducted at the end of the session indicated that, after having committed themselves, Ss in all four of the control conditions had silently started to think about supporting arguments, in anticipation of having to execute the role-playing task. Hence the controls apparently had engaged in *implicit* role-playing. But the attitude-change data provide no evidence at all that the control condition of nonovert role-playing produced any attitude changes, since none of the four control means in Table 1 differs significantly from zero. This finding cannot be taken at face value, however, because we did not have an additional "uncommitted" control group (given all the relevant background information but without any role-playing instructions at all) to compare with the nonovert role-playing condition. We cannot be sure that the latter condition was totally ineffective because, for example, the background information given about the Soviet-sponsored proposal might have had the effect of shifting attitudes in the negative direction, which would be manifested by a significant change in the negative direction by an "uncommitted" control group; the implicit role-playing that occurred among the Ss in our control groups, therefore, might have prevented them from changing in the anti-Soviet direction, resulting in manifestly zero change. What can be said with certainty, however, is that the nonovert role-playing condition was *relatively ineffective* as compared with overt role-playing carried out under favorable incentive conditions.

The large mean attitude-change score noted in the group of overt role-players given the favorable sponsorship information and the large monetary reward indicates that attitude change can be induced by role-playing even for a counter-norm type of attitude. Quite aside from the implications this finding has for opposing theories of attitude change, it helps to substantiate an empirical generalization inferred from prior role-playing experiments dealing with more innocuous types of opinion changes. The generalization in question is that the technique of improvised role-playing can exert a powerful influence to modify existing attitudes, including those anchored in social norms, which ordinarily are highly resistant to the usual forms of persuasive pressures.

Our finding that the greatest gain in attitude change was produced by overt role-playing under conditions of favorable sponsorship and large reward is similar to the outcome of the earlier experiment by Janis and Gilmore. In that experiment, too, the greatest amount of attitude change occurred in the group of overt role-players given favorable (public welfare) sponsorship and a large ($20) reward. The analysis of variance, however, showed that the only significant interaction effect arose from the sponsorship and the overt vs. nonovert role-playing variables, indicating that more attitude change occurred when overt role-playing was carried out under favorable sponsorship than under unfavorable conditions; the amount of attitude change was not significantly affected by the amount of financial reward. The incentive theory analysis was further borne out by the finding that, in the favorable sponsorship condition, the overt role-players improvised arguments of better quality than in the unfavorable sponsorship condition, as judged by two psychologists who made blind, independent ratings of all statements in the written essays.

The attitude change results of the present experiment are similar in that we again find that positive incentive conditions make for more attitude change. The sponsorship variable alone was found to have a positive effect on the amount of attitude change among the overt role-playing groups, but this effect was subordinate to the interaction of favorable sponsorship with the large monetary reward. This outcome, although somewhat different from that of the earlier experiment, bears out the prediction made by Janis and Gilmore for counter-norm role-playing, i.e., that a large monetary reward will have a positive effect on attitude change only when the role-playing task is sponsored by an acceptable group and is oriented toward a goal perceived by S as being consonant with his own; but the same large reward will tend to create suspicion, guilt, and other interfering responses that make for less attitude change when the role-playing task is sponsored by a distrusted sponsor and is perceived as having a purpose antithetical to one's own values. Thus, the findings from both experiments contradict the predictions from dissonance theory and support predictions from incentive theory concerning the conditions under which role-playing will be more effective in modifying attitudes.

There is one respect, however, in which the present experiment fails to parallel the earlier experiment: judgments of the quality of the essays written by the overt role-players did not yield the expected significant differences. Blind ratings of the essays by two independent judges revealed that every one of the overt role-players conformed with the demands of the task to write out arguments that were strongly in favor of the alleged proposal by the Soviet Union. Under favorable sponsorship conditions, the average number of "good quality" arguments was 4.2 in the group paid $10.00 as against 3.2 in the group paid $0.50; under unfavorable sponsorship conditions, the corresponding difference was approximately zero, both groups showing an average of about 3.9 "good quality" arguments. Although this second-order difference is in the expected direction and roughly parallels the attitude-change findings, an analysis of variance indicated that the interaction effect was not strong enough to be statistically significant at the 10% confidence level. The self-ratings of the arguments by the four groups of overt role-players showed uniformly high scores in all four groups, with no significant increases attributable to the variations in incentive conditions. The only significant difference found in the essays written by the four experimental groups is in the mean total number of words produced. On this variable, a significant main effect was found for the financial reward variable ($p < .01$), indicating that in both sponsorship conditions the large financial reward elicited more verbose essays than the small reward.

According to "incentive theory," the attitude changes produced by role-playing are mediated by intensive "biased scanning" of positive incentives, which involves two types of verbal responses: (1) fulfilling the demands of the role-playing task by recalling and inventing arguments that are capable of functioning as positive incentives for accepting a new attitude position, and

(2) appraising the recalled and improvised arguments with a psychological set that fosters *open-minded cognitive exploration of their potential incentive value,* rather than a negativistic set of the type engendered by the arousal of feelings of hostility, resentment, or suspicion. Thus, for example, it would be expected that many intelligent American soldiers who were captured by the Chinese Communists during the Korean War could comply with the role-playing demands of their despised "brain-washing" captors and nevertheless remain uninfluenced: While verbalizing "good" pro-Communist arguments, the prisoners could privately label all the improvised arguments with negative epithets or could think about counterarguments that would refute the statements they were overtly verbalizing (see Lifton, 1961; Schein, 1956).

In experimental research on role-playing effects, the first of the two types of response essential for effective biased scanning can be readily assessed by examining the manifest content of the role-playing performance to see if plausible-sounding arguments were improvised, but the second type is difficult to assess because it involves private verbalizations that occur silently, along with the overt statements that are being made. Judgments of the quality of written essays, as in the present experiment, are at best an indirect measure of the second type of response, based on the assumption that a hostile or closed-minded role-player will tend to be more perfunctory in his role-playing performance and hence produce arguments of poorer quality. On this indirect measure, our ratings of the essays fail to show that the incentive variables had a significant effect on the quality of the role-playing performance. But it is quite possible, of course, that this indirect measure is too crude to detect differences in psychological sets, and that research on this problem requires much more subtle measures, such as those provided by a content analysis of detailed interviews in which each S is asked to report on his covert subjective thoughts during the role-playing performance itself.

In summary, the predictions from "incentive" theory are borne out by the main results from this experiment, which show that a gain in attitude change was produced by overt role-playing under favorable inducement conditions. Our supplementary data on the quality of the essays, however, do not provide evidence that the gain was mediated by a corresponding increase in biased scanning while Ss were improvising arguments in favor of the assigned position. Obviously, the question of how the positive inducements lead to increased attitude change remains an open question to be settled by subsequent research.

Summary

One hundred and twenty-five college students were asked to invent arguments in favor of a counter-norm proposal, allededly put forth by the Soviet

Union, to allow American students to go to Russia for their entire 4-year college education. A three-dimensional factorial design was used in order to test hypotheses about attitude change as a function of (1) overt versus nonovert role-playing; (2) unfavorable (Soviet Union) vs. favorable (U.S. Government) sponsorship of the role-playing task; and (3) small vs. large monetary reward for the role-playing performance. Analysis of variance of attitude-change scores showed a significant triple interaction effect: a high degree of acceptance of the counter-norm proposal occurred only under conditions of overt role-playing when acceptable justification and large rewards were given. These findings bear out predictions from an "incentive" theory of attitude change and contradict predictions from "dissonance" theory.

10

Comment on "Counter-Norm Attitudes Induced by Consonant versus Dissonant Conditions of Role-Playing"

Brehm does not accept Elms and Janis' conclusion (in Chapter 9) that their data contradict the hypothesis from dissonance theory, and he offers his own interpretation of their research findings.*

Jack W. Brehm

The two apparent conclusions of Elms and Janis are (1) to accept incentive theory as an explanation of at least the major effects of role-playing on attitudes, and (2) to reject dissonance theory as an explanation of *any* of the effects of role-playing on attitudes. It may therefore be useful to remind the reader that dissonance theory takes a relatively limited position; under certain conditions, positive incentives reduce dissonance and the consequent pressure to change an attitude. The theory does *not* say that positive incentives have no other effects, and therefore incentive theory could be "true" at the same time that dissonance theory is "true." Leventhal (1964), for example, has proposed that incentives which have a value appropriate to an instrumental task result in no change in attitude toward the task, while those that are inappropriately low result in dissonance and positive attitude change, and those that are inappropriately high result in direct positive attitude change (following Peak, 1955).

In their discussion of previous relevant research, Elms and Janis dismiss an experiment by Cohen (Brehm and Cohen, 1962, pp. 73-78) on the basis of a report by Rosenberg which provides less than convincing evidence that Cohen's study is weak in the ways specified. What primarily is missing is the establishment by Rosenberg that his experimental conditions would in fact produce the effects obtained by Cohen. For example, Rosenberg reports *S*s in all

*The paper following this editorial introduction is excerpted and slightly abridged from J. W. Brehm, Comment on "Counter-norm attitudes induced by consonant versus dissonant conditions of role-playing," *Journal of Experimental Research in Personality,* 1965, *1,* 61-64, by permission of the author and the publisher, Academic Press.

his conditions indicated they were relatively free to refuse to write the discrepant essay. On the other hand, Cohen reports (Brehm and Cohen, 1962, p. 204) a fairly strong inverse relationship between amount of incentive and reported freedom to choose. Since Brehm and Cohen have taken the position that perceived choice may be a necessary condition for the arousal of dissonance, and that the magnitude of dissonance is therefore a function of the magnitude of perceived choice, it may not be so strange that Rosenberg failed to obtain attitudinal effects similar to those of Cohen. While Rosenberg's paper does point out a possible alternative interpretation of Cohen's experiment, it fails to provide convincing evidence that the alternative is the best explanation. The experiment by Cohen should not be so easily dismissed; it provides support for the assertion that dissonance and consequent attitude change are inversely proportional to the incentive used to obtain role-playing compliance.

A similar point can be made in regard to the criticism Elms and Janis make of the experiment by Festinger and Carlsmith (1959). After suggesting that $20 may have created suspicion, they cite as evidence a study by Janis and Gilmore (1965). In that study, Ss who were offered $20 "expressed a great deal of puzzlement. . . ." There is no doubt that Ss can be offered $20 in such a way as to be puzzling, but neither is there doubt that the same reward can be made to seem reasonable. An incentive which arouses suspicion entails processes other than consonant cognition, and would provide a poor way to contrive a "low dissonance" condition. Since Festinger and Carlsmith were trying to establish a low dissonance condition by offering $20, we may assume that they tried to make the amount seem reasonable. Specifically, they informed all experimental Ss that the money was not only for performing the immediate task but also to be on call in case their services should be needed again. The effect of "being on call" would be to make the $20 seem relatively reasonable and the $1 rather little. Personal communications from both Festinger and Carlsmith have indicated that there was little or no suspiciousness on the part of Ss about the $20. While the possibility that suspicion was aroused cannot be completely ruled out, there is good reason to believe that this factor does not account for the results.

Disproving a dissonance hypothesis should be no more difficult, nor easy, than disproving other reasonable hypotheses about the same class of events. In the case of "forced compliance" one must be able to show that there are cognitions which lead the person not to comply, that there are cognitions which lead the person to comply, and (to insure relatively high dissonance) that the weighted cognitions leading to compliance are barely sufficient to obtain it. Furthermore, research (Brehm and Cohen, 1962; Festinger, 1964) has shown that dissonance effects may be clear only when the individual is committed to an alternative, an outcome, etc., so the disproof of dissonance must also rest upon a clear demonstration of commitment. If it can be shown that dissonance effects do not occur under these stipulated conditions, and if confounding effects can be ruled out, then the dissonance hypothesis tested would certainly tend to be disconfirmed.

What truth is there, then, in the assertion by Elms and Janis that "The outcome clearly contradicts the dissonance-theory prediction . . ."? Aside from the possibility that the assertion is true, three answers might be given: (1) dissonance was not aroused by the experimental conditions; (2) dissonance was aroused but did not affect the attitude measured; and (3) dissonance was aroused and did in fact affect the attitude in a way consistent with the theory.

It is likely that dissonance was aroused, as Elms and Janis endeavored to show, because it seems that Ss in the unfavorable sponsorship condition were resistant to writing the essay and were quite uncomfortable about doing so. But a question may certainly be raised whether or not the aroused dissonance could be expected to result in positive change of the attitude measured. It will be recalled that the way in which dissonance is reduced is through change (or addition) of relevant cognitions, and those cognitions which are least resistant to change would be those most likely to exhibit change. Elms and Janis take pains to point out that the position of the essay is quite distasteful to the Ss and is clearly at variance with the popular position on the issue. Furthermore, the unfavorable sponsorship manipulation makes it even more difficult for Ss to favor the position of the essay since it highlights the negative aspects of the sponsor, e.g., propagandizing, dishonesty, ulterior motives, etc. Under these conditions, then, S's attitude would be highly resistant to change toward the position of the essay. Hence, if he did experience dissonance from agreeing to write the discrepant essay, he would have difficulty reducing the dissonance by becoming more favorable toward the discrepant stand. He would then be expected to attempt dissonance reduction in other ways.

Several ways of reducing dissonance can be distinguished in a relatively complex situation such as that used by Elms and Janis, and it is plausible that Ss used one or more of them. For example, a person might have subjectively magnified the pressure from E to comply, or the approval of the project by our own government, or the belief that other students would not be taken in by one's own arguments. Similarly, an S might simply have admitted that he was wrong to write the essay, or he also might have attempted to belittle the importance of his role in the study, or the likely success of the study. The anecdotal evidence cited by Elms and Janis indicates not only tension but also attempts at dissociation and avoidance of responsibility for the decision; such attempts, if successful, would help to reduce dissonance. It is also interesting to note that Ss showed "marked relief" when they were "dehoaxed." This indicates not only that they experienced dissonance, but also that they had failed to reduce their dissonance successfully. In summary, the second answer concerning the truth of the Elms and Janis assertion that the data contradict the dissonance theory prediction seems at least partly true: since Ss found it difficult to become more positive toward the position of the essay, they attempted to reduce dissonance in other ways and were not altogether successful in their attempts at dissonance reduction.

When a person holds two cognitions or sets of cognitions which are dissonant with each other, and when each set is highly resistant to change, then dissonance can be reduced by adding cognitions consonant with one of the two sets (see Brehm and Cohen, 1962, pp. 55-59). In effect, this means that in the forced verbal compliance setting the individual bolsters his original position, or else he bolsters the act of writing the discrepant essay (or making a discrepant speech). As we have seen, the procedure in the Elms and Janis experiment made it difficult for Ss in the unfavorable sponsorship condition to change positively toward the position of the essay even though they experienced dissonance upon agreeing to write the essay. Thus, it would not be surprising to find these Ss attempting to bolster their original position, that is, changing negatively rather than positively in respect to the position of the essay. This effect would, of course, be greater where commitment to writing the essay was relatively low (control condition), and it would be greater in a high dissonance (low payment) than in a low dissonance (high payment) condition. In Table 1 of the Elms and Janis article there is a negative change in the appropriate condition: unfavorable sponsorship, low payment, no overt role-playing. Although, as Elms and Janis noted, one cannot be sure that this is true negative change, it is nevertheless clear that the low payment condition change (-2.0) is reliably different from the corresponding high payment change (+1.6) with $p = .05$, an effect which Elms and Janis were unable to account for.

The effect of actually writing the essay is, of course, to increase commitment toward the position of the essay and thereby to make it more likely that an S would attempt to reduce dissonance by changing his attitude positively rather than negatively. The same Table 1 reveals the expected effect. For Ss who wrote the essay in the unfavorable sponsorship condition, there was a tendency for those who received low payment to change more positively than those who received high payment. While this tendency was not reliable in itself, it appears reliably different from the corresponding difference in the condition where Ss did not write the essay — again, an effect for which Elms and Janis give no explanation. In summary, the data in the unfavorable sponsorship condition are consistent with the view that writing a discrepant essay is dissonance-arousing, and the tendency to reduce dissonance by changing one's attitude negatively rather than positively (toward the essay position) is an inverse function of the strength of one's commitment to the essay position. It is reasonable to say, then, that Elms and Janis were incorrect in asserting that the outcome clearly contradicts the dissonance theory prediction. It seems more likely that dissonance was aroused and did in fact affect attitudes in a way consistent with the theory.

The problem here is not so much in how one reads the data, because the present analysis is post hoc and is admittedly in defense of dissonance theory; rather, the primary problem is in providing an adequate test of the dissonance hypothesis of central interest. In attempting to obtain positive evidence for a hypothesis, an investigator must immerse himself in the relevant theory and must be sure that the methods provide an adequate test. But to *disprove* a hypothesis is even more demanding of an investigator in terms of familiarity with the theory and providing adequate methods. He must be able to make a case, quite independently of the expected outcome of "no effect," that his use of the theory is accurate, his manipulation effective, his measures sensitive, and confounding factors are absent. In the experiment under discussion, the dissonance manipulation of unfavorable sponsorship also made the dependent attitude relatively resistant to positive change. Thus, the conditions for an adequate test of the dissonance hypothesis were not provided. The fact that dissonance effects apparently did occur is then due more to accident than to the experiment's having provided a good test.

Perhaps in practice the person best equipped to disprove a dissonance hypothesis is one who has been successful in supporting it. When such a person designs a test, he is more likely to do so in a sensitive and adequate way and is thus in a position to produce and to recognize disconfirming evidence when it appears. An example is Walster's experiment (in Festinger, 1964, pp. 112-127) in which she found that postdecisional re-evaluation of choice alternatives disappeared rather soon after the choice.

The application of dissonance theory to role-playing must take into account not only the decision to play the counter-norm role but also the effect of inventing, and perhaps publicly stating, the arguments themselves. If the decision to comply arouses relatively low dissonance because the force to comply is great, the behavior of inventing or stating arguments, or both, may in itself arouse further and significant amount of dissonance and consequent attitude change. However, where a considerable amount of dissonance is aroused by the decision to comply, the invention or statement of arguments could on the one hand contribute to the dissonance, but may, on the other, simply help to reduce dissonance by facilitating attitude change. The relevant data are ambiguous (Brehm and Cohen, 1962, pp. 248-258).

This attempt by Elms and Janis to disprove a dissonance hypothesis serves to point up the methodological problems which must be solved if this type of disproof is to be produced. More valuable, however, is their test of the application of incentive theory. For it is apparent that the relatively obvious implications of dissonance theory for the understanding of role-playing effects on attitudes have been tested and supported, and if there is to be a confrontation of dissonance and incentive theories, incentive theory must be made more explicit and tenable through this type of empirical demonstration.*

Summary

The conclusion by Elms and Janis that their data contradict dissonance theory is not borne out by close inspection of their methods and data. Their method for creating high dissonance (unfavorable sponsorship) probably makes the relevant attitude relatively resistant to change toward the position of the discrepant essay, thus forcing subjects who agree to write a discrepant essay to bolster their initial positions in order to reduce dissonance. Subjects who actually write the discrepant essay, and are thereby more committed to the discrepant position, respond quite differently and tend to show the usual dissonance reduction effects of change toward the discrepant position.

*Elms has replied to Brehm's comment in a review article entitled "Role-playing, incentive, and dissonance," which appears in the *Psychological Bulletin,* 1967, *68,* 132-143, especially on pages 137-138. Elms also comments on Bem's critical analysis of dissonance, theory (which appears earlier in this volume) on page 142 of his article.

11

Inducing Resistance to Persuasion: Some Contemporary Approaches

William J. McGuire

Up to this point, all the papers in this volume have concentrated on the problem of *changing* attitudes. McGuire considers the problem from the other side — preventing attitude change. He outlines various approaches to this question and points out that many studies that are nominally investigations of attitude change often inadvertently demonstrate means of inducing resistance to change. Some of his illustrations are drawn from theoretical approaches to attitude change already presented in this volume, such as the functional and dissonance theory approaches.

Only the theoretical portions of McGuire's paper are presented here, including his own "inoculation" model. The part omitted contains detailed reports of several studies of McGuire's model. References to these studies appear at the end of the selection.*

Introduction

Several years ago I thought of doing research on ways of inducing resistance to persuasion, under the impression that while much experimental work was being done on factors that increased persuasive effectiveness, little was being

---

*The paper following this editorial introduction is excerpted and slightly abridged from W. J. McGuire, Inducing resistance to persuasion: Some contemporary approaches, *Advances in Experimental Soc; 1 Psychology*, 1964, *1*, 192-202, by permission of the author and the publisher, Academic Press.

done on ways of producing resistance to persuasion. As I considered the problem further, however, I realized that there are many people investigating resistance to persuasion, only they — like M. Jourdain speaking prose — haven't always been aware of it. The first part of this chapter briefly sketches a dozen or so approaches to producing resistance to persuasion currently under active study; the balance of the chapter presents an introduction to our own work in the area.

Before reviewing the theories and findings regarding inducing resistance to persuasion, it would be useful to make explicit several points regarding our conceptualization of the process, since this conceptualization has determined the range of coverage. The scope of this inquiry is the uncovering of pretreatments which, when applied to the person, make him less susceptible to persuasive messages than he is found to be without these pretreatments. Hence, studying resistance to persuasion is not simply the inverse of studying persuasion itself. Suppose, for example, persuasive messages are known to be more effective if they are presented with their conclusions explicitly drawn, rather than left to be drawn by the recipient. This fact would not imply that resistance to persuasion — in the sense used here — could be enhanced by presenting messages whose conclusions are left to the recipient to draw. Rather, our interest is in pretreatments which would lessen the effectiveness of any given persuasive message (with or without its conclusion explicitly drawn).

A second preliminary point concerns the "healthiness" of resistance to persuasion. In our society we are inclined to accept the romantic notion that the autonomous man is admirable, while the man easily swayed by argument is weak and deplorable. Such a view suggests that we should look for resistance-conferring treatment among healthy processes. However, a consideration of the close psychological relation between susceptibility to persuasion and ability to learn, a closeness that makes it difficult to distinguish (at least on the basis of the psychological processes involved) between propaganda and education, shows that this resistance is not always "healthy." Anyone can be made impervious to the most skillful propaganda if we reduce him to catatonic schizophrenia and anyone can, with a bare bodkin, be made forever free from influence. The best of both worlds would be to discover pretreatments that would make the person receptive to the true and resistant to the false. But since the distinction between truth and falsity is not strictly germane to the psychological processes under discussion, such a consideration will be ignored here. Hence, as ways of inducing resistance to persuasion some possibly "unhealthy" pretreatments — like enhancing the person's tendency to use perceptual distortion in the defense of his preconceptions — are included.

A final preliminary point deals with the generality of the induced resistance to persuasion. The most general type would involve making the person resistant to the change toward any side of all issues, regardless of the variables (source, channel, message, etc.) involved. The technique involving enhancing self-esteem comes the nearest to such a panacea against persuasion, and even this procedure tends to have limitations. A more specific type of conferred resistance is restricted to a certain type of issue, or to only one of the two sides of an issue. For example, inducing aggressiveness tends to make the person less susceptible to benevolent appeals but, if anything, more vulnerable to malevolent ones.

Other resistance-inducing techniques tend to be specific to certain sources, for example, pairing that source in advance with unpopular stands on other issues. Another form of specificity involves conferring resistance to any argument on either side from any source but restricted to a given issue. An example of a technique which does this is sensitizing the person in advance of the persuasive attack to how closely his belief on the given issue is tied with his beliefs on other issues. This chapter concentrates on techniques that are general to the extent that the resistance they induce is not specific to certain sources or to just one side of the issue. At least on a given issue, these treatments make the subject more resistant to any kind of a persuasive attempt.

The next section briefly reviews four general approaches to the problem of inducing resistance to persuasion, and mentions a number of variations on each approach. The limited space available permits little more than a statement of the main points involved, along with a few illustrative experiments.

Some Contemporary Approaches to the Problem

The Behavioral Commitment Approach

The "behavioral commitment" approaches to inducing resistance to persuasion all involve the believer's taking some more or less irrevocable step on the basis of his belief, thereby committing himself to it. Insofar as commitment makes changing the belief dangerous, costly, awkward, or at least harmful to self-esteem, it strengthens the believer's tendency to resist social influence attempts aimed at this belief. The approaches that fall under this rubric can be grouped into several classes differing among themselves with respect to the nature of the committing behavior or the way of eliciting it. Below are four subclasses, listed in order of increasing externality of the commitment.

Private decision. The most tenuous kind of commitment to the belief is created simply by having the person come to a private decision that he does indeed hold the belief. Bennett (1955) found a significant tendency for subjects who are asked to come to a private (or at least anonymous) decision to persist longer in their intention than those not so requested. Such enhanced persistence may readily be interpreted as an increased resistance to the contrary pressures occurring in the interim. Lewin (1951, 1958) felt that decision-making, even of this anonymous sort, would have a "freezing" effect which could result in the belief's being maintained more firmly in the face of subsequent events. However, it appears that such private decision-making fails to confer any resistance under some conditions. Studies on the primacy-recency effect* have generally yielded negative results (Hovland and Mandell, 1957; Anderson, 1959).

2 * Public announcement of one's belief.* It has also been suggested (e.g., Lewin, 1958) that public identification of one's belief should constitute a firmer commitment than that established by private decision-making. To the extent this is so, more resistance to subsequent persuasive attempts should follow a public rather than private statement of one's beliefs. Confirmatory evidence has been reported by a number of experimenters (Deutsch and Gerard, 1955; Hovland *et al.,* 1957; Cohen *et al.,* 1959). On the other hand, Bennett (1955) found private decision-making to be at least as effective as publicly identified decisions. Fisher and associates (1956) found that the public decisions did confer resistance to peer conformity pressures on the specific point decided upon, but that accommodations of a basic sort were made so that subsequently the person tended to anticipate and submit in advance to the expected, disparate judgment of the group.

3 * Active participation on the basis of the belief.* Still more committing, it would seem, than simply stating one's belief is to take some further action on the basis of this belief. A typical action of this type which has been widely studied is the overt defense of one's belief by writing an essay or delivering a speech in support of it. McGuire's studies on the efficacy of active participation are examples (McGuire, 1963a, c; McGuire and Papageorgis, 1961). Another somewhat relevant set of experiments are the studies dealing with "overt compliance" (Kelman, 1953; King and Janis, 1956; Festinger, 1957; Cohen *et al.,* 1958). These latter studies suggest some conditions under which such

*Primacy-recency studies are those in which two or more sides of an argument are presented to a recipient in an attempt to discover whether the temporal arrangement of the presentations is a determinant of which effects the greater attitude change (the one first presented or the one most recently presented). Presumably, for the purposes of McGuire's comment, this means that after the first side is presented, the recipient may privately commit himself to the first, and, if such commitment does result in resistance to attitude change, the second presentation will be much less effective — Eds.

compliance has the greatest committing effect (e.g., when elicited with the least pressure; when many alternatives were available).

The use of belief-defensive essays as the form of active participation is somewhat unfortunate for it leaves a theoretical ambiguity: Is the increased resistance resulting from such behavior due simply to acting overtly on the basis of the belief, or is it due to the self-indoctrination and rehearsal of one's defenses involved in this particular type of activity? Fortunately, there have been a number of "forced compliance" studies in which the active participation did take other forms, forms that did not involve this rehearsal of one's defenses (Brehm, 1960a; Smith, 1961; Raven and Fishbein, 1961). These studies yield the same implications as did the rehearsal ones just considered.

4· External commitment. The final type of commitment, and by far the most tenuous of those considered here, is that called "external commitment." Rosenbaum (see Rosenbaum and Franc, 1960; Rosenbaum and Zimmerman, 1959) has shown that if the person is committed to a belief "externally," by being told someone else thinks the person holds that belief, the person does indeed show an increased adherence to the belief. It seems rather surprising that so mild a commitment could have a detectable effect; and yet, when confronted by the data, the phenomenon seems provocative rather than inexplicable.

B· Anchoring the Belief to Other Cognitions

A second family of approaches to inducing resistance to persuasion can be classified as "anchoring the belief to other cognitions." They have in common the notion of somehow linking the belief in question to other cognitions, or at least sensitizing the believer to the fact that such links exist. This procedure makes it more difficult for the person to change his belief because such a change would require his changing all the linked beliefs correspondingly. Otherwise, he would have to endure the discomfort of cognitive inconsistency. It will be recognized that this analysis accepts the basic assumption of the many current balance theories. Three such anchoring approaches, which differ regarding the type of cognitions to which a given belief is to be linked, are considered below.

1· Linking to valued goals. A number of theorists have suggested that a belief is held firmly to the extent that it is perceived as instrumental to the attainment of positively valenced goals, and/or as facilitating avoidance of negatively valenced goals (Carlson, 1956; Rosenberg, 1956; Zajonc, 1960b). According to this approach, any pretreatment that would strengthen the believer's perception that his opinion did have such linkage to valenced goals (or, alternatively, made him increase the valence of the goals involved in the perceived instrumentality relationship) would enhance his adherence to the belief, making him more resistant to subsequently received pressures to change.

2. *Linking to other beliefs.* A very popular area in this anchoring category of studies involves the linkage of the given beliefs to other beliefs in the person's cognitive system. The various balance theories are all relevant to this point. The general idea is that sensitizing the person to the fact that the given belief is logically related to many beliefs which he holds will make him adhere to it more strongly. Changing it will introduce a whole series of imbalances into his cognitive system, and these imbalances cause psychological discomfort. Much of the work so far has been confined to showing that this reasoning is indeed correct (Abelson and Rosenberg, 1958; Harary, 1959). However, some studies have actually manipulated these belief linkages (see Rosenberg and Hovland, 1960). McGuire's "Socratic effect" studies are also pertinent. They suggest that merely asking the person to rehearse the related beliefs which he already possesses makes more salient these linkages to the given belief, and thereby confers enhanced resistance to subsequent attacks — at least to the extent that such attacks will introduce inconsistencies into his belief system (McGuire, 1960a, b).

3. *Linking to valenced sources and reference groups.* A final class of anchoring effects considered here involves tying the given belief to positively valenced sources of one kind or another. The general assumption is that if the believer is made to see that his opinion is shared by others whom he values highly, the opinion will be more resistant to subsequent attacks. Many experiments have demonstrated the importance of this "source" variable in persuasion. Even anonymous individuals and groups have been shown to confer such resistance when the believer is made to recognize that they share his belief (Schachter and Hall, 1952; Bennett, 1955). The effect has also been demonstrated for positively valenced reference groups (Kelley and Volkhart, 1952; Kelley and Woodruff, 1956; Dittes and Kelley, 1956; Charters and Newcomb, 1958; Newcomb, 1961). Still other experimenters have demonstrated that tying the belief to highly regarded, specific individuals establishes the belief more firmly (Tannenbaum, 1956; Kelman and Hovland, 1953).

Each anchoring approach can be utilized to confer resistance in two ways. The believer can be provided with new information which connects the given belief with the other cognitions he already holds. Alternatively, work can be done within his already existing cognitive system by making more salient to him the linkages that already exist. For example, he might be questioned so as to call his attention to these linkages (as in the "Socratic effect" study cited above) or the social setting might be manipulated (as in the "salience of reference groups" studies cited above).

C. Inducing Resistant Cognitive States

It has been proposed that certain personality, motivational, or ideological states are correlated with resistance to social influence pressures. Hence, any treatment that induces such states in the believer should enhance his resistance to persuasion. One difficulty in applying this approach is that, despite very extensive work on the problem, few states have been discovered which are generally effective in predisposing the person to resist persuasion. Let us now examine a rather heterogeneous set of such variables.

1. *Inducing anxiety about the issue.* A good deal of research has been done on the use of fear-arousing appeals in persuasion usually with the notion that when we attach anxiety to a given issue, the person is subsequently inclined to avoid the topic. He should therefore avoid exposure to subsequent messages (including those attacking his position) on the issue and, consequently, should be less influenced by them. Nunnally and Bobren (1959) found that people do say they are less willing to receive further information on the topic after reading an anxiety-arousing message on it. On the other hand, Janis and Feshbach (1953) found that the greater the prior anxiety arousal, the *less* the resistance to a subsequent attack on the issue. Indeed, other studies (e.g., Berkowitz and Cottingham, 1960) have suggested that the effects of fear appeals are more complex than indicated by the original formulation.

2. *Inducing aggressiveness.* We might also think that the person who has been made hostile to others would be more resistant to influence attempts. Contrary to such an expectation, Weiss and Fine (1956) have shown that the actual result of inducing aggressiveness is quite different: This treatment does increase the person's resistance to benevolent arguments but makes him *more* susceptible to misanthropic arguments. Nevertheless, since several studies do indicate that chronic hostility is associated (at least in males) with resistance to persuasion, this proposition apparently deserves further study (Lesser and Abelson, 1959; Linton and Graham, 1959; Janis and Rife, 1959; Janis and Field, 1959).

3. *Raising self-esteem.* Perhaps the most successful demonstrations of induced resistance to persuasion via personality restructuring are those in which the person's self-esteem is manipulated. A number of investigators have demonstrated that a prior success experience enhances the believer's resistance to subsequent social influence attempts (Kelman, 1950; Mausner, 1954; Samelson,

1957). Resistance is increased, even when the task on which the individual succeeds is quite different from the task employed in the influence attempt.

4. *Ideological preconditioning.* The suggestion by some students of the "brainwashing" process that "ideological preconditioning" can induce resistance to influence attempts is also relevant here. This method involves giving the individual certain cognitive content that will increase his ideological autonomy. Among the contents that have been suggested are: pervasive ideologies, such as well-worked-out sets of religious beliefs that allow the person to counter the subsequent indoctrinator's ideology with his own; the belief that he has supporters as well as others dependent on his resisting (e.g., by inculcating esprit-de-corps); the consciousness that he has secret resources of which the indoctrinator is unaware, etc. (U.S. Senate, 1956). Little if any experimental work has been done to test these notions. Such support as they have received comes from anecdotal reports. The success with which Westerners have resisted indoctrination attempts by the Chinese is greater for clergymen than for businessmen; for those who identify with their parents than for those who reject them; for Marines than for Army personnel, etc.

This technique of inducing cognitive states which produce resistance to persuasion calls for further study. There is a double problem involved here: Identifying states that do indeed enhance resistance, and discovering ways of creating these states. The approach seems promising if pursued creatively, but to date confirmatory evidence is scant.

D. Prior Training in Resisting Persuasive Attempts

A final approach to conferring resistance to persuasion considered here involves giving the person some specific training that would enhance his ability to adhere to his belief when subsequently confronted with influence attempts. We shall mention briefly a number of such educational procedures that have been suggested and evaluated.

The most generic method involves general education. It has often been claimed that with better education the individual becomes more resistant to persuasion. However, empirical research does not consistently support such a proposition. Weitzenhoffer's (1953) review of the suggestibility literature shows there is no simple, negative relationship between intelligence and resistance to suggestion. There is some evidence that the more intelligent are more resistant to conformity pressures from peers (Crutchfield, 1955; Stukát, 1958); but they also seem to be, if anything, more susceptible to the mass-media kind of persuasion attempts (Hovland *et al.,* 1949; Janis and Rife, 1959). Hence, it is by no means clear that any general-education manipulation (i.e., such as would increase scores on IQ tests) would have the effect of increasing resistance to persuasion.

Training more specifically tailored to reduce susceptibility to persuasion might be more successful. One type of such training has an aura of unhealthiness: Namely, training that will enhance the selective avoidance or perceptual distortion of information that is at variance with one's beliefs. For selective avoidance to be effective, the believer must learn to recognize that the attacking message will be dissonant with his beliefs. Training to perceive the indexing characteristics of the message (Tannenbaum, 1955) would be an approach to this end. Perceptual distortion has also been shown to facilitate resistance to persuasion (Kendall and Wolf, 1949; Cooper and Dinerman, 1951; Kelley, 1957; Cantril, 1958). As with other defense mechanisms, facility in the use of such perceptual distortion can probably be acquired, although the training procedure would no doubt require considerable time and ingenuity. The effectiveness of this particular "clinical" approach remains in the realm of conjecture.

A presumably "healthier" type of specific pretraining involves enhancing the person's critical capacities so that he will be better able to recognize and discount persuasive attempts. A number of studies have shown that training in the critical evaluation of propaganda can increase the person's resistance to such material when he subsequently encounters these communications (Collier, 1944; Allport and Lepkin, 1945; Citron and Harding, 1950). Also effective in this regard is providing the person with special instruction which urges him to be critical just before the attack on his beliefs (Das *et al.,* 1955; Luchins, 1957). In these cases, the conferred resistance tends to be small. The work by McGuire stemming from inoculation theory, which is introduced in the subsequent section, probes more deeply into the immunizing effectiveness of such prior training and warnings.

The Inoculation Approach

Use of Cultural Truisms

McGuire's series of experiments on inducing resistance to persuasion stems from a biological analogy, whence the term "inoculation theory." In the biological situation, the person is typically made resistant to some attacking virus by pre-exposure to a weakened dose of the virus. This mild dose stimulates his defenses so that he will be better able to overcome any massive viral attack to which he is later exposed, but is not so strong that this pre-exposure will itself cause the disease. Alternatively, biological resistance can be augmented by supportive therapy such as adequate rest, good diet, and vitamin supplements. Inoculation is likely to be superior to supportive therapy to the extent that the person has previously been brought up in a germ-free environment. It is a seeming paradox that individuals raised aseptically tend to appear vigorously healthy (even without supportive therapy) but are highly vulnerable when suddenly exposed to massive doses of the disease virus.

Since the experimenter wished to make heuristic use of the inoculation analogy in deriving hypotheses about producing resistance to persuasion, he chose to deal as far as possible with beliefs that had been maintained in a "germ-free" ideological environment, that is, beliefs that the person has seldom, if ever, heard attacked. Nearly all beliefs should be of this sort, according to the selective-avoidance postulate, which implies that a person avoids dissonant information wherever possible. While this has been widely accepted (Festinger, 1957; Klapper, 1949, 1960), the empirical evidence for it is not clear-cut (Steiner, 1962). Hence, to be more certain that the beliefs used in these experiments met the conditions of inoculation theory, "cultural truisms" were used as the beliefs to be made resistant to persuasive attacks. "Cultural truisms" are beliefs that are so widely shared within the person's social milieu that he would not have heard them attacked, and indeed, would doubt that an attack were possible. Beliefs maintained in so monolithic an ideological environment would approximate, as regards inoculation theory, the health status of an organism raised in a germ-free environment.

After much pretesting (which showed that cultural truisms were rarer in our college samples than had been expected), one area was finally found that abounded in almost unanimously accepted propositions, namely, health beliefs. Upwards of 75% of the student samples checked "15" on a 15-point scale to indicate their agreement with propositions like: "It's a good idea to brush your teeth after every meal if at all possible"; "Mental illness is not contagious"; "The effects of penicillin have been, almost without exception, of great benefit to mankind"; "Everyone should get a yearly chest X-ray to detect any signs of TB at an early stage." These truisms (which proved quite vulnerable when exposed to massive attacks without any prior "immunizing" treatment) were used as the beliefs to be made resistant to persuasion by procedures derived by analogy from biological inoculation.

Basic Assumptions and Relevant Variables

Underlying assumptions. McGuire's version of the inoculation theory assumes that pretreatments designed to make truisms resistant to subsequent persuasive attacks will be effective to the extent that they overcome two basic difficulties: one, the believer is unpracticed in defending his belief; and two, he is unmotivated to undertake the necessary practice. He is unpracticed because he has never been called upon to defend the truism. He is unmotivated to start practicing because he regards the belief as unassailable.

It follows that any prior treatment designed to improve the believer's defenses must motivate him to develop a defense of a truism whose validity he regards as obvious. Motivation can be supplied by making him aware of the vulnerability of the truism. That is, to be effective the prior defense of a truism presumably should be threatening rather than reassuring about the belief. An obvious way of threatening him is by pre-exposure to weakened forms of the attacking arguments.

It also follows that supplying motivation alone is inadequate for an effective defense. Because of the believer's lack of prior practice, he may not be able to bolster his belief sufficiently unless he is given careful guidance in developing defensive material; or, if he is required to develop such material on his own initiative, he must at least be given considerable time to do so.*

*The studies which McGuire proceeds to describe can be found in the original source (McGuire, 1964) or individually by the following references: McGuire, 1961a, b, 1962, 1963a, b, c; McGuire and Papageorgis, 1961, 1962; Papageorgis and McGuire, 1961; Anderson 1965.

12

Reconciling Conflicting Results Derived from Experimental and Survey Studies of Attitude Change

Carl I. Hovland

Carl Hovland's classic critique of the state of research on attitude change is a logical concluding statement for this volume. The theoretical approaches we have presented are derived from and have led to empirical research. An evaluation of the relative merits of these approaches must be qualified by an evaluation of the procedures used to substantiate them.

Hovland compares two basic types of research design. He calls one the *experiment*, in which the investigator examines the effects of controlled exposure to information on the "amount of attitude change or opinion produced." Most of the research described in this volume is of this nature. The second basic design is the *sample survey*. It differs from the experiment in that the exposure to information is not controlled but occurs in the natural course of events — for example, television advertising and political candidates' brochures — and attitude change is assessed by means of interviews or general questionnaires of a sample of the people receiving this information. An opinion poll studying the effect of an advertising campaign on consumers' attitudes is a sample survey.

Hovland notes that studies of attitude change often present conflicting results. He discusses the possibility that part of the divergence in these results can be attributed to

184

differences in the research design, and he suggests conceptual means of reconciling some of the divergent conclusions.*

Two quite different types of research design are characteristically used to study the modification of attitudes through communication. In the first type, the *experiment*, individuals are given a controlled exposure to a communication and the effects evaluated in terms of the amount of change in attitude or opinion produced. A base line is provided by means of a control group not exposed to the communication. The study of Gosnell (1927) on the influence of leaflets designed to get voters to the polls is a classic example of the controlled experiment.

In the alternative research design, the *sample survey*, information is secured through interviews of questionnaires both concerning the respondent's exposure to various communications and his attitudes and opinions on various issues. Generalizations are then derived from the correlations obtained between reports of exposure and measurements of attitude. In a variant of this method, measurements of attitude and of exposure to communication are obtained during repeated interviews with the same individual over a period of weeks or months. This is the "panel method" extensively utilized in studying the impact of various mass media on political attitudes and on voting behavior (cf., e.g., Kendall and Lazarsfeld, 1950).

Generalizations derived from experimental and from correlational studies of communication effects are usually both reported in chapters on the effects of mass media and in other summaries of research on attitude, typically without much stress of the type of study from which the conclusion was derived. Close scrutiny of the results obtained from the two methods, however, suggests a marked difference in the picture of communication effects obtained from each. The object of my paper is to consider the conclusions derived from these two types of design, to suggest some of the factors responsible for the frequent divergence in results, and then to formulate principles aimed at reconciling some of the apparent conflicts.

Divergence

The picture of mass communication effects which emerges from correlational studies is one in which few individuals are seen as being affected by

*Reprinted from C. I. Hovland, Reconciling conflicting results derived from experimental and survey studies of attitude change, *American Psychologist*, 1959, *14*, 8-17, by permission of the publisher, the American Psychological Association.

communications. One of the most thorough correlational studies of the effects of mass media on attitudes is that of Lazarsfeld, Berelson, and Gaudet published in *The People's Choice* (1944). In this report there is an extensive chapter devoted to the effects of various media, particularly radio, newspapers, and magazines. The authors conclude that few changes in attitudes were produced. They estimate that the political positions of only about 5% of their respondents were changed by the election campaign, and they are inclined to attribute even this small amount of change more to personal influence than to the mass media. A similar evaluation of mass media is made in the *Handbook of Social Psychology* by Lipset and his collaborators (1954).

Research using experimental procedures, on the other hand, indicates the possibility of considerable modifiability of attitudes through exposure to communication. In both Klapper's survey (1949) and in my chapter in the *Handbook of Social Psychology* (Hovland, 1954) a number of experimental studies are discussed in which the opinions of a third to a half or more of the audience are changed.

The discrepancy between the results derived from these two methodologies raises some fascinating problems for analysis. This divergence in outcome appears to me to be largely attributable to two kinds of factors: One, the difference in research design itself; and, two, the historical and traditional differences in general approach to evaluation characteristic of researchers using the experimental as contrasted with the correlational or survey method. I would like to discuss, first, the influence these factors have on the estimation of overall effects of communications and, then, turn to other divergences in outcome characteristically found by the use of the experimental and survey methodology.

Undoubtedly the most critical and interesting variation in the research *design* involved in the two procedures is that resulting from differences in definition of exposure. In an experiment the audience on whom the effects are being evaluated is one which is fully exposed to the communication. On the other hand, in naturalistic situations with which surveys are typically concerned, the outstanding phenomenon is the limitation of the audience to those who *expose themselves* to the communication. Some of the individuals in a captive audience experiment would, of course, expose themselves in the course of natural events to a communication of the type studied; but many others would not. The group which does expose itself is usually a highly biased one, since most individuals "expose themselves most of the time to a kind of material with which they agree to begin with" (Lipset *et al.*, 1954, p. 1158). Thus one reason for the difference in results between experiments and correlational studies is that experiments describe the effects of exposure on the whole range of individuals studied, some of whom are initially in favor of the position being advocated and some who are opposed, whereas surveys primarily describe the effects produced on those already in favor of the point of view advocated in the communication. The amount of change is thus, of course, much smaller in surveys. Lipset and his collaborators make this same evaluation, stating that:

> As long as we test a program in the laboratory we always find that it has great effect on the attitudes and interests of the experimental subjects. But when we put the program on as a regular broadcast, we then note that the people who are most influenced in the laboratory tests are those who, in a realistic situation, do not listen to the program. The controlled experiment always greatly overrates effects, as compared with those that really occur, because of the self-selection of audiences (Lipset *et al.*, 1954, p. 1158).

Differences in the second category are not inherent in the design of the two alternatives, but are characteristic of the way researchers using the two methods typically proceed.

The first difference within this class is in the size of the communication unit typically studied. In the majority of survey studies the unit evaluated is an entire program of communication. For example, in studies of political behavior an attempt is made to assess the effects of all newspaper reading and television viewing on attitudes toward the major parties. In the typical experiment, on the other hand, the interest is usually in some particular variation in the content of the communications, and experimental evaluations much more frequently involve single communications. On this point results are thus not directly comparable.

Another characteristic difference between the two methods is in the time interval used in evaluation. In the typical experiment the time at which the effect is observed is usually rather soon after exposure to the communication. In the survey study, on the other hand, the time perspective is such that much more remote effects are usually evaluated. When effects decline with the passage of time, the net outcome will, of course, be that of accentuating the effect obtained in experimental studies as compared with those obtained in survey researches. Again it must be stressed that the difference is not inherent in the designs as such. Several experiments, including our own on the effects of motion pictures (Hovland, Lumsdaine, and Sheffield, 1949) and later studies on the "sleeper effect" (Hovland and Weiss, 1951; Kelman and Hovland, 1953), have studied retention over considerable periods of time.

Some of the difference in outcome may be attributable to the types of communicators characteristically used and to the motive-incentive conditions operative in the two situations. In experimental studies communications are frequently presented in a classroom situation. This may involve quite different types of factors from those operative in the more naturalistic communication situation with which the survey researchers are concerned. In the classroom there may be some implicit sponsorship of the communication by the teacher and the school administration. In the survey studies the communicators may often be remote individuals either unfamiliar to the recipients, or outgroupers clearly known to espouse a point of view opposed to that held by many members of the audience. Thus there may be real differences in communicator credibility in the laboratory and survey researches. The net effect of the differences will typically be in the direction of increasing the likelihood of change in the experimental as compared with the survey study.

There is sometimes an additional situational difference. Communications to the type studies by survey researchers usually involve reaching the individual in his natural habitat, with consequent supplementary effects produced by discussion with friends and family. In the laboratory studies a classroom situation with low postcommunication interaction is more typically involved. Several studies, including one by Harold Kelley reported in our volume on *Communication and Persuasion* (Hovland, Janis, and Kelley, 1953), indicate that, when a communication is presented in a situation which makes group membership salient, the individual is typically more resistant to counternorm influence than when the communication is presented under conditions of low salience of group membership (cf. also, Katz and Lazarsfeld, 1955, pp. 48-133).

A difference which is almost wholly adventitious is in the types of populations utilized. In the survey design there is, typically, considerable emphasis on a random sample of the entire population. In the typical experiment, on the other hand, there is a consistent overrepresentation of high school students and college sophomores, primarily on the basis of their greater accessibility. But as Tolman has said: "College sophomores may not be people." Whether differences in the type of audience studied contribute to the differences in effect obtained with the two methods is not known.

Finally, there is an extremely important difference in the studies of the experimental and correlational variety with respect to the type of issue discussed in the communications. In the typical experiment we are interested in studying a set of factors or conditions which are expected on the basis of theory to influence the extent of effect of the communication. We usually deliberately try to find types of issues involving attitudes which are susceptible to modification through communication. Otherwise, we run the risk of no measurable effects, particularly with small-scale experiments. In the survey procedures, on the other hand, socially significant attitudes which are deeply rooted in prior experience and involve much personal commitment are typically involved. This is especially true in voting studies which have provided us with so many of our present results on social influence. I shall have considerably more to say about this problem a little later.

The differences so far discussed have primarily concerned the extent of overall effectiveness indicated by the two methods: why survey results typically show little modification of attitudes by communication while experiments indicate marked changes. Let me now turn to some of the other differences in generalizations derived from the two alternative designs. Let me take as the second main area of disparate results the research on the effect of varying distances between the position taken by the communicator and that held by the recipient of the communication. Here it is a matter of comparing changes for persons who at the outset closely agree with the communicator with those for others who are mildly or strongly in disagreement with him. In the naturalistic situation studied in surveys the typical procedure is to determine changes in opinion following reported exposure to communication for individuals differing from the communicator by varying amounts. This gives rise to two possible artifacts. When the communication is at one end of a continuum, there is little room for improvement for those who differ from the communication by small amounts, but a great deal of room for movement among those with large discrepancies. This gives rise to a spurious degree of positive relationship between the degree of discrepancy and the amount of change. Regression effects will also operate in the direction of increasing the correlation. What is needed is a situation in which the distance factor can be manipulated independently of the subject's initial position. An attempt to set up these conditions experimentally was made in a study by Pritzker and the writer (1957). The method involved preparing individual communications presented in booklet form so that the position of the communicator could be set at any desired distance from the subject's initial position. Communicators highly acceptable to the subjects were used. A number of different topics were employed, including the likelihood of a cure for cancer within five years, the desirability of compulsory voting, and the adequacy of five hours of sleep per night.

The amount of change for each degree of advocated change is shown in Figure 1. It will be seen that there is a fairly clear progression, such that the greater the amount of change advocated the greater the average amount of opinion change produced. Similar results have been reported by Goldberg (1954) and by French (1956).

But these results are not in line with our hunches as to what would happen in a naturalistic situation with important social issues. We felt that here other types of response than change in attitude would occur. So Muzafer Sherif, O. J. Harvey, and the writer (1957) set up a situation to simulate as closely as possible the conditions typically involved when individuals are exposed to major social issue communications at differing distances from their own position. The issue used was the desirability of prohibition. The study was done in two states

(Oklahoma and Texas) where there is prohibition or local option, so that the wet-dry issue is hotly debated. We concentrated on three aspects of the problem: How favorably will the communicator be received when his position is at varying distances from that of the recipient? How will what the communicator says be perceived and interpreted by individuals at varying distances from his position? What will be the amount of opinion change produced when small and large deviations in position of communication and recipient are involved?

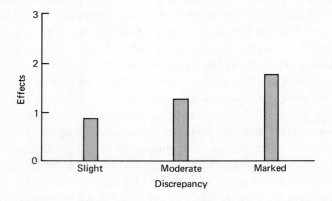

Figure 1. Mean opinion change score with three degrees of discrepancy (deviation between subject's position and position advocated in communication) (from Hovland and Pritzker, 1957).

Three communications, one strongly wet, one strongly dry, and one moderately wet, were employed. The results bearing on the first problem, of *reception*, are presented in Figure 2. The positions of the subjects are indicated on the abscissa in letters from *A* (extreme dry) to *H* (strongly wet). The positions of the communication are also indicated in the same letters, *B* indicating a strongly dry communication, *H* a strongly wet, and *F* a moderately wet. Along the ordinate there is plotted the percentage of subjects with each position on the issue who described the communication as "fair" and "unbiased." It will be seen that the degree of distance between the recipient and the communicator greatly influences the evaluation of the fairness of the communication. When a communication is directed at the pro-dry position, nearly all of the dry subjects consider it fair and impartial, but only a few per cent of the wet subjects consider the identical communication fair. The reverse is true at the other end of the scale. When an intermediate position is adopted, the percentages fall off sharply on each side. Thus under the present conditions with a relatively ambiguous communicator one of the ways of dealing with strongly discrepant positions is to *discredit* the communicator, considering him unfair and biased.

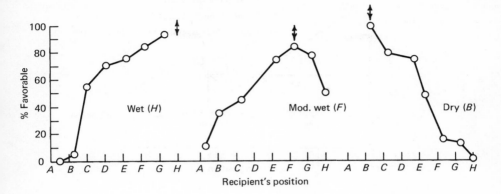

Figure 2. Percentage of favorable evaluations ("fair," "unbiased," etc.) of wet (*H*), moderately wet (*F*), and dry (*B*) communications for subjects holding various positions on prohibition. Recipients' positions range from *A* (very dry) to *H* (very wet). Position of communications indicated by arrow (from Hovland, Harvey, and Sherif, 1957).

A second way in which an individual can deal with discrepancy is by distortion of what is said by the communicator. This is a phenomenon extensively studied by Cooper and Jahoda (1947). In the present study, subjects were asked to state what position they thought was taken by the communicator on the prohibition question. Their evaluation of his position could then be analyzed in relation to their own position. These results are shown in Figure 3 for the moderately wet communication. It will be observed that there is a tendency for individuals whose position is close to that of the communicator to report the communicator's position quite accurately, for individuals a little bit removed to report his position to be substantially more like their own (which we call an "assimilation effect"), and for those with more discrepant positions to report the communicator's position as more extreme than it really was. This we refer to as a "contrast effect."

Now to our primary results on opinion change. It was found that individuals whose position was only slightly discrepant from the communicator's were influenced to a greater extent than those whose positions deviated to a larger extent. When a wet position was espoused, 28% of the middle-of-the-road subjects were changed in the direction of the communicator, as compared with only 4% of the drys. With the dry communication 14% of the middle-of-the-roaders were changed, while only 4% of the wets were changed. Thus, more of the subjects with small discrepancies were changed than were those with large discrepancies.

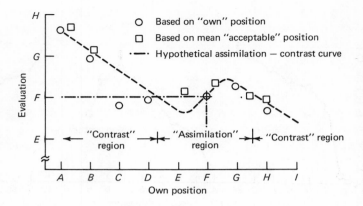

Figure 3. Average placement of position of moderately wet communication (F) by subjects holding various positions on the issue, plotted against hypothetical assimilation-contrast curve (from Hovland, Harvey, and Sherif, 1957).

These results appear to indicate that, under conditions when there is some ambiguity about the credibility of the communicator and when the subject is deeply involved with the issue, the greater the attempt at change the higher the resistance. On the other hand, with highly respected communicators, as in the previous study with Pritzker using issues of lower involvement, the greater the discrepancy the greater the effect. A study related to ours has been completed by Zimbardo (1959) which indicated that, when an influence attempt is made by a strongly positive communicator (i.e., a close personal friend), the greater the discrepancy the greater the opinion change, even when the experimenter made a point of stressing the great importance of the subject's opinion.

The implication of these results for our primary problem of conflicting results is clear. The types of issues with which most experiments deal are relatively uninvolving and are often of the variety where expert opinion is highly relevant, as for example, on topics of health, science, and the like. Here we should expect that opinion would be considerably affected by communications and furthermore that advocacy of positions quite discrepant from the individual's own position would have a marked effect. On the other hand, the types of issues most often utilized in survey studies are ones which are very basic and involve deep commitment. As a consequence small changes in opinion due to communication would be expected. Here communication may have little effect on those who disagree at the outset and function merely to strengthen the position already held, in line with survey findings.

A third area of research in which somewhat discrepant results are obtained by the experimental and survey methods is in the role of order of presentation. From naturalistic studies the generalization has been widely adopted that primacy is an extremely important factor in persuasion. Numerous writers have reported that what we experience first has a critical role in what we believe. This is particularly stressed in studies of propaganda effects in various countries when the nation getting across its message first is alleged to have a great advantage and in commercial advertising where "getting a beat on the field" is stressed. The importance of primacy in political propaganda is indicated in the following quotation from Doob:

> The propagandist scores an initial advantage whenever his propaganda reaches people before that of his rivals. Readers or listeners are then biased to comprehend, forever after, the event as it has been initially portrayed to them. If they are told in a headline or a flash that the battle has been won, the criminal has been caught, or the bill is certain to pass the legislature, they will usually expect subsequent information to substantiate this first impression. When later facts prove otherwise, they may be loath to abandon what they believe to be true until perhaps the evidence becomes overwhelming (Doob, 1948, pp. 421-422).

A study by Katz and Lazarsfeld (1955) utilizing the survey method compares the extent to which respondents attribute major impact on their decisions about fashions and movie attendance to the presentations to which they were first exposed. Strong primacy effects are shown in their analyses of the data.

We have ourselves recently completed a series of experiments oriented toward this problem. These are reported in our monograph on *Order of Presentation in Persuasion* (Hovland, Mandell, Campbell, Brock, Luchins, Cohen, McGuire, Janis, Feierabend, and Anderson, 1957). We find that primacy is often *not* a very significant factor when the relative effectiveness of the first side of an issue is compared experimentally with that of the second. The research suggests that differences in design may account for much of the discrepancy. A key variable is whether there is exposure to both sides or whether only one side is actually received. In naturalistic studies the advantage of the first side is often not only that it is first but that it is often the only side of the issue to which the individual is exposed. Having once been influenced, many individuals make up their mind and are no longer interested in other communications on the issue. In most experiments on order of presentation, on the other hand, the audience is systematically exposed to both sides. Thus under survey conditions, self-exposure tends to increase the impact of primacy.

Two other factors to which I have already alluded appear significant in determining the amount of primacy effect. One is the nature of the communicator, the other the setting in which the communication is received. In our volume Luchins presents results indicating that, when the same communicator presents contradictory material, the point of view read first has more influence. On the other hand, Mandell and I show that, when two different communicators present opposing views successively, little primacy effect is obtained. The communications setting factor operates similarly. When the issue and the conditions of presentation make clear that the points of view are controversial, little primacy is obtained.

Thus in many of the situations with which there had been great concern as to undesirable effects of primacy, such as in legal trials, election campaigns, and political debate, the role of primacy appears to have been exaggerated, since the conditions there are those least conducive to primacy effects: the issue is clearly defined as controversial, the partisanship of the communicator is usually established, and different communicators present the opposing sides.

Time does not permit me to discuss other divergences in results obtained in survey and experimental studies, such as those concerned with the effects of repetition of presentation, the relationship between level of intelligence and susceptibility to attitude change, or the relative impact of mass media and personal influence. Again, however, I am sure that detailed analysis will reveal differential factors at work which can account for the apparent disparity in the generalizations derived.

Integration

On the basis of the foregoing survey of results I reach the conclusion that no contradiction has been established between the data provided by experimental and correlational studies. Instead it appears that the seeming divergence can be satisfacrorily accounted for on the basis of a different definition of the communication situation (including the phenomenon of self-selection) and differences in the type of communicator, audience, and kind of issue utilized.

But there remains the task of better integrating the findings associated with the two methodologies. This is a problem closely akin to that considered by the members of the Social Science Research Council seminar on *Narrowing the Gap Between Field Studies and Laboratory Studies in Social Psychology* (Riecken, 1954). Many of their recommendations are pertinent to our present problem.

What seems to me quite apparent is that a genuine understanding of the effects of communications on attitudes requires both the survey and the experimental methodologies. At the same time there appear to be certain inherent limitations of each method which must be understood by the researcher if he is not to be blinded by his preoccupation with one or the other type of design. Integration of the two methodologies will require on the part of the experimentalist an awareness of the narrowness of the laboratory in interpreting the larger and more comprehensive effects of communication. It will require on the part of the survey researcher a greater awareness of the limitations of the correlational method as a basis for establishing causal relationships.

The framework within which survey research operates is most adequately and explicitly dealt with by Berelson, Lazarsfeld, and McPhee in their book on *Voting* (1954). The model which they use, taken over by them from the economist Tinbergen, is reproduced in the top half of Figure 4. For comparison, the model used by experimentalists is presented in the lower half of the figure. It will be seen that the model used by the survey researcher, particularly when he employs the "panel" method, stresses the large number of simultaneous and interacting influences affecting attitudes and opinions. Even more significant is its provision for a variety of "feedback" phenomena in which consequences wrought by previous influences affect processes normally considered as

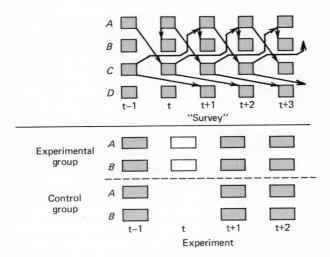

Figure 4. Top Half: "Process analysis" schema used in panel research. (Successive time intervals are indicated along abscissa. Letters indicate the variables under observation. Arrows represent relations between the variables) (from Berelson, Lazarsfeld, and McPhee, 1954).
Bottom Half: Design of experimental research. (Letters on vertical axis again indicate variables being measured. Unshaded box indicates experimentally manipulated treatment and blank absence of such treatment. Time periods indicated as in top half of chart.)

occurring earlier in the sequence. The various types of interaction are indicated by the placement of arrows showing direction of effect. In contrast the experimentalist frequently tends to view the communication process as one in which some single manipulative variable is the primary determinant of the subsequent attitude change. He is, of course, aware in a general way of the importance of context, and he frequently studies interaction effects as well as main effects; but he still is less attentive than he might be to the complexity of the influence situation and the numerous possibilities for feedback loops. Undoubtedly the real life communication situation is better described in terms of the survey type of model. We are all familiar, for example, with the interactions in which attitudes predispose one to acquire certain types of information, that this often leads to changes in attitude which may result in further acquisition of knowledge, which in turn produces more attitude change, and so on. Certainly the narrow question sometimes posed by experiments as to the effect of knowledge on attitudes greatly underestimates these interactive effects.

But while the conceptualization of the survey researcher is often very valuable, his correlational research design leaves much to be desired. Advocates of correlational analysis often cite the example of a science built on observation exclusively without experiment: astronomy. But here a very limited number of space-time concepts are involved and the number of competing theoretical formulations is relatively small so that it is possible to limit alternative theories rather drastically through correlational evidence. But in the area of communication effects and social psychology generally the variables are so numerous and so intertwined that the correlational methodology is primarily useful to suggest hypotheses and not to establish causal relationships (Hovland *et. al.*, 1949, pp. 329-340; Maccoby, 1956). Even with the much simpler relationships involved in biological systems there are grave difficulties of which we are all aware these days when we realize how difficult it is to establish through correlation whether eating of fats is or is not a cause of heart disease or whether or not smoking is a cause of lung cancer. In communications research the complexity of the problem makes it inherently difficult to derive causal relationships from correlational analysis where experimental control of exposure is not possible. And I do not agree with my friends the Lazarsfelds (Kendall and Lazarsfeld, 1950) concerning the effectiveness of the panel method in circumventing this problem since parallel difficulties are raised when the relationships occur over a time span.

These difficulties constitute a challenge to the experimentalist in this area of research to utilize the broad framework for studying communication effects suggested by the survey researcher, but to employ well controlled experimental design to work on those aspects of the field which are amenable to experimental manipulation and control. It is, of course, apparent that there are important communication problems which cannot be attacked directly by experimental methods. It is not, for example, feasible to modify voting behavior by manipulation of the issues discussed by the opposed parties during a particular campaign. It is not feasible to assess the effects of communications over a very long span of time. For example, one cannot visualize experimental procedures for answering the question of what has been the impact of the reading of *Das Kapital* or *Uncle Tom's Cabin*. These are questions which can be illuminated by historical and sociological study but cannot be evaluated in any rigorous experimental fashion.

But the scope of problems which do lend themselves to experimental attack is very broad. Even complex interactions can be fruitfully attacked by experiment. The possibilities are clearly shown in studies like that of Sherif and Sherif (1953) on factors influencing cooperative and competitive behavior in a camp for adolescent boys. They were able to bring under manipulative control many of the types of interpersonal relationships ordinarily considered impossible to modify experimentally, and to develop motivations of an intensity characteristic of real-life situations. It should be possible to do similar studies in the communication area with a number of the variables heretofore only investigated in uncontrolled naturalistic settings by survey procedures.

In any case it appears eminently practical to minimize many of the differences which were discussed above as being not inherent in design but more or less adventitiously linked with one or the other method. Thus there is no reason why more complex and deeply-involving social issues cannot be employed in experiments rather than the more superficial ones more commonly used. The resistance to change of socially important issues may be a handicap in studying certain types of attitude change; but, on the other hand, it is important to understand the lack of modifiability of opinion with highly-involving issues. Greater representation of the diverse types of communicators found in naturalistic situations can also be achieved. In addition, it should be possible to do experiments with a wider range of populations to reduce the possibility that many of our present generalizations from experiments are unduly affected by their heavy weighting of college student characteristics, including high literacy, alertness, and rationality.

A more difficult task is that of experimentally evaluating communications under conditions of self-selection of exposure. But this is not at all impossible in theory. It should be possible to assess what demographic and personality factors predispose one to expose oneself to particular communications and then to utilize experimental and control groups having these characteristics. Under some circumstances the evaluation could be made on only those who select themselves, with both experimental and control groups coming from the self-selected audience.

Undoubtedly many of the types of experiments which could be set up involving or simulating naturalistic conditions will be too ambitious and costly to be feasible even if possible in principle. This suggests the continued use of small-scale experiments which seek to isolate some of the key variables operative in complex situations. From synthesis of component factors, prediction of complex outcomes may be practicable. It is to this analytic procedure for narrowing the gap between laboratory and field research that we have devoted major attention in our research program. I will merely indicate briefly here some of the ties between our past work and the present problem.

We have attempted to assess the influence of the communicator by varying his expertness and attractiveness, as in the studies by Kelman, Weiss, and the writer (Hovland and Weiss, 1951; Kelman and Hovland, 1953). Further data on this topic were presented earlier in this paper.

We have also been concerned with evaluating social interaction effects. Some of the experiments on group affiliation as a factor affecting resistance to counternorm communication and the role of salience of group membership by Hal Kelley and others are reported in *Communication and Persuasion* (Hovland *et al.*, 1953).

Starting with the studies carried out during the war on orientation films by Art Lumsdaine, Fred Sheffield, and the writer (1949), we have had a strong interest in the duration of communication effects. Investigation of effects at various time intervals has helped to bridge the gap between assessment of immediate changes with those of longer duration like those involved in survey studies. Extensions of this work have indicated the close relationship between the credibility of the communicator and the extent of post-communication increments, of "sleeper effects" (Hovland and Weiss, 1951; Kelman and Hovland, 1953).

The nature of individual differences in susceptibility to persuasion via communication has been the subject of a number of our recent studies. The generality of persuasibility has been investigated by Janis and collaborators and the development of persuasibility in children has been studied by Abelson and Lesser. A volume concerned with these audience factors to which Janis, Abelson, Lesser, Field, Rife, King, Cohen, Linton, Graham, and the writer have contributed appears under the title *Personality and Persuasibility* (Hovland and Janis, 1959).

Lastly, there remains the question on how the nature of the issues used in the communication affects the extent of change in attitude. We have only made a small beginning on these problems. In the research reported in *Experiments on*

Mass Communication, we showed that the magnitude of effects was directly related to the type of attitude involved: film communications had a significant effect on opinions related to straightforward interpretations of policies and events, but had little or no effect on more deeply intrenched attitudes and motivations. Further work on the nature of issues is represented in the study by Sherif, Harvey, and the writer (1957) which was discussed above. There we found a marked contrast between susceptibility to influence and the amount of ego-involvement in the issue. But the whole concept of ego-involvement is a fuzzy one, and here is an excellent area for further work seeking to determine the theoretical factors involved in different types of issues.

With this brief survey of possible ways to bridge the gap between experiment and survey I must close. I should like to stress in summary the mutual importance of the two approaches to the problem of communication effectiveness. Neither is a royal road to wisdom, but each represents an important emphasis. The challenge of future work is one of fruitfully combining their virtues so that we may develop a social psychology of communication with the conceptual breadth provided by correlational study of process and with the rigorous but more delimited methodology of the experiment.

References

Abelson, R. P., and M. J. Rosenberg. Symbolic psycho-logic: A model of attitudinal cognition. *Behavioral Science*, 1958, *3*, 1-13.

Adams, J. S. Reduction of cognitive dissonance by seeking consonant information. *Journal of Abnormal and Social Psychology,* 1961, *62*, 74-78.

Adams, J. S. Inequity in social exchange. In L. Berkowitz (Ed.), *Advances in experimental social psychology*. Vol. 2. New York: Academic Press, 1965. Pp. 267-300.

Adams, J. S., and P. R. Jacobsen. Effects of wage inequities on work quality. *Journal of Abnormal and Social Psychology*, 1964, *69*, 19-25.

Adorno, T. W., *et al. The authoritarian personality*. New York: Harper, 1950.

Allport, F., and M. Lepkin. Wartime rumors of waste and special privilege: Why some people believe them. *Journal of Abnormal and Social Psychology*, 1945, *40*, 3-36.

Allport, G. W. *ABC's of scapegoating*. Chicago: Central Y.M.C.A. College, 1944.

Allport, G. W. The historical background of modern social psychology. In G. Lindzey (Ed.), *Handbook of social psychology*. Vol. 1. Cambridge, Mass.: Addison-Wesley, 1954. Pp. 3-56.

Anderson, L. R., and W. J. McGuire. Prior reassurance of group consensus as a factor in producing resistance to persuasion. *Sociometry*, 1965, *28*, 44-56.

Anderson, N. H. Test of a model for opinion change. *Journal of Abnormal and Social Psychology*, 1959, *59*, 371-381.

Aronson, E., and J. M. Carlsmith. Performance expectancy as a determinant of actual performance. *Journal of Abnormal and Social Psychology*, 1962, *65*, 178-182.

Aronson, E., and J. M. Carlsmith. Effect of the severity of threat on the devaluation of forbidden behavior. *Journal of Abnormal and Social Psychology*, 1963, *66*, 584-588.

Aronson, E., and L. Festinger. Some attempts to measure tolerance for dissonance. USAF WADC Technical Report, 1958, No. 58-492.

Asch, S. E. *Social psychology*. Englewood Cliffs, N. J.: Prentice-Hall, 1952.

Asch, S. E. Review of L. Festinger, *A theory of cognitive dissonance. Contemporary Psychology*, 1958, *3*, 194-195.

Barlow, M. F. Security and group approval as value systems related to attitude change. Unpublished doctoral dissertation, University of Michigan, 1954.

Bem, D. J. An experimental analysis of self-persuasion. *Journal of Experimental Social Psychology*, 1965, *1*, 199-218.

Bem, D. J. Inducing belief in false confessions. *Journal of Personality and Social Psychology*, 1966, *3*, 707-710.

Bem, D. J. Self-perception: An alternative interpretation of cognitive dissonance phenomena. *Psychological Review*, 1967, *74*, 183-200.

Bennett, E. B. Discussion, decision commitment, and consensus in "group decision." *Human Relations*, 1955, *8*, 251-273.

Berelson, B. R., P. F. Lazarsfeld, and W. N. McPhee. *Voting: A study of opinion formation in a presidential campaign.* Chicago: Univ. Chicago Press, 1954.

Berkowitz, L. The expression and reduction of hostility. *Psychological Bulletin*, 1958, *55*, 257-283.

Berkowitz, L. Anti-Semitism and the displacement of aggression. *Journal of Abnormal and Social Psychology*, 1959, *59*, 182-188.

Berkowitz, L., and D. R. Cottingham. The interest value and relevance of fear arousing communications. *Journal of Abnormal and Social Psychology*, 1960, *60*, 37-43.

Berkowitz, L., and D. S. Holmes. The generalization of hostility to disliked objects. *Journal of Personality*, 1959, *27*, 565-577.

Berkowitz, L., and R. M. Lundy. Personality characteristics related to susceptibility to influence by peers or authority figures. *Journal of Personality*, 1957, *25*, 306-316.

Berlyne, D. *Conflict, arousal, and curiosity.* New York: McGraw-Hill, 1960.

Bettelheim, B., and M. Janowitz. *Dynamics of prejudice.* New York: Harper, 1950.

Birch, H. G. The effect of socially disapproved labeling upon well-structured attitudes. *Journal of Abnormal and Social Psychology*, 1945, *40*, 301-310.

Bramel, D. A dissonance theory approach to defensive projection. *Journal of Abnormal and Social Psychology*, 1962, *64*, 121-129.

Brasfield, C., and D. Papageorgis. Manifest anxiety and the effects of a dissonant self-relevant communication on self-perception. *Proceedings of the 73rd Annual Convention of the American Psychological Association*, 1965, 193-194.

Brehm, J. W. Post-decision changes in the desirability of alternatives. *Journal of Abnormal and Social Psychology*, 1956, *52*, 384-389.

Brehm, J. W. A dissonance analysis of attitude-discrepant behavior. In C. I. Hovland and M. J. Rosenberg (Eds.), *Attitude organization and change.* New Haven, Conn.: Yale Univ. Press, 1960. Pp. 164-197. *(a)*

Brehm, J. W. Attitudinal consequences of commitment to unpleasant behavior. *Journal of Abnormal and Social Psychology*, 1960, *60*, 379-383. *(b)*

Brehm, J. W. Comment on "Counter-norm attitudes induced by consonant versus dissonant conditions of role-playing." *Journal of Experimental Research in Personality*, 1965, *1*, 61-64.

Brehm, J. W., and A. R. Cohen. Choice and chance relative deprivation as determinants of cognitive dissonance. *Journal of Abnormal and Social Psychology*, 1959, *58*, 383-387. *(a)*

Brehm, J. W., and A. R. Cohen. Re-evaluation of choice alternatives as a function of their number and qualitative similarity. *Journal of Abnormal and Social Psychology*, 1959, *58*, 373-378. *(b)*

Brehm, J. W., and A. R. Cohen. *Explorations in cognitive dissonance.* New York: Wiley, 1962.

Brewster, G. W. Attitude change as a function of cognitive dissonance due to attitude ambivalence, field independence, resolving ambivalence, and discrepant compliance. *Dissertation Abstracts*, 1966, *27*, 248-249.

Brock, T. C. Cognitive restructuring and attitude change. *Journal of Abnormal and Social Psychology,* 1962, *64,* 264-271.

Brock, T. C. Commitment to exposure as a determinant of information receptivity. *Journal of Abnormal and Social Psychology,* 1965, *2,* 10-19.

Brock, T.C., and A. H. Buss. Dissonance, aggression, and evaluation of pain. *Journal of Abnormal and Social Psychology,* 1962, *65,* 197-202.

Campbell, A. A., *et al. The American voter.* New York: Wiley, 1960.

Campbell, A. A., G. Gurin, and W. Miller. *The voter decides.* New York: Harper, 1954.

Canon, L. K. Self-confidence and selective exposure to information. In L. Festinger (Ed.), *Conflict, decision, and dissonance.* Stanford, Calif.: Stanford Univ. Press, 1964. Pp. 83-95.

Cantril, H. The invasion from Mars. In E. Maccoby, T. M. Newcomb, and E. Hartley (Eds.), *Readings in social psychology.* 3rd ed. New York: Holt, 1958. Pp. 291-300.

Carlson, E. R. A study of attitude change and attitude structure. Unpublished doctoral dissertation, University of Michigan, 1953.

Carlson, E. R. Attitude change through modification of attitude structure. *Journal of Abnormal and Social Psychology,* 1956, *52,* 256-261.

Cartwright, D. Some principles of mass persuasion. *Human Relations,* 1946, *2,* 253-268.

Cartwright, D., and F. Harary. Structural balance: A generalization of Heider's theory. *Psychological Review,* 1956, *63,* 277-293.

Chapanis, N. P., and A. Chapanis. Cognitive dissonance: Five years later. *Psychological Bulletin,* 1964, *61,* 1-22.

Charters, W. W., and T. M. Newcomb. Some attitudinal effects of experimentally increased salience of a membership group. In E. Maccoby, T. M. Newcomb, and E. Hartley (Eds.), *Readings in social psychology.* 3rd ed. New York: Holt, 1958. Pp. 276-281.

Chein, I. Behavior theory and the behavior of attitudes. *Psychological Review,* 1948, *55,* 175-188.

Citron, A. F., and J. Harding. An experiment in training volunteers to answer anti-minority remarks. *Journal of Abnormal and Social Psychology,* 1950, *45,* 310-328.

Cohen, A. R. Need for cognition and order of communication as determinants of opinion change. In C. I. Hovland (Ed.), *The order of presentation in persuasion.* New Haven, Conn.: Yale Univ. Press, 1957.

Cohen, A. R., J. W. Brehm, and W. H. Fleming. Attitude change and justification for compliance. *Journal of Abnormal and Social Psychology,* 1958, *56,* 276-278.

Cohen, A. R., J. W. Brehm, and B. Latane. Choice of strategy and voluntary exposure to information under public and private conditions. *Journal of Personality,* 1959, *27,* 63-73.

Collier, R. M. The effect of propaganda upon attitude following a critical examination of the propaganda itself. *Journal of Social Psychology,* 1944, *20,* 3-17.

Cooper, E., and H. Dinerman. Analysis of the film "Don't be a sucker": A study in communication. *Public Opinion Quarterly,* 1951, *15,* 243-264.

Cooper, E., and M. Jahoda. The evasion of propaganda: How prejudiced people respond to anti-prejudiced propaganda. *Journal of Psychology,* 1947, *23,* 15-25.

Crockett, W. H. The effect of attitude change on cognitive differentiation, under conditions of norm-presentation with and without counter-argument. Unpublished doctoral dissertation, University of Michigan, 1953.

Crutchfield, R. S. Conformity and character. *American Psychologist,* 1955, *10,* 191-198.

Culbertson, F. M. Modification of an emotionally held attitude through role playing. *Journal of Abnormal and Social Psychology,* 1957, *54,* 230-233.

Das, J. P., R. Rath, and R. S. Das. Understanding versus suggestion in the judgment of literary passages. *Journal of Abnormal and Social Psychology,* 1955, *51,* 624-628.

Davis, M. Community attitudes toward fluoridation. *Public Opinion Quarterly,* 1959, *23,* 474-482.

Deutsch, M., and H. Gerard. A study of normative and informational social influence upon individual judgment. *Journal of Abnormal and Social Psychology,* 1955, *51,* 629-636.

Deutsch, M., R. M. Krauss, and N. Rosenau. Dissonance or defensiveness? *Journal of Personality,* 1962, *30,* 16-28.

Dewey, J. *How we think.* New York: Macmillan, 1910.

Dittes, J. E., and H. H. Kelley. Effects of different conditions of acceptance upon conformity to group norms. *Journal of Abnormal and Social Psychology,* 1956, *53,* 100-107.

Doob, L. W. *Public opinion and propaganda.* New York: Holt, 1948.

Ehrlich, D., *et al.* Postdecision exposure to relevant information. *Journal of Abnormal and Social Psychology,* 1957, *54,* 98-112.

Elms, A. C., and I. L. Janis. Counter-norm attitudes induced by consonant versus dissonant conditions of role playing. *Journal of Experimental Research in Personality,* 1965, *1,* 50-61.

Feather, N. T. Cognitive dissonance, sensitivity, and evaluation. *Journal of Abnormal and Social Psychology,* 1963, *66,* 157-163.

Feldman, S. (Ed.). *Cognitive consistency.* New York: Academic Press, 1966.

Festinger, L. *A theory of cognitive dissonance.* New York: Harper, 1957.

Festinger, L. (Ed.). *Conflict, decision and dissonance.* Stanford, Calif.: Stanford Univ. Press, 1964.

Festinger, L., and J. M. Carlsmith. Cognitive consequences of forced compliance. *Journal of Abnormal and Social Psychology,* 1959, *58,* 203-210.

Fillenbaum, S. Dogmatism and individual differences in reduction of dissonance. *Psychological Reports,* 1964, *14,* 47-50.

Fischer, L. In R. Crossman (Ed.), *The god that failed.* New York: Bantam, 1949. Pp. 198-231.

Fisher, S., I. Rubenstein, and R. W. Freeman. Intertrial effects of immediate self-committal in a continuous social influence situation. *Journal of Abnormal and Social Psychology*, 1956, *52*, 200-207.

Fiske, D., and S. Maddi. *Functions of varied experience.* Homewood, Ill.: Dorsey, 1961.

Fitch, H. G. Dissonance theory and research: A complete bibliography. Unpublished manuscript, Purdue University, 1967.

Flesch, R. *The art of plain talk.* New York: Harper, 1946.

Fowler, H. *Curiosity and exploratory behavior.* New York: Macmillan, 1965.

Freedman, J. L., and D. O. Sears. Selective exposure. *Advances in Experimental Social Psychology*, 1965, *2*, 57-97.

French, J. R. P., Jr. A formal theory of social power. *Psychological Review*, 1956, *63*, 181-194.

Gallimore, R. G. Reduction styles and dissonance-associated autonomic activity. *Dissertation Abstracts*, 1965, *25*, 6759.

Gladstone, A. I., and M. A. Taylor. Threat-related attitudes and reactions to communication about international events. *Journal of Conflict Resolution*, 1958, *2*, 17-28.

Goldberg, S. C. Three situational determinants of conformity to social norms. *Journal of Abnormal and Social Psychology*, 1954, *49*, 325-329.

Gosnell, H. F. *Getting out the vote: An experiment in the stimulation of voting.* Chicago: Univ. Chicago Press, 1927.

Greenblum, J., and L. I. Pearlin. Vertical mobility and prejudice. In R. Bendix and S. M. Lipset (Eds.), *Class, status, and power.* New York: Free Press, 1953.

Harary, F. On the measurement of structural balance. *Behavioral Science*, 1959, *4*, 316-323.

Hartley, E. L. *Problems in prejudice.* New York: King's Crown Press, 1946.

Harvey, O. J. Some situational and cognitive determinants of dissonance resolution. *Journal of Personality and Social Psychology*, 1965, *1*, 349-355.

Harvey, O. J., and G. Beverly. Some personality correlates of concept change through role playing. *Journal of Abnormal and Social Psychology*, 1961, *63*, 125-130.

Heider, F. Attitudes and cognitive organization. *Journal of Psychology*, 1946, *21*, 107-112.

Herzog, H. What do we really know about daytime serial listeners? In P. F. Lazarsfeld and F. N. Stanton (Eds.), *Radio research, 1942-1943.* New York: Duell, Sloan, & Pearce, 1944. Pp. 3-33.

Hovland, C. I. Effects of the mass media of communication. In G. Lindzey (Ed.), *Handbook of social psychology.* Vol. 2. Cambridge, Mass.: Addison-Wesley, 1954, Pp. 1062-1103.

Hovland, C. I. Reconciling conflicting results derived from experimental and survey studies of attitude change. *American Psychologist*, 1959, *14*, 8-17.

Hovland, C. I., E. Campbell, and R. Brock. The effects of "commitment" on opinion change following communication. In C. I. Hovland (Ed.), *Order of presentation in persuasion.* New Haven, Conn.: Yale Univ. Press, 1957. Pp. 23-32.

Hovland, C. I., O. J. Harvey, and M. Sherif. Assimilation and contrast effects in reactions to communication and attitude change. *Journal of Abnormal and Social Psychology,* 1957, *55,* 244-252.

Hovland, C. I., and I. L. Janis (Eds.). *Personality and persuasibility.* New Haven, Conn.: Yale Univ. Press, 1959.

Hovland, C. I., I. L. Janis, and H. H. Kelley. *Communication and persuasion.* New Haven, Conn.: Yale Univ. Press, 1953.

Hovland, C. I., A. A. Lumsdaine, and F. D. Sheffield. *Experiments on mass communication.* Princeton, N.J.: Princeton Univ. Press, 1949.

Hovland, C. I., and W. Mandell. An experimental comparison of conclusion-drawing by the communicator and by the audience. *Journal of Abnormal and Social Psychology,* 1952, *47,* 581-588.

Hovland, C. I., *et al. The order of presentation in persuasion.* New Haven, Conn.: Yale Univ. Press, 1957.

Hovland, C. I., and H. A. Pritzker. Extent of opinion change as a function of amount of change advocated. *Journal of Abnormal and Social Psychology,* 1957, *54,* 257-261.

Hovland, C. I., and W. Weiss. The influence of source credibility on communication effectiveness. *Public Opinion Quarterly,* 1951, *15,* 635-650.

Hyman, H. H. *Political socialization.* New York: Free Press, 1959.

Janis, I. L. Personality correlates of susceptibility to persuasion. *Journal of Personality,* 1954, *22,* 504-518.

Janis, I. L. Motivational factors in the resolution of decisional conflicts. In M. R. Jones (Ed.), *Nebraska symposium on motivation, 1959.* Lincoln, Neb.: Univ. Nebraska Press, 1959.

Janis, I. L., and S. Feshbach. Effects of fear-arousing communications. *Journal of Abnormal and Social Psychology,* 1953, *48,* 78-92.

Janis, I. L., and S. Feshbach. Personality differences associated with responsiveness to fear-arousing communications. *Journal of Personality,* 1954, *23,* 154-166.

Janis, I. L., and P. B. Field. Sex differences and personality factors related to persuasibility. In C. I. Hovland and I. L. Janis (Eds.), *Personality and persuasibility.* New Haven, Conn.: Yale Univ. Press, 1959. Pp. 55-68.

Janis, I. L., and J. B. Gilmore. The influence of incentive conditions on the success of role-playing in modifying attitudes. *Journal of Personality and Social Psychology,* 1965, *1,* 17-27.

Janis, I. L., and C. I. Hovland. An overview of persuasibility research. In C. I. Hovland and I. L. Janis (Eds.), *Personality and persuasibility.* New Haven, Conn.: Yale Univ. Press, 1959. Pp. 1-16.

Janis, I. L., and B. T. King. The influence of role playing on opinion change. *Journal of Abnormal and Social Psychology*, 1954, *49*, 211-218.

Janis, I. L., A. A. Lumsdaine, and A. I. Gladstone. Effects of preparatory communications on reactions to a subsequent news event. *Public Opinion Quarterly*, 1951, *15*, 487-518.

Janis, I. L., and D. Rife. Persuasibility and emotional disorders. In C. I. Hovland and I. L. Janis (Eds.), *Personality and persuasibility*. New Haven, Conn.: Yale Univ. Press, 1959. Pp. 121-140.

Jenkins, W. O., and J. C. Stanley. Partial reinforcement: A review and critique. *Psychological Bulletin*, 1950, *47*, 193-234.

Johnson, W., The communication process and general semantic principles. In W. Schramm (Ed.), *Mass communications*. Urbana, Ill.: Univ. Illinois Press, 1949. Pp. 261-274.

Jones, R. G. Forced compliance dissonance predictions: Obvious, non-obvious, or non-sense? Paper read at American Psychological Association, New York, September 1966.

Katz, D. The functional approach to the study of attitudes. *Public Opinion Quarterly*, 1960, *24*, 163-204.

Katz, D., and S. J. Eldersveld. The impact of local party activity upon the electorate. *Public Opinion Quarterly*, 1961, *25*, 1-24.

Katz, D., C. McClintock, and I. Sarnoff. The measurement of ego-defense as related to attitude change. *Journal of Personality*, 1957, *25*, 465-474.

Katz, D., I. Sarnoff, and C. McClintock. Ego-defense and attitude change. *Human Relations*, 1956, *9*, 27-45.

Katz, D., and E. Stotland. A preliminary statement to a theory of attitude structure and change. In S. Koch (Ed.), *Psychology: A study of a science*. Vol. 3. New York: McGraw-Hill, 1959. Pp. 423-475.

Katz, E., and P. F. Lazarsfeld. *Personal influence*. New York: Free Press, 1955.

Kelley, H. H. Salience of membership and resistance to change of group-anchored attitudes. *Human Relations*, 1955, *8*, 275-289.

Kelley, H. H. Resistance to change and the effects of persuasive communications. In M. Sherif and M. O. Wilson (Eds.), *Emerging problems in social psychology*. Norman, Okla.: Univ. Oklahoma Press, 1957. Pp. 229-248.

Kelley, H. H., and J. W. Thibaut. Experimental studies of group problem solving and process. In G. Lindzey (Ed.), *Handbook of social psychology*. Vol. 2. Cambridge, Mass.: Addison-Wesley, 1954.

Kelley, H. H., and E. H. Volkart. The resistance to change of group-anchored attitudes. *American Sociological Review*, 1952, *17*, 453-465.

Kelley, H. H., and C. L. Woodruff. Members' reactions to apparent group approval of a counter-norm communication. *Journal of Abnormal and Social Psychology*, 1956, *52*, 67-74.

Kelman, H. C. Effects of success and failure on "suggestibility" in the autokinetic situation. *Journal of Abnormal and Social Psychology*, 1950, *45*, 267-285.

Kelman, H. C. Attitude change as a function of response restriction. *Human Relations*, 1953, *6*, 185-214.

Kelman, H. C. Compliance, identification, and internalization: Three processes of attitude change. *Journal of Conflict Resolution*, 1958, *2*, 51-60.

Kelman, H. C. Social influence and personal belief: A theoretical and experimental approach to the study of behavior change. Unpublished manuscript, 1959.

Kelman, H. C. Processes of opinion change. *Public Opinion Quarterly*, 1961, *25*, 57-78.

Kelman, H. C., and C. I. Hovland. "Reinstatement" of the communicator in delayed measurement of opinion change. *Journal of Abnormal and Social Psychology*, 1953, *48*, 327-335.

Kendall, P. L., and P. F. Lazarsfeld. Problems of survey analysis. In R. K. Merton and P. F. Lazarsfeld (Eds.), *Continuities in social research: Studies in the scope and method of "The American Soldier."* New York: Free Press, 1950. Pp. 133-196.

Kendall, P. L., and K. M. Wolf. The analysis of deviant cases in communications research. In P. F. Lazarsfeld and F. N. Stanton (Eds.), *Communication research, 1948-1949*. New York: Harper, 1949. Pp. 152-179.

King, B. T., and I. L. Janis. Comparison of the effectiveness of improvised versus nonimprovised role-playing in producing opinion change. *Human Relations*, 1956, *9*, 177-186.

Klapper, J. T. The effects of mass media. New York: Columbia Univ. Bureau of Applied Social Research, 1949. (Mimeo.)

Klapper, J. T. *Effects of mass communication.* New York: Free Press, 1960.

Krech, D., and R. S. Crutchfield. *Theory and problems of social psychology.* New York: McGraw-Hill, 1948.

Lane, R. E. Political personality and electoral choice. *American Political Science Review*, 1955, *49*, 173-190.

LaPiere, R. T. Attitudes versus actions. *Social Forces*, 1934, *13*, 230-237.

Lawrence, D. H., and L. Festinger. *Deterrents and reinforcement.* Stanford, Calif.: Stanford Univ. Press, 1962.

Lazarsfeld, P. F., B. Berelson, and H. Gaudet. *The people's choice.* New York: Duell, Sloan, & Pearce, 1944.

Lesser, G. S., and R. P. Abelson. Personality correlates of persuasibility in children. In C. I. Hovland and I. L. Janis (Eds.), *Personality and persuasibility*. New Haven, Conn.: Yale Univ. Press, 1959. Pp. 187-206.

Leventhal, G. S. Reward magnitude, task attractiveness, and liking for instrumental activity. *Journal of Abnormal and Social Psychology*, 1964, *68*, 460-463.

Levinson, D. J. Authoritarian personality and foreign personality. *Journal of Conflict Resolution*, 1957, *1*, 37-47.

Lewin, K. In D. Cartwright (Ed.), *Field theory in social science.* New York: Harper, 1951.

Lewin, K. Group decision and social change. In E. Maccoby, T. M. Newcomb, and E. Hartley (Eds.), *Readings in social psychology.* 3rd ed. New York: Holt, 1958. Pp. 197-211.

Lifton, R. J. Thought reform of Chinese intellectuals: A psychiatric evaluation. *Journal of Social Issues,* 1957, *13,* 5-20.

Lifton, R. J. *Thought reform and the psychology of totalism.* New York: Norton, 1961.

Linder, D., J. Cooper, and E. E. Jones. Decision freedom as a determinant of the role of incentive magnitude in attitude change. *Journal of Personality and Social Psychology,* 1967, *6,* 245-254.

Linton, H., and E. Graham. Personality correlates of persuasibility. In C. I. Hovland and I. L. Janis (Eds.), *Personality and persuasibility.* New Haven, Conn.: Yale Univ. Press, 1959. Pp. 69-101.

Lippmann, W. *Public opinion.* New York: Macmillan, 1922.

Lipset, S. M., *et al.* The psychology of voting: An analysis of political behavior. In G. Lindzey (Ed.), *Handbook of social psychology.* Vol. 2. Cambridge, Mass.: Addison-Wesley, 1954. Pp. 1124-1175.

Luchins, A. S. Primacy-recency in impression formation. In C. I. Hovland (Ed.), *The order of presentation in persuasion.* New Haven, Conn.: Yale Univ. Press, 1957. Pp. 33-61.

Lumsdaine, A. A., and I. L. Janis. Resistance to "counterpropaganda" produced by a one-sided versus a two-sided presentation. *Public Opinion Quarterly,* 1953, *17,* 311-318.

Maccoby, E. E. Pitfalls in the analysis of panel data: A research note on some technical aspects of voting. *American Journal of Sociology,* 1956, *59,* 359-362.

Mausner, B. The effect of prior reinforcement on the interaction of observer pairs. *Journal of Abnormal and Social Psychology,* 1954, *49,* 65-68.

McClintock, C. Personality syndromes and attitude change. *Journal of Personality,* 1958, *26,* 479-493.

McGuire, W. J. Cognitive consistency and attitude change. *Journal of Abnormal and Social Psychology,* 1960, *60,* 345-353. (a)

McGuire, W. J. Direct and indirect persuasive effects of dissonance producing messages. *Journal of Abnormal and Social Psychology,* 1960, *60,* 354-358. (b)

McGuire, W. J. Resistance to persuasion conferred by active and passive prior refutation of the same and alternate counter-arguments. *Journal of Abnormal and Social Psychology,* 1961, *63,* 326-332. (a)

McGuire, W. J. The effectiveness of supportive and refutational defenses in immunizing and restoring beliefs against persuasion. *Sociometry,* 1961, *24,* 184-197. (b)

McGuire, W. J. Persistence of the resistance to persuasion induced by various types of prior belief defenses. *Journal of Abnormal and Social Psychology,* 1962, *64,* 241-248.

McGuire, W. J. Threat and reassurance as factors in conferring resistance to persuasion. Unpublished manuscript, 1963. (a)

McGuire, W. J. Comparative persistence of actively and passively conferred resistance to persuasion. Unpublished manuscript, 1963. (b)

McGuire, W. J. Cross-issue generalization of conferred resistance to persuasion. Unpublished manuscript, 1963. (c)

McGuire, W. J. Inducing resistance to persuasion: Some contemporary approaches. In L. Berkowitz (Ed.), *Advances in experimental social psychology,* 1964, *1,* 191-229.

McGuire, W. J. Attitudes and opinions. *Annual Review of Psychology,* 1966, *17,* 475-514. (a)

McGuire, W. J. The current status of cognitive consistency theories. In S. Feldman (Ed.), *Cognitive consistency.* New York: Academic Press, 1966. Pp. 1-46. (b)

McGuire, W. J., and D. Papageorgis. The relative efficacy of various types of prior belief-defense in producing immunity against persuasion. *Journal of Abnormal and Social Psychology,* 1961, *62,* 327-337.

McGuire, W. J., and D. Papageorgis. Effectiveness of forewarning in developing resistance to persuasion. *Public Opinion Quarterly,* 1962, *26,* 24-34.

Mead, G. H. *Mind, self, and society.* Chicago: Univ. Chicago Press, 1934.

Miller, D. R., and G. E. Swanson. *Inner conflict and defense.* New York: Holt, 1960.

Mills, J. Changes in moral attitudes following temptation. *Journal of Personality,* 1958, *26,* 517-531.

Mills, J., E. Aronson, and H. Robinson. Selectivity in exposure to information. *Journal of Abnormal and Social Psychology,* 1959, *59,* 250-253.

Newcomb, T. M. *Personality and social change.* New York: Dryden, 1943.

Newcomb, T. M. An approach to the study of communicative acts. *Psychological Review,* 1953, *60,* 393-404.

Newcomb, T. M. *The acquaintance process.* New York: Holt, 1961.

Nunnally, J. C., and H. Bobren. Variables governing the willingness to receive communications on mental health. *Journal of Personality,* 1959, *27,* 38-46.

Osgood, C. E. The nature and measurement of meaning. *Psychological Bulletin,* 1952, *49,* 197-237.

Osgood, C. E. Report on development and application of the semantic differential. Unpublished manuscript, Institute of Communications Research, University of Illinois, 1953.

Osgood, C. E., and P. H. Tannenbaum. The principle of congruity in the prediction of attitude change. *Psychological Review,* 1955, *62,* 42-55.

Papageorgis, D., and W. J. McGuire. The generality of immunity to persuasion produced by pre-exposure to weakened counter-arguments. *Journal of Abnormal and Social Psychology,* 1961, *62,* 475-481.

Peak, H. Attitude and motivation. In M. Jones (Ed.), *Nebraska symposium on motivation, 1955.* Lincoln, Neb.: Univ. Nebraska Press, 1955.

Peak, H. The effects of aroused motivation on attitudes. Technical Report to the Office of Naval Research, 1959. (Mimeo.)

Pettigrew, T. F. Personality and socio-cultural factors in intergroup attitudes: A cross-national comparison. *Journal of Conflict Resolution,* 1958, *2,* 29-42.

Rabbie, J. M., J. W. Brehm, and A. R. Cohen. Verbalization and reactions to cognitive dissonance. *Journal of Personality,* 1959, *27,* 407-417.

Raven, B. H., and M. Fishbein. Acceptance of punishment and change in belief. *Journal of Abnormal and Social Psychology,* 1961, *63,* 411-416.

Razran, G. H. S. Conditioned response changes in rating and appraising sociopolitical slogans. *Psychological Bulletin,* 1940, *37,* 481. (Abstract.)

Remmers, H. H. (Ed.). Generalized attitude scales: Studies in socio-psychological measurements. *Bulletin of Purdue University Studies in Higher Education,* 1934, *36,* No. 4.

Remmers, H. H., and E. B. Silance. Generalized attitude scales. *Journal of Social Psychology,* 1934, *5,* 298-312.

Riecken, H. W. (Chairman). Narrowing the gap between field studies and laboratory experiments in social psychology: A statement by the summer seminar. *Items of the Social Science Research Council,* 1954, *8,* 37-42.

Rosen, S. Postdecision affinity for incompatible information. *Journal of Abnormal and Social Psychology,* 1961, *63,* 188-190.

Rosenbaum, M. E., and D. E. Franc. Opinion change as a function of external commitment and amount of discrepancy from the opinion of another. *Journal of Abnormal and Social Psychology,* 1960, *61,* 15-20.

Rosenbaum, M. E., and I. M. Zimmerman. The effect of internal commitment on response to an attempt to change opinions. *Public Opinion Quarterly,* 1959, *23,* 247-254.

Rosenberg, M. J. The experimental investigation of a value theory of attitude structure. Unpublished doctoral dissertation, University of Michigan, 1953.

Rosenberg, M. J. Cognitive structure and attitudinal affect. *Journal of Abnormal and Social Psychology,* 1956, *53,* 367-372.

Rosenberg, M. J. Affect and cognition in attitude structure and attitude change. Paper read at Eastern Psychological Association, April 1957.

Rosenberg, M. J. A structural theory of attitude dynamics. *Public Opinion Quarterly,* 1960, *24,* 319-341. (a)

Rosenberg, M. J. Cognitive reorganization in response to the hypnotic reversal of attitudinal affect. *Journal of Personality,* 1960, *28,* 39-63. (b)

Rosenberg, M. J. When dissonance fails: On eliminating evaluation apprehension from attitude measurement. *Journal of Personality and Social Psychology,* 1965, *1,* 28-42.

Rosenberg, M. J., and R. P. Abelson. An analysis of cognitive balancing. In M. J. Rosenberg, *et al.* (Eds.), *Attitude organization and change.* New Haven, Conn.: Yale Univ. Press, 1960. Pp. 112-163.

Rosenberg, M. J., and C. W. Gardner. Some dynamic aspects of posthypnotic compliance. *Journal of Abnormal and Social Psychology,* 1958, *57,* 351-366.

Rosenberg, M. J., *et al.* (Eds.). *Attitude organization and change.* New Haven, Conn.: Yale Univ. Press, 1960.

Ryle, G. *The concept of mind.* London: Hutchinson, 1949.

Samelson, F. Conforming behavior under two conditions of conflict in the cognitive field. *Journal of Abnormal and Social Psychology,* 1957, *55,* 181-187.

Sarnoff, I. Identification with the aggressor: Some personality correlates of anti-Semitism among Jews. *Journal of Personality,* 1951, *20,* 199-218.

Sarnoff, I. Psychoanalytic theory and social attitudes. *Public Opinion Quarterly,* 1960, *24,* 251-279.

Sarnoff, I., and D. Katz. The motivational bases of attitude change. *Journal of Abnormal and Social Psychology,* 1954, *49,* 115-124.

Schachter, S., and R. Hall. Group derived restraints and audience persuasion. *Human Relations,* 1952, *5,* 397-406.

Schachter, S., and J. Singer. Cognitive, social, and physiological determinants of emotional state. *Psychological Review,* 1962, *69,* 379-399.

Schein, E. H. The Chinese indoctrination program for prisoners of war: A study of attempted "brain washing." *Psychiatry,* 1956, *19,* 149-172.

Schein, E. H. Reaction patterns to severe, chronic stress in American Army prisoners of war of the Chinese. *Journal of Social Issues,* 1957, *13,* 21-30.

Scott, W. A. Attitude change through reward of verbal behavior. *Journal of Abnormal and Social Psychology,* 1957, *55,* 72-75.

Scott, W. A. Attitude change by response reinforcement: Replication and extension. *Sociometry,* 1959, *22,* 328-335. (a)

Scott, W. A. Cognitive consistency, response reinforcement, and attitude change. *Sociometry,* 1959, *22,* 219-229. (b)

Scriven, M. A study of radical behaviorism. In H. Feigl and M. Scriven (Eds.), *Minnesota studies in philosophy of science.* Vol. 1. *Foundations of science and the concepts of psychology and psychoanalysis.* Minneapolis: Univ. Minnesota Press, 1956. Pp. 88-131.

Segal, J. Correlates of collaboration and resistance behavior among U.S. Army POW's in Korea. *Journal of Social Issues,* 1957, *13,* 31-40.

Sherif, M., and C. W. Sherif. *Groups in harmony and tension: An integration of studies on intergroup relations.* New York: Harper, 1953.

Sherif, M., and C. W. Sherif. *An outline of social psychology.* New York: Harper, 1956.

Siegel, S. *Non-parametric statistics for the behavioral sciences.* New York: McGraw-Hill, 1956.

Skinner, B. F. *Science and human behavior.* New York: Macmillan, 1953.

Skinner, B. F. *Verbal behavior.* New York: Appleton-Century-Crofts, 1957.

Smith, E. E. The power of dissonance techniques to change attitudes. *Public Opinion Quarterly,* 1961, *25,* 626-639.

Smith, H. P., and E. W. Rosen. Some psychological correlates of world-mindedness and authoritarianism. *Journal of Personality,* 1958, *26,* 170-183.

Smith, M. B. Personal values as determinants of a political attitude. *Journal of Personality*, 1949, *23*, 477-486.

Smith, M. B., J. S. Bruner, and R. W. White. *Opinions and personality*. New York: Wiley, 1956.

Stack, J. J. Individual differences in the reduction of cognitive dissonance: An exploratory study. *Dissertation Abstracts*, 1964, *24*, 4806-4807.

Stagner, R., and C. E. Osgood. An experimental analysis of a nationalistic frame of reference. *Journal of Social Psychology*, 1941, *14*, 389-401.

Steiner, I. D. Receptivity to supportive versus nonsupportive communications. *Journal of Abnormal and Social Psychology*, 1962, *65*, 266-267.

Stotland, E., D. Katz, and M. Patchen. The reduction of prejudice through the arousal of self-insight. *Journal of Personality*, 1959, *27*, 507-531.

Stukát, K. G. *"Suggestibility": A factorial and experimental analysis*. Stockholm: Almqvist & Wiksell, 1958.

Suinn, R. M. Anxiety and cognitive dissonance. *Journal of General Psychology*, 1965, *73*, 113-116.

Tannenbaum, P. H. Attitudes toward source and concept as factors in attitude change through communications. Unpublished doctoral dissertation, University of Illinois, 1953.

Tannenbaum, P. H. The indexing process in communication. *Public Opinion Quarterly*, 1955, *19*, 292-302.

Tannenbaum, P. H. Initial attitude toward source and concept as factors in attitude change through communication. *Public Opinion Quarterly*, 1956, *20*, 413-425.

Thomas, W. I., and F. Znaniecki. *The Polish peasant in Europe and America*. Vols. 1-5. Boston: Badger, 1918-1920.

Titus, H. E., and E. P. Hollander. The California F-scale in psychological research: 1950-1955. *Psychological Bulletin*, 1957, *54*, 47-64.

Tolman, E. C. A psychological model. In T. Parsons and E. A. Shils (Eds.), *Toward a general theory of action*. Cambridge, Mass.: Harvard Univ. Press, 1951.

U.S. Senate, Committee on Government operations. *The interrogation, indoctrination, and exploitation of American military and civilian prisoners*. Washington: U.S. Government Printing Office, 1956.

Wagman, M. An investigation of the effectiveness of authoritarian suggestion and non-authoritarian information as methods of changing the prejudiced attitudes of relatively authoritarian and non-authoritarian personalities. Unpublished doctoral dissertation, University of Michigan, 1953.

Wagman, M. Attitude change and the authoritarian personality. *Journal of Psychology*, 1955, *40*, 3-24.

Weick, K. E. Reduction of cognitive dissonance through task enhancement and effort expenditure. *Journal of Abnormal and Social Psychology*, 1964, *68*, 533-539.

Weick, K. E. When prophecy pales: The fate of dissonance theory. *Psychological Reports*, 1965, *16*, 1261-1275.

Weiss, W. A "sleeper" effect in opinion change. *Journal of Abnormal and Social Psychology*, 1953, *48*, 173-180.

Weiss, W., and B. J. Fine. Opinion change as a function of some intrapersonal attributes of the communicatees. *Journal of Abnormal and Social Psychology*, 1955, *51*, 246-253.

Weiss, W., and B. J. Fine. The effect of induced aggressiveness on opinion change. *Journal of Abnormal and Social Psychology*, 1956, *52*, 109-114.

Weitzenhoffer, A. M. *Hypnotism.* New York: Wiley, 1953.

Woodruff, A. D., and F. J. DiVesta. The relationship between values, concepts, and attitudes. *Educational and Psychological Measurement,* 1948, *8*, 645-660.

Yaryan, R. B., and L. Festinger. Preparatory action and belief in the probable occurrence of future events. *Journal of Abnormal and Social Psychology,* 1961, *63*, 603-606.

Zajonc, R. B. The concepts of balance, congruity, and dissonance. *Public Opinion Quarterly,* 1960, *24*, 280-296. (a)

Zajonc, R. B. The process of cognitive tuning in communication. *Journal of Abnormal and Social Psychology,* 1960, *61*, 159-167. (b)

Zimbardo, P. G. Involvement and communication discrepancy as determinants of opinion change. Unpublished doctoral dissertation, Yale University, 1959.